Hold the Roses

Hold the Roses

Rose Marie

THE UNIVERSITY PRESS OF KENTUCKY

Publication of this volume was made possible in part by a grant
from the National Endowment for the Humanities.

Editorial and Sales Offices: The University Press of Kentucky
663 South Limestone Street, Lexington, Kentucky 40508–4008

02 03 04 05 06   5 4 3 2 1

All photos from author's personal collection.

Library of Congress Cataloging-in-Publication Data

Rose Marie, 1923-
Hold the roses / Rose Marie.
p. cm.
Includes index.
ISBN: 978-0-8131-6800-5
1. Rose Marie, 1923- 2. Entertainers—United States—Biography.
I. Title.
PN2287.R7575 A3 2002
791'.092—dc21   2002152552

This book is printed on acid-free recycled paper meeting
the requirements of the American National Standard
for Permanence in Paper for Printed Library Materials.

Isn't it the truth!

By CARL RIBLET JR.

There are six women of generations past and present that you can't forget — Helen of Troy, Betsy Ross, Mata Hari, Betty Grable, Baby Rose Marie.

"There are few women whose charm survives their beauty."

—LaRochefoucauld

I am third.
First comes God,
then everybody else
...and I am third.

To my mother and my husband,
the two people who loved me the most
and made me the woman I am today.
And to my Noop...
My baby, my love, my life.

Contents

❦

List of Illustrations   xi

Prologue   1

One   And Here She Is, Folks   3

Two   Baby Rose Marie, the Child Wonder   11

Three   Springtime in the Rockies   20

Four   Baby Meets "Uncle Al" and the Boys   29

Five   Hollywood—the First Time   33

Six   Tastyeast Is Tempting   38

Seven   From Baby to Miss Rose Marie   47

Eight   Sweet Sixteen…or Eighteen?   50

Nine   The Love of My Life   58

Ten   *Spring in Brazil* and Berle   66

Eleven   Courtship in Hell   76

Twelve   Heavenly Honeymoon   90

Thirteen   Hollywood—Love, Home, and Work   96

Fourteen   The Flamingo Opening   105

Fifteen   Presenting Georgiana Marie Guy   111

Sixteen   Florida and the Ski School   117

Seventeen   Our Social Life—California Style   121

Eighteen   Phil Silvers and Broadway…Again   125

Nineteen   The Singer's Curse—Nodes   135

Twenty   My Illustrious Movie Career   142

Twenty-One   *The Dick Van Dyke Show*   149

Twenty-Two   My Dear Friends—My Angels   159

Twenty-Three   When "Tom" Became "Tim" Conway   166

Twenty-Four   Life Is a Three-Legged Chair   175

Twenty-Five   *Hollywood Squares*   185

Twenty-Six   An Affair Not to Remember   193

Twenty-Seven   Doris Day and Australia   200

Twenty-Eight   The Theater—Dinner and Otherwise   209

Twenty-Nine   The Pussycat Theaters and Vince   215

Thirty   *Up a Tree*, or Ring around Rosie   221

Thirty-One   *4 Girls 4*   226

Thirty-Two   Noop's Wedding   237

Thirty-Three   *4 Girls 4*, the Second Time   241

Epilogue   Things I Forgot to Tell You   251

Appearances   263

Acknowledgments   269

Index   271

Illustrations

❦

Clipping from my scrapbook   v

Father and Mother   4

Mother and me   5

At age four   7

Early media coverage   8

With Rudy Vallee   9

From *The Child Wonder*   12

Ticket to the radio show   14

At NBC microphone before a program   15

My brocade Mary Jane shoes   17

With Dick Powell   19

Orpheum   21

Song sheets   22

"Have You Ever Been Lonely?"   23

The Andrews Sisters   25

With George Burns and Gracie Allen   26

With Milton Berle   27

With Jimmy Durante   34

With radio sponsor "Tastyeast"   39

Mini-biography NBC sent to fans   40-41

About to leave the "Baby" behind   45

Miss Rose Marie at sweet sixteen   51

My husband, William Robert Guy   62

A cherished telegram from Durante   78

With Frank Sinatra and Rocky Graziano   79

Miss Rose Marie's first club date   101

Flamingo Hotel table card   106

On stage at the Flamingo Hotel   107

From the *Las Vegas Review*   108

Georgiana Marie at nine months old   113

Bobby and me at waterskiing school   119

Noopy and Daddy   122

Noopy, Bobby, Stella, and Nan   126

With Phil Silvers in *Top Banana*   127

With Audrey Meadows in *Top Banana*   128

With Zero Mostel   133

With Bobby, showing off our matching suits   140

With Milton Berle   146

With Dick Van Dyke   150

With Morey Amsterdam and Dick Van Dyke   151

Sally and Buddy   152

Morey and I dance it up for TV Guide   154

Letter from Tim Conway   174

Hollywood Squares   187

With Ethel Merman   191

With Doris Day   201

With Ethel Merman and Richard Deacon   211

4 Girls 4   229

Noopy at her wedding   238

Noopy and Steve Rodrigues   240

Mother and me   248

Noopy, Stella, and Rose Marie   249

Getting my star   259

Prologue

It was the last day of *The Dick Van Dyke Show*. We had been together five years. We were so close. We have been through divorces, marriages, sicknesses, and deaths together, and now it was all coming to an end. Would we stay in touch with one another? Would we be as close as we had been for the past five years? No one knew. We kept looking at one another and trying to keep from crying.

How we ever got through that show was a miracle. Mary would say, "That's the last time I will get made up in that room." "This is the last time I will walk through that door." Morey was trying to make jokes at every turn, but he too had a lump in his throat. Everyone was so keyed up. No one would admit that we all felt like kids losing our best friends. I kept trying to think that it wouldn't end. We were too close for this to just stop.

We had done our run-through. We got our notes from Carl Reiner and our director Jerry Paris. We went to dinner, just as we had done for five years. No one ate. We were all in the dumps. We tried to kid around and act as crazy as we always did, but we were all acting. I sat in my dressing room...cried...and went to our makeup man, Tom Tuttle, to fix my makeup. He smiled....He knew. Even he had tears in his eyes. I got dressed, and Marge Mullen, our script girl, came to me, hugged me, and said, "This is the last time I give you notes. Let's make it a good one."

The audience came in and we went on to do the last *Dick Van Dyke Show*. What wonderful memories I would have of that show. Five years...So much had happened in those five years.

I began to think of my life before the Van Dyke Show, before all the other TV shows and performances I had done during my lifetime, before I grew up. My mind took me back to the first time I ever stepped on a stage to perform.

I was three years old. My mother always said I was two years and nine months, but you know how mothers like to exaggerate, so let's go for three years old. I won an amateur contest at the Mecca Theatre on 14th Street in New York City. I sang "What Can I Say, Dear, After I Say I'm Sorry?"

I don't remember too much of that night, except that I sang and ran off the stage. When I got to the wings, somebody put a bouquet of roses in one of my arms and another bouquet in the other arm. I could hear the audience applauding and screaming and someone yelling, "Bring the kid back! Let her sing! We want the kid to sing!" When I heard this commotion, I threw the roses down and said, "Hold the roses—I can't take my bow!"

It has been like that ever since. Hence the title of this book.

Chapter One

And Here She Is, Folks

I was born, illegitimately, on August 15 in New York City. A holy day…the Feast of the Assumption. I was named Rose Marie: Marie because it was a holy day, so my grandmother said I would be named either Mary or Marie. The choice was not a difficult one for my mother, since she never did like the name Mary. My father decided I should be named after his mother, Rose. So, to please everybody, I was named Rose Marie. A musical entitled "Rose-Marie" had opened on Broadway the night I was born, and my mother liked the name as two words rather than one. Little did she know how many times in my life I would be called "Rosemary" or "Miss Marie."

My mother's name was Stella Gluscak. My father was Frank Mazzetta. They never married because my father already was married to a woman in Brooklyn—he also had two children with her. I think my mother knew, but what could she do—I had arrived. We lived in a three-story railroad tenement at 616 East 17th Street—the first high stoop on the right, across the street from the dumps. At least that's what we used to say when we could afford to take a cab.

I don't remember my father ever living with us. I lived with my mother and her mother and father, Ursula and Michael Gluscak. My grandmother cleaned office buildings and my grandfather was a shoemaker. He made all my shoes until he passed away when I was about five. My mother had various jobs (telephone company, pencil factory, and so on). I remember my grandmother saying to my mother, "Don't worry: when you're working, I'll take care of her. And when I'm working, you'll take care of her.

My father, Frank Mazzetta, and my mother, Stella Gluscak

We'll get along." My grandparents were from Kraków, Poland. My mother was born in New York on Christmas (also a holy day).

On my father's side, both of his parents were born in Italy...Rose and Joseph Mazzetta. My father was born in New York. He had many jobs during his lifetime. He was a suit cutter, and was with "the boys" when they were trying to get everybody to join the union. Anybody who didn't join, they would go and bomb that person's place. He also claimed to be part of a trio that played with George M. Cohan in one of his big shows, but I never did believe that. Another of my father's "positions" was manager, or owner, or bouncer, of the Diana Ballroom.

My mother was a happy-go-lucky girl, weighing 90 pounds soaking wet, and quite attractive. She loved the theater, music, dancing, and all the glitter of show business. She used to go to the Diana Ballroom to dance, but she always went with a bunch of girls. My father saw her, a cute girl of seventeen, and took a liking to her. He would set up contests so my mother would win. Bless her heart, at that time she was so gullible and naive. This guy had her dance with George Raft (I checked this out with George when I went to Hollywood ... you'll hear more about this later) and Rudolph

Mother and me, Atlantic City, New Jersey

Valentino (I couldn't check this out; he was long gone by then). My mother always swore that she did indeed dance with Valentino.

My mother used to take me to the Jefferson Theater on 14th Street and to the Academy of Music to see the movies and vaudeville shows. I would come home and sing all of the songs I had heard for my grandparents. They would applaud, fuss over me and say how wonderful I was. I would say, "I have to go upstairs and sing for the Polish people on the third floor." It was those wonderful Polish neighbors who entered me in the amateur contest at the Mecca Theater. In fact, they bought the dress I wore and the gold-brocaded Mary Jane shoes—which I still have. (I treasure them very much, and I smile whenever I look at them.)

My mother was petrified. "I don't know if she'll sing in front of a lot of people or cry or just not want to sing."

The neighbors said, "She sings for us and we're an audience. She'll sing."

Well, I won the contest. How can you beat a three-year-old kid who sings like Sophie Tucker? I think the prize was twenty dollars. My father heard about my victory and quickly became part of the picture. He took my mother and me to Atlantic City. He had relatives there. We stayed for a little while. In those days, nightclubs were family restaurants, with dancing and a floor show.

One night we went to the Little Club. Evelyn Nesbit was a showgirl who was known as "The Girl in the Red Velvet Swing" and was also involved in what was later called the biggest scandal of the early years of the century. Her boyfriend had shot her husband over her. Evelyn was the star of the show. While she was singing, I of course started to sing with her. She was very upset, but I kept on singing with her. She finally came over, took me by the hand and led me to the microphone, and I sang. Boy, did I sing! Everybody started throwing money on the stage—lots of money. I was such a big hit. Some of the waiters picked up the money and gave it to my mother. I think that's the only time she got every penny of what I earned.

Backstage, Evelyn Nesbit said to my father, "What's her name?"

My father said, "Dainty Rose Marie."

She said, "She is a baby, call her Baby Rose Marie." And that's how I became Baby Rose Marie! (Until I was fifteen!)

My mother immediately went on the Boardwalk and bought me a red felt coat with large, white angora polka dots with a cloche hat and bag to match. It must have cost everything I made at the Little Club. Whether it did or not, I wore it until the polka dots fell off.

Word got around town about this three-year-old kid who sounded like Sophie Tucker, with a raspy, grown-up voice. I never sounded like the Shirley Temple "Good Ship Lollipop" type. I have the voice today that I had when I was a child. I started singing at parties, clubs and the Ambassador Hotel, one of the finest hotels in Atlantic City. In fact, I sang there in a big show on New Year's Eve.

By now, Radio Station WPG asked my father to come and talk to them about me. I remember it was at the Steel Pier, which is still a big attraction in Atlantic City. We went over and I sang. They wanted me to go on the radio twice a week. I stood in a glass booth, facing the Boardwalk so that everyone could see this child singing on the radio. They say I received one hundred fan letters a week, which in those days was unbelievable. I continued with WPG, my very first "real" job, for a few months.

My mother wanted to go back to New York, so we went home to

At age four, WPG Radio, Steel Pier, Atlantic City, New Jersey

17th Street. WMCA Radio Station in New York called and wanted me to sing on their weekly variety show called The Orhbach Hour. (Yes, Orhbach's, the department store.) I did that show every week for about three months, and I was becoming very well known. I was also making quite a bit of money, and we could now afford to move to a better place. My grandmother, who had decided that we should move; my father, who by now had appointed himself my manager; and my sweet but oh-so-naive mother and I moved to Sunnyside, New York. We had the bottom floor of a two-

Baby Rose Marie, youngest contract star in radio, and Papa Frank Curley are pictured at the left as they returned to their east-side home after a visit to the studios of the National Broadcasting Company. Next she is shown taking the new doll out for an airing, and in the third picture with a group of playmates on the steps of the Curley apartment. At the right the 3-year-old prodigy is boop-boop-a-oing before the microphone.

Early media coverage

Baby Rose Marie, a celebrity herself, likes other well known people. Here you see her before the microphone with her friends Graham McNamee, left, and Rudy Vallee, right.

With Rudy Vallee

story house, which was like a mansion compared to our railroad flat. Looking back now, maybe we should have stayed on 17th Street; I understand it now has become a very exclusive area. Very, very avant-garde!

After the Orhbach Hour, NBC Radio Network called my parents and wanted to talk to them about signing me to a seven-year contract. This was quite unusual because NBC had only a few artists signed—Rudy Vallee, Amos and Andy, symphony conductor Leo Reisman, Vincent Lopez, and announcer Graham McNamara. We went to 711 Fifth Avenue to see a Mr. Ed Schewing, the head of the NBC Artists Bureau. Miss MacDonald, his secretary, led us into this huge office—big oak desk, humongous chairs with red leather and an entire wall of windows overlooking Fifth Avenue. I will never forget that day!

Mr. Schewing was tall, slender, and very kind. He asked us to sit down, and then he talked to my father about signing me to a seven-year contract, assuring my mother throughout the conversation that he would look out for me. After my father signed the contract and they shook hands, Mr. Schewing came over and gave me a big hug, saying, "Now honey, even if you spit, you'll get paid." He then went over to my mother, shook her hand and gave her a Chinese red-lacquered box of Schrafft's Candy. I think it was the most expensive gift my mother had ever received. She still has that red-lacquered box. It's been used as a sewing box, a button box, and so on. Every time I look at that box I think of that day—when my career really started to move into the "Big Time."

Chapter Two

✣

Baby Rose Marie, the Child Wonder

The first big thing NBC did was put me in a Vitaphone movie short. These were fifteen-minute short subjects that went on before the features. Many of the big stars of the day made these shorts. Harry Richman, Georgie Price, Georgie Jessel, Sophie Tucker, to name a few. If you remember these names, you're an "Alta Cocka" like I am. But remember: I was five years old!

I wore my polka-dot coat and hat and a pink ruffled dress. I sang two songs. My short was the one that played the Winter Garden Theater on Broadway at the opening of *The Jazz Singer* starring Al Jolson. I went to the premiere with my mother and father and met Mr. Jolson. He was very angry about having to follow my short. My short was all singing, and *The Jazz Singer* was part talk and part singing. He made such a fuss that I thought he was going to hit someone. He kept raving and ranting, but finally he went into the theater.

When the show was over, I saw him being congratulated. I ran over to him and said, "Oh, Mr. Jolson, you were so great, you made me cry."

He looked at me and said, "You were great too, ya little runt."

Nice man! However, every time we would appear together at benefits, like the Milk Fund at Madison Square Garden, he would spot me with my father, come over and say, "Hi, ya little runt. You gonna go out and kill the people?"

I would look up at him and say, "I hope so."

He would give me a little kiss on the cheek and say, "Tell 'em they ain't seen nothin' yet till they see Uncle Al." Go figure!

By now I was five years old and doing a lot of guest appearances on

From Vitaphone short, *The Child Wonder,* 1928

the NBC shows. I sang with the NBC Symphony Orchestra conducted by Leo Reisman; after one rehearsal, he threw down his baton and said, "I can't believe this child. She has such a knowledge of tempo and rhythm. She can't be five years old! She's a midget." And he stormed off the podium. (More on the midget bit later.)

I sang on the *RKO Theater of the Air, The Rudy Vallee Show,* which was the biggest hit on the radio at that time. We did his show in the basement of the Brooklyn Paramount Theater. Rudy was a wonderful friend to me, and when I went to California in 1945, I did his show again. In fact, it was the first show I did after I got married.

Being with NBC was a blessing because I was given the opportunity to do so many things. I started making records on the Brunswick label. I did songs like, "Come Out, Come Out, Wherever You Are," "Take a Picture of the Moon" and "Say That You Were Teasing Me," to name a few. All cute songs.

Bernie Cummings and His Orchestra were playing at the New Yorker Hotel on 34th Street in Manhattan. They played there every night and had two radio shows a night broadcast coast to coast as well. Those were the days when most of the big bands had radio shows from the places where they were appearing. "Radio remotes," they were called.

Some of you will remember when an announcer would say over the music, "Ladies and Gentlemen, from the Aragon Ballroom, Lawrence Welk and his orchestra." This was, "Ladies and Gentlemen, here's Bernie Cummings and his Orchestra from the New Yorker Hotel in the heart of Manhattan, starring Baby Rose Marie." I sang on these radio shows twice a night for several months.

I was six years old when the New York Society for the Prevention of Cruelty to Children started to bother us about the child labor laws. Sometimes known as the Gerry Society, it was created to enforce the child labor laws. The laws in the state of New York about children working were very strict. It came about back when there were children working in the factories day and night, with no proper meals, schooling and time to sleep. Hell, it wasn't work for me—I loved it.

Nevertheless, we had to meet the head man of the Gerry Society, who said, "So many mothers have called to complain: 'How come she can work and sing on the radio and you won't allow my daughter or son to do that?'" Apparently it was all right to sing on the radio, but you couldn't sing or dance in a show. Children could talk on the stage in plays, but no singing or dancing. It was really a strange law, because African American children *were* allowed to sing and dance on stage. I specifically remember the Nicholas Brothers, a brilliant dance act who were always working. We became very good friends, and we did a lot of club dates together when we were young.

Being six years old, I quickly learned that life couldn't be all fun and no work. It was time to go to school! Actually, school was fun for me. When I began school, I attended Professional Children's School on 61st Street in Manhattan, at the old Daddy Browning Building. The school consisted of three floors: one floor was an auditorium, and the other two floors were classrooms. It went up to the 8th grade. Many children who were in plays on Broadway attended the school. Children who were on the road would do "correspondence schoolwork," and send the finished lessons back to the school. Some very famous people went to this school: Milton Berle, Anne Baxter, Peter McDonald and many, many more. The girl who played Kim, the child in *Showboat,* was in my kindergarten class. Many of the "radio children," who did radio soap operas, were also in attendance. The hours for the school were 10:00 A.M. to 2:00 P.M.

I did my first play in school with Peter McDonald and Jack Jorden. It was a children's play, written especially for the commencement of that year. Being primarily a singer, I was very flattered and proud to have

National Broadcasting Company, Inc.
Fifth Avenue at Fifty-fifth Street
New York City

invites

Admit One

M _iss Helen Hoatainer_

to visit its Studios

JUN 4 - 1933

on...th Floor

Program .... BABY ROSE MARIE

Sunday 12 to 12:15 P.M.

Joe Geralticon

THIS INVITATION IS GOOD FOR THIS DATE AND PROGRAM ONLY
VISITORS MUST NOT LEAVE STUDIO UNTIL THE CONCLUSION OF THE PROGRAM

Ticket to the Baby Rose Marie Radio Show at NBC Studios

been chosen to appear in a play with a cast of already accomplished actors and actresses. Imagine my delight when I received the letter from the principal.

I was still doing radio guest shots and club dates about once a week. The Gerry Society would call and say, "How is she? What do you feed her? Where do you buy her clothes?" My clothes for work were either hand-made for me by my mother's cousin, or selected and purchased by my mother from a dear lady, Mrs. Kowalski. From time to time, Mrs. Kowalski would bring several dresses for my mother to see.

My mother got very disgusted and asked someone at the Gary Society if there wasn't something we could do to keep from getting the calls and checkups. The man said, "You could move to Jersey, we can't touch you there!" So we moved to East Orange, New Jersey. Another two-family house; we were on the bottom floor again.

It was about this time that NBC told us of the plans they had for me: my own fifteen-minute, coast-to-coast radio show on Sunday mornings at 12:00 P.M. on WJZ, New York's NBC radio station. They even had the sponsor all set up! Julius Grossman Shoes. They had one store at 5th Avenue and 39th Street in Manhattan. It's still there! I could never under-

Looking up at NBC microphone before a
program

stand why the show was coast-to-coast and the sponsor had only one store
… in New York City. Remember, I was only six years old. The show consisted of my own piano player, Herbie Steiner; the announcer, Clyde Kitel;
and me. No orchestra, just a piano. My theme song was "Baby Shoes":
"Baby Shoes…mother remembers. She still has a pair of Julius Grossman
Shoes."

Talk about the commercials today, we had a beaut: "Julius Grossman
Shoes…bad feet need 'em and good feet deserve 'em."

The show was a smash. I was on for two years. The fan mail was
unbelievable, which brings us back to the midget bit. People kept writing,
"She can't be a child, she's gotta be a 45-year-old midget.…No child sings
like that." I told you that I never sounded like a child. During the two

At NBC

years I was on the air, I was named "Princess of the Radio." (Rudy Vallee was named King and Ruth Etting was the Queen.) I was still making records and they were selling like crazy.

To dispel the midget myth, NBC decided that I had to go on tour to prove that I was a child. RKO was affiliated with NBC, and I was set to do a 52-week tour in RKO theaters all over the county. I would do my act, which consisted of singing about four songs and talking to the audience. The whole thing lasted about twenty-five minutes.

My father traveled with me for the entire tour. My mother divided her time between home and coming out to certain cities to visit with me. We really missed each other, and mother felt that 52 weeks was much too long for us not to see each other. During one of her visits, she became pregnant with my brother Frank. He too was born on a special day: June 14, Flag Day, a holiday! Years later, I asked her why she allowed herself to

My brocade Mary Jane shoes, still a treasure today

become pregnant again since she had had me illegitimately. She told me that my father had threatened her by saying he'd take me away from her if she didn't have a second baby. My dear mother—she was so naive, she believed everything he told her.

Dear readers, here's something you will learn about for the very first time. I was very fortunate that nobody has discussed this "scandal" during all these years. I myself just recently learned some of the other details of this "scandal." The "other woman" refused to give my father a divorce. The two children they had together were also named Rose and Frank. I was supporting two families for years! How do you like that, boys and girls?

The first few cities on the tour went smoothly, and I was having a ball seeing all the sights and traveling. It was quite an education. Speaking of education, I also had my formal schooling correspondence courses to work on each day. I was very proud of myself. I got all A's while on my tour.

When we hit Rochester, New York, they got us with the child labor laws again. I couldn't go on. Tapping my foot in tempo was considered dancing, and the singing was "hard labor." Can you believe that? The authorities came backstage and made sure I didn't go on. The manager of the theater was heartsick. We had a full house, and the people were very disappointed. They tried to work out some sort of an agreement where the theater would pay a percentage to a children's hospital, but the authorities wouldn't budge. Si Wills, who was the second act on the bill, with his wife Joan Davis (who went on to become a big star), asked my father if we had any records of mine. My father said "yes." Si then went over to the authorities and asked them if I could go on stage and just move my mouth to the recording. They thought about that for about an hour, and finally said okay—but no toe-tapping!

They got a phonograph (actually a Victrola), put it on the stage, and Si went out and told the audience what had happened with the law. "You'll see her," he said, "and she'll be singing her records." They all applauded. He introduced me. I went on and lip-synced about four of my records, and it all went over just fine. Another first! I did the first record/pantomime act.

After Rochester, I went to Syracuse, Columbus, Philadelphia and Pittsburgh, where I played the Stanley Theater with Dick Powell, the year-round MC. I would do my act, then Dick would call me back and we would do a duet. I sat on his lap and sang "You Don't Know What You're Doing." It was a cute song, during which I would mess up his hair and say, "What do you do with the sardines?" (His hair was oily.) It got a big laugh, believe it or not.

One afternoon I was doing the number with Dick on the extended stage, in front of the regular stage. I guess the spotlight was very strong. I lost my balance and fell into the orchestra pit where the organist, who was watching the show, caught me and lifted me back up onto the stage. I was crying.

Dick asked, "Do you want to go off?"

I said, "No, we'll finish the song."

We did and I ran off…with a broken arm.

Small world department: Many years later, while in Hawaii promoting a telethon, I was doing some radio interviews when one of the listeners called in and said, "Do you remember falling off a stage in Pittsburgh? I was the one who caught you, lo those many years ago."

The next big spot was Cleveland. My father was arrested 127 times. Child labor laws again.

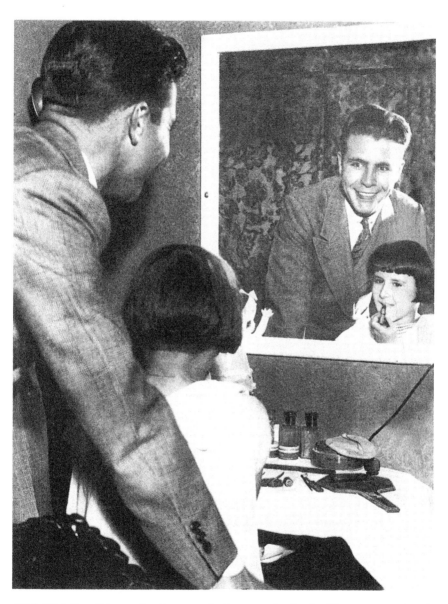

With Dick Powell in my dressing room backstage at the Stanley Theatre in Pittsburgh

Chapter Three

Springtime in the Rockies

I had arrived for my engagement at the Palace Theater and the law said they wouldn't let me go on. It was funny, because Mitzi Green, the great performer and impressionist who also had made some movies, was about thirteen years old when she was working at the 105th Street Theater in another part of Cleveland. Mitzi and I became very good friends and remained so until the day she passed away. The management asked why Mitzi could perform and I couldn't. The law said she did impressions; she didn't sing and dance. So here we went again! The management tried, just as they had at the theater in Rochester, to work out some sort of arrangement whereby a children's hospital and/or local orphanages would get some financial aid as a result of our shows. I thought, from what little I heard and understood about this discussion, it was a pretty nice idea. The authorities would have none of it. Instead they decided they would arrest my father after each show. Nice people, eh?

Frankly, it was a little scary to me, but nevertheless, I would do my show and immediately after I took my last bow, they would take my father downtown, arrest him, let him go, and he would come back to the theater. I would do my next show—they'd arrest him and let him go again. This went on seven days a week for the two weeks I was there. In addition to arresting my father, the authorities thought it would be a good idea for me to visit the children in the hospital and the orphanages. Perhaps they thought that the people of Cleveland would view the constant arrests of my father less harshly. I loved these visits because it gave me a chance to spend a little time with children, but more importantly,

it made me realize how lucky I really was. At least I had a mother and father and I was healthy.

I was still doing my radio show on Sunday mornings from each town in which I played. We'd go to the radio station—NBC would send some kind of script to go by, we'd rehearse, and I would do the show at 12:15. Immediately afterward, I would go back to the theater and do my shows. I think at this point I was doing six shows a day. Sounds like a lot, I know, but I didn't mind because I learned so much from the other acts. Being the only child in the show, the rest of the cast members thought I should have playtime in between shows. Sometimes we all played games together, but the most fun for me was learning all of their crafts. The juggler taught me how to juggle; I learned how to jump on a trampoline, walk on a gigantic wooden ball, and do all of the wonderful tricks with a yo-yo.

Years later when my daughter got a yo-yo—I think she was seven—I

HAVE YOU EVER BEEN LONELY

(HAVE YOU EVER BEEN BLUE)

WORDS BY
GEORGE BROWN

MUSIC BY
PETER DE ROSE

Baby ROSE MARIE

Shapiro Bernstein & Co. MUSIC PUBLISHERS Capitol Theatre Building 1 Broadway & 51st Street New York.

showed her all the tricks. She stood there, eyes wide as saucers, mouth open, and said, "Gee mother, where did you learn how to do that?"

I told her, "I worked with some very talented and wonderful people when I was six and a half years old, and they taught me all these things."

There was a great act called "Panzy the Horse," which consisted of two guys in a horse costume. One was the head of the horse; the other was the back end of the horse. They were the Mayo Brothers. They had a girl with them, dressed as a ringmaster. She had long legs, blonde hair, a short skirt, a tall hat, and a whip. She was beautiful. She would put "the horse" through its paces: Sit up, fall down, and roll over. Very funny and very clever. It was what we used to call in vaudeville a "number-two act," meaning a novelty act.

One night Sam Goldwyn came in to see the show. When it was over, he came backstage to see the girl in the horse act. He told her he would make her a star and wanted her to come to California.

She said, "What about the boys?"

He replied, "No, I don't want them, just you."

He asked her name and she said, "Virginia Rittinshroud."

"That's too long, it won't look good on the marquee," he said.

With that, she replied, "Okay, I'll take the boys' name."

And that's how she became Virginia Mayo. She did become a motion-picture star and appeared in quite a few movies with Danny Kaye and James Cagney (the best picture was *White Heat*). *White Heat* really showed Virginia to be not only beautiful, but also a damn good actress. She, of course, did many more movies and is now retired. She does a great deal of charity work, which keeps her busy.

Virginia and I live about a half hour away from each other and manage to see each other at least once or twice a month. We sometimes go to dinner together and attend various charity parties. And yes, dear readers, she is still as lovely as she always was.

Larry Rich was a variety-type act. There was an orchestra, a couple of acts, and three sisters called The Andrews Sisters! It was like a show within a show, and it was usually the finale of the stage show. The girls and I became good friends; even though they were a little older than I was, we spent a lot of time together. We got along beautifully, and they always looked out for me. I often went to their hotel room, where we would sit on the bed, talk, and eat sandwiches. They were like my sisters. We were on the road quite a bit, and I always spent time with them. When their first

The Andrews Sisters with some words of praise for me

big hit record came out, I was so proud of them; it was like it was my family. They made so many hit records and appeared in wonderful movies, which brought them to the height of their marvelous career.

Later in life, we'd all see one another here and there. La Verne, the eldest, died many years ago; Maxene only a few years ago. Patty, who is now retired, still looks the same. I see her and her husband, Wally Welscher, all the time. They are both animal lovers, as I am, and we attend a good many charitable events in connection with our four-legged friends. We always manage to sit together so we can talk and get caught up on everything that is going on. Patty, Wally, and I have become good friends, and she and I enjoy talking about the "good old days" of show business and vaudeville ... especially the difference of talent then and now!

My next stop on this tour was the Steel Pier in Atlantic City, with Georgie Jessel. We did such great business that the management took pictures and had them made into postcards, which are still selling today.

With George Burns and Gracie Allen

During the tour, someone had a wonderful promotional idea: There would be a Baby Rose Marie contest on Saturday mornings in each of the theaters at which I appeared. It didn't take too long for me to decide this was one of the few things that I didn't like. As a matter of fact, it was just awful. Every so-called talented child in each town (and I cannot think of even one parent in any town who doesn't think his or her child has an overabundance of talent) sang "Springtime in the Rockies." Believe me, if I never hear that song again, it will be too soon—and I'm being kind. In addition to the contest, they now had Baby Rose Marie clothes, hair bows, and dolls. I would go to the leading department store in each town, model the clothes, sign autographs, and have pictures taken. This part was fun for me. I enjoyed it.

I think now of all the money that was made and my poor mother

With Milton Berle, Palace Theatre, Chicago

who would maybe get one-quarter of it (the "other family" got the rest). My mother thought she was rich—even the little bit she got, she thought it was a fortune. Between gambling on everything and taking care of two families, I'm sure my father manipulated several hundred thousand dollars. Remember that there was no income tax at that time! This was only the beginning—I was only six and a half years old.

Next stop, Chicago. The Palace Theater with Milton Berle! We would work together quite a lot during my career. Milton was a genius. He taught me so much. He just didn't know how to express himself in a calm, normal way. He ranted and raved, but damn it, he was always right. When I was younger, I played the Steel Pier with Milton, and again we broke all records. Milton always kidded me. He used to say that he was the only man who saw me on the beach, in Atlantic City, in a bathing suit with no top! (Hey, I was six and a half years old!) Milton wrote some special material for my act from time to time. He was a great songwriter and wrote many hit songs. There's a lot of Milton throughout this book—and throughout my career. And no—I never slept with him!

Chapter Four

⤧

Baby Meets "Uncle Al" and the Boys

We arrived in Chicago for my engagement at the Palace Theater on a Saturday evening. Our first show was at 10:00 A.M. Sunday morning. Immediately after my first show, we had to go to the radio station for my NBC Sunday radio show at noon. My regular piano player, Jack Carrol, had not yet arrived from New York. We went up to the radio station office to tell them about Jack, and they told us not to worry. We could use the NBC Orchestra piano player who was there in Chicago. Great! His name? David Rose. Not too bad, huh? Little did I know then that he and his wife Betty would become good friends with my husband and me many years later in Hollywood. I would also work with David again when I did *The Red Skelton Show* and he was the musical conductor. Talk about a small world!

After we finished the radio show, my father and I went back to the Palace for my second show. When we got to the backstage door, there was a *big* black car in the alley. A man was leaning against the car. He came over and said very softly to my father, "Al's in the car—wants to talk to you."

My father went over to the car and I heard someone say from the back seat, "Hiya, Happy." (My father had the nickname "Happy Hank" with the boys in those days.)

My father said, "She's doing five shows a day and we only have about two and a half hours between shows."

The voice said, "We'll send a car to pick you up after the show, say four or five o'clock, have dinner, and we'll drive you back in time for the next show."

My father said, "Okay, Al, how about tomorrow?"

The voice said, "See you tomorrow, Happy."

I was standing by the backstage door listening to all of this. When the car drove away, I said, "Who was that?"

My father said, "A very good friend. We're gonna have dinner with him and his wife tomorrow."

I said, "What's his name?"

My father said, "Never mind, I'll tell you tomorrow."

The next day after the third show (which was called the supper show), it was about 5:00 P.M. I went to my dressing room, changed my clothes, met my father at the stage door, and we went outside. There it was—the big black car. I had never seen such a large car in my life. The guy was standing by the driver's side. He opened the door for us and we got in the backseat of the car. He drove for about thirty-five minutes to a place called Cicero, Illinois. The car stopped at a beautiful, big mansion-type house. We went in and there were about twenty or thirty people milling around (all Italian, may I add!).

A large, heavyset man with a long scar across the left side of his face came over, picked me up and said, "Hi, sweetheart, I'm your Uncle Al!"

Then this very nice lady with reddish-blonde hair came over. She was slight of build and very well dressed. She took me from "Uncle Al" and gave me a hug and a kiss and said, "Hello, Baby, I'm Mrs. C." (What? Not Aunt something?) She took me by the hand and started to introduce me to all the other people: Uncle Al's brother "Mimie," "Dutch," "Blackjack," and many other funny names. No one had a regular name like Joe, Sam or Fred! Oh, wait—there was a Louie.

The house was very large and ornate. Big lamps with fringe, overstuffed couches, large mirrors with wide, gold fancy frames, religious pictures on the walls, and figurines all over the place. I was afraid to move for fear of breaking one of them. We all walked into the dining room where I saw what must have been the longest dining table in the world! It sat about twenty-five people. The table was set with the most beautiful china and crystal I had ever seen. All the chairs matched the hand-carved table. No bridge chairs! It looked like the Last Supper—with the original cast!

Everyone was talking to me, saying how cute I was. They had all listened to my radio show and they were planning to see the show at the Palace Theater.

Uncle Al and Mrs. C. were seated next to me. I was in the middle, and my father was to the right of Mrs. C.

My father said, "We don't have too much time, Al—we've got two more shows to do."

With that, we all began eating one of the most elaborate dinners I can ever remember eating. Antipasto, macaroni, roast chicken, vegetables—God, what a feast!

As soon as we finished dinner, my father said, "Al, we have to go."

We got up from the table, said our thank-yous and good nights, and Uncle Al came to the door with us. He called out, "Dom, take them to the theater."

By now, Mrs. C. had come to the door. She gave me a kiss and a box of chocolates.

Uncle Al picked me up and gave me a kiss on the cheek and said to my father, "Happy, we gotta talk. We gotta protect the kid…She's one of us."

My father smiled and said, "Anytime, Al. Thanks for everything."

We left for the theater. When we got to my dressing room, I said, "Who is 'Uncle Al' and 'Mrs. C.'?"

He said, "Al Capone and his wife, and keep your mouth shut!"

That wasn't the only time we saw the Capones and had dinner with them. Uncle Al came to the theater one day, and he and my father spoke for about an hour. They came into my dressing room and talked.

Uncle Al said, "Ya gotta change the last name, Happy. It could lead to a lot of unnecessary trouble. Find an easy name to use. How about your uncle Dick Curley? That sounds like an easy name and no trouble with the 'other family.'" My father gulped a little. I guess he realized that Al and the boys knew the whole story.

So my father said, "Okay, we'll use Curley." Right then and there, we changed our last name to Curley.

We stayed in Chicago an extra day at the end of my engagement because Uncle Al and Mrs. C. wanted to throw a party for me … like a going-away party. This time "the boys" and their wives came. It was a beautiful party and of course I had to sing. Mrs. C. came over to me and gave me a little package. I opened it. It was a dinner ring, white gold with three little diamonds. I was absolutely thrilled.

"Uncle Al" came over, picked me up (he always did that, until I became too big to pick up), gave me a kiss and said, "If you ever need me for anything, tell your father to call me."

I said, "Okay."

He put me down and looked at my father and said, "Don't forget, Happy, she's one of us, so be careful. We will be keeping tabs on you."

Well, my father just about fell down. I could see he was a little scared. They shook hands and they drove us back to the hotel.

Chapter Five

✤

Hollywood—The First Time

After Chicago, we went to New Orleans to play the RKO Theater. It was August, so it was time for my seventh birthday. We opened the day after we arrived. Evidently Antoine's, one of the most famous restaurants in the world, read the rave reviews of the show and learned of my birthday. They invited my father and me to celebrate by having dinner there. What a night it was! The dinner they served us was simply out of this world. The pièce de résistance, however, was the special birthday cake they made for me. It had almost life-size white sugar doves all over it, some of them seemingly in flight. I will never forget that cake, or New Orleans, for that matter. I love that town in more ways than one.

On to Fort Worth, Texas, and a week at their RKO Theater. Shortly after our arrival, the governor called and invited my father and me to the capitol. In his office, Governor Lovejoy made me a Deputy Sheriff and presented me with a little pearl-handled gun...a real one! I still have it. Next stop, San Antonio, where I signed the guest book at the Alamo! Talk about an education, I had the best. I was there!

Then it was on to many other towns: St. Louis, Denver, Portland, Seattle—you name it, I played it. We landed in Los Angeles. I played the Paramount Theater in downtown L.A. Rube Wolfe was the permanent MC there. I did my act and a song with him, just like I did with Dick Powell. We were terrific.

While we were working in Los Angeles, my father decided we should stay an extra week or two and see about the possibility of a contract at one of the studios. So after the gig, we stayed at the Franklin Apartments on

With Jimmy Durante

Franklin Avenue in Hollywood. Every day we went to a different studio and tried to see the people we knew. At Paramount, we went to see Bing Crosby, who was very kind and cordial and that was about it. We went to Warner Bros. and saw Dick Powell. He was doing a scene in a boat. When he saw me, he jumped out of the boat and came over to give me a hug and a kiss. He was so glad to see us.

He asked my father if we were going to be in town for a while.

My father said, "No, unless something happens with one of the studios."

So Dick said, "The big *L.A. Examiner* benefit is in about two weeks and each studio goes on with their contract stars. I want her to go on with me, let her sing a song and we'll do the duet just like we did in Pittsburgh."

My father said, "Okay."

We stayed on for another two weeks. My mother thought it was time for me to come home, but since we decided to stay, she felt I should go to school while I was in Hollywood. There was a Professional Children's School like in New York called Miss Lawlor's Professional School. It was located just around the corner from where we were staying, so it was easy to get there. We went over and I was enrolled immediately. The next day I was in school with Mickey Rooney and Judy Garland, who were still known there as Joe Yule Jr. and Frances Gumm. We quickly became friends, and we had a lot of fun together. It was only later that Mickey and I became really good friends, and we still are to this day. Judy and I only saw each other a few times.

The benefit was coming and California was having a serious drought. My father decided I should sing "Rain (When Ya Gonna Rain Again)." It was a popular song of the day, and what a great way to use the song at the benefit. My piano player Jack Carrol went down to the Shrine Auditorium and rehearsed the band. We went down about seven o'clock. The show was at eight. We went backstage, where I had never seen so many movie stars in my whole life. All the big stars from MGM, Paramount, and Universal Studios were there.

I saw Jackie Cooper. We smiled and he came over to me and said, "Hi! I'm Jackie Cooper."

I said "Hi! I'm Baby Rose Marie."

He said, "I know, I listen to you on the radio."

My father went over to the stage manager or producer—I don't know which, but he looked like he was running the whole show—and said, "I'm here with Baby Rose Marie. She's going on with the Warner Bros. Studio's Dick Powell."

He said, "One song, that's it. We have no more time to spare."

My father said, "Fine."

We looked for Dick Powell. He finally came into the "green room"— every theater and TV show has one. It's the place where the acts go prior to going on stage. He saw us and said, "I'm going to introduce her."

"Fine," my father said.

We waited there until they called "Warner Bros. Studio up next."

Dick grabbed my hand and said, "Come on, honey."

We waited in the wings until they introduced him. He went on stage and sang two songs from his movies. He killed them. He then introduced me. I went on and belted out "Rain." The house came down, whistling, stomping—unbelievable.

I ran off the stage to the wings. My father was there and said, "Stay here."

"I gotta take my bow," I said.

The stage manager guy came over and said, "Get her out there."

My father said, "No, you said one song."

The guy said, "I've changed my mind, don't you hear that audience? Get her out there."

Finally Dick came over and grabbed my hand and we went on stage. He was wearing a white suit (I've never forgotten that) and we did our little silly song—the same one we did in Pittsburgh—and when I said, "What do you do with the sardines?" he fell flat on his back with that white suit!

We were a smash. When the number was over, I took many bows. Dick picked me up and kissed me and I ran off into the wings. Everybody started to grab me to take pictures.

Jackie Cooper came over and said, "You were wonderful."

"Thanks," I said.

He said, "They want some pictures of us."

I said, "Okay."

What a night! Everyone was talking to my father about me. Guys came up to him saying, "I'm from Paramount," "I'm from Universal," "Who's her agent?"

My father said, "I am her manager."

They all said, "Give us your number, we'll call you tomorrow." And they left.

Dick came over and said, "I'm going to talk to the people at Warner's and see what I can do."

My father said, "Thank you so much for everything."

It was getting late and everybody was leaving, so my father, Jack Carrol and I got my music and we left. We stopped for a bite to eat and went back to the hotel.

The next day, we were expecting all kinds of calls … and nothing happened. My father called the guy at Paramount.

The Paramount guy said, "There's nothing right now, but keep in touch."

He then called Universal … same thing: "Who's her agent? She should have an agent."

My father said, "I'm her manager."

"No, she needs a big agent. Call us when she's signed with someone."

Then Dick called and said he was sorry. He did everything he could, but they weren't interested in kids right now. He felt awful and asked, "How long are you going to be here?"

My father said, "I don't think we'll stay too long. We're running out of money, her mother is pregnant and wants her home for Christmas. It's been a long tour."

Dick said, "Call me before you leave and I'll keep trying."

My father thanked him and that was that.

Three days later we went back to Jersey and NBC had called. What a nice Christmas present!

Chapter Six

Tastyeast Is Tempting

We arrived back in New Jersey about a week before Christmas. It was good to see my mother again after such a long tour, and to see the house all decorated for the holidays. Christmas was always very important to my mother, and I know now that I inherited her love for this special time of the year—I especially love preparing for it. Today, no corner of my house goes undecorated. There have only been two times in my life that I have agreed to be away from home to work at Christmas.

NBC had been calling for about two weeks, and my mother said it was very important to return the call. My father called and was told that they had come up with another coast-to-coast radio show. Same time and day ... 12:15 Sunday afternoon for fifteen minutes. Just a piano player, an announcer, and me. This time the sponsor was Tastyeast, a nutritious candy bar intended to stimulate children's appetites. We didn't have the same kind of junk food then, and kids just didn't care about eating. The idea was that this candy bar would increase their appetite. At least it was a national product known and available over the entire country. Not like Julius Grossman Shoes, with the one store in New York. They felt I would be a walking example of how good this candy bar was, since I ate it, liked it, and was even gaining weight from eating it.

We moved again. This time to 729 Kingsland Avenue in Grantwood, New Jersey. It was close to New York City and NBC (five minutes to the George Washington Bridge and then thirty minutes into the city). Another double-decker. We lived on the bottom floor. My grandmother, God love her, kept after my mother about getting our own home, to have some-

With my radio sponsor, "Tastyeast"

thing solid. She believed in knowing where you're going to sleep every night and knowing where you'll sleep when you die. I remember her words, and when I got my own home, I immediately bought cemetery plots.

We started making preparations for my new NBC show. It was only January and the show wouldn't start until May. There was a lot to be done. My father called my old piano player Herbie Steiner and got Sammy Ward, a well-known writer of special material. We were getting the new songs from music publishers and picking the ones we liked. Sammy would change the lyrics to some of the songs. They were mostly love songs—he would make them "mother" songs so they didn't sound too grown-up for me to sing. Herbie and I would make a little arrangement for the songs. We went to Shapiro Bernstein Music Publishers, where we had some sort of half-assed office in which I rehearsed every day.

Now that I would be working at NBC and not traveling for a while,

BABY ROSE MARIE
WITH PETE THE DOG
COURTESY OF OUR GANG COMEDIES

BABY ROSE MARIE
Tastyeast Radio Star

ABY ROSE MARIE, popularly known as the Child Wonder of Song, was born on New York's lower east side August 15, 1924. Her off-the-radio name is Rose Marie Curley and her father, Frank Curley, was formerly on the stage, playing the banjo and dancing in vaudeville and in several of George M. Cohan's productions. Her mother is not a professional.

Her first public appearance was at the age of six months when she won first prize in a baby contest. Her first stage appearance was at the age of two years when she appeared in an amateur night performance at a neighborhood theatre and carried off premier honors. Baby Rose Marie still loves to sing the song she sang upon that occasion. It was "What Can I Say, Dear, After I Say I'm Sorry."

The little "starlet's" radio career began at the age of three, and entirely by accident. Her parents had taken her to Atlantic City and while laughing and singing with a group of children on the beach her voice attracted the attention of an official of one of the local broadcasting stations. The proud father and mother were induced to bring Rose Marie to the studio and her first broadcast was followed by a flood of letters and telegrams asking when she would sing again. At that tender age she knew the words and music of 72 songs.

From that time forward, her career on the radio, on the stage and, recently, in the "talkies" has been one of phenomenal success. She lately appeared with Peggy Hopkins Joyce and a galaxy of famous co-stars in "International House." Her repertoire has been increased to 200 songs for which special arrangements have been made in keeping with Baby Rose Marie's inimitable style and manner. Her favorite songs are "Got the World on a String" and "Baby Shoes."

As the little radio star stands on tip-toes before the microphone singing the songs that have thrilled millions of listeners, she presents an entrancing picture of a happy, healthy little girl who is having the time of her life singing the songs she loves just for the fun of doing it. A little tanned body is set on sturdy little legs, a cunning rounded face is framed by a Dutch bob of jet black hair, and the

Two-page mini-biography NBC sent to fans who wrote in about my weekly radio show

I was enrolled once again in Professional Children's School. My mother would pick me up at 2:00 P.M. We'd walk to Lindy's, the famous New York restaurant/delicatessen, to have lunch and then go to Shapiro Bernstein to rehearse. We'd go over many songs, always making sure the lyrics were suitable for me. This was pretty much my daily routine, unless something else came up—as it did with Paramount Studios.

Someone called from Paramount's New York office and said that "the coast" wanted to audition me for a part in a picture. Arrangements were made. We called Herbie to play for me, and both my parents came along with me. We went to Paramount's New York offices and were shown into one of the suites, which had been turned into a screening room and was also used for auditions.

I sang "If I Only Had a Five Cent Piece." ("Enough to buy a cup of coffee.... I'd drink water instead and go beggin' for bread, 'cuz I'd give the

loveliest of deep brown eyes twinkle with mischief and mer-
riment. She weighs 74 pounds, is 3 feet 6 inches in height
and virtually radiates health and well-being.

In the studio or at home Baby Rose Marie is best
described as a "regular kid"—no different from your own
fun-loving Mary or little Junior. Officials of a large broadcasting station recently learned this to their consternation.
The announcer had concluded his introduction, an eager
public awaited but Baby Rose Marie was nowhere to be
found. She had slipped off to play hide-and-seek with several children who had been invited to the broadcast. The
entire studio crew had to be enlisted in a serious playing
of the game before a little black head was found peeping
out from behind a heavy curtain that had been hung in
deaden sound.

Although the adulation of a little queen has been hers,
Baby Rose Marie is true to her first love, a teddy bear
which she takes to bed with her each night. She admits,
however, a growing partiality toward Jackie Cooper, with
whom she expects some day to appear in pictures.

Next to her teddy bear, Baby Rose Marie loves dolls.
The Curley home, now located in a New Jersey suburb, is
filled from top to bottom with them in various shapes, con-
ditions and sizes. In all, she has 300 dolls, many of which
were given to her by celebrities of the radio, stage and
screen. When she travels, she takes some of her dolls and
toys with her, just like any other little girl.

Despite Baby Rose Marie's busy little life, her professional work has not been allowed to interfere with her
schooling. She attends the Professional Children's School in
New York City and stands at the head of her class. Upon
her return from school she spends the rest of the afternoon,
when not rehearsing, playing with her baby brother, who is
just three years old, and with the children of the neighborhood. Rehearsals are directed by her father who proudly
states that Baby Rose Marie can memorize the words and
music of a new song in from five to ten minutes.

Baby Rose Marie's hobbies are those of any other normal, healthy child. She particularly likes swimming, roller
skating and bicycling. Despite the fact that she is radio's
highest paid juvenile, the little star is quite content with the
sensible allowance allotted her by her parents. Given a
dime to go shopping in a five-and-ten she is as happy as any
child in the world.

All in all, Baby Rose Marie is just a sweet, natural
little miss to whom singing over the radio is only another
game to be interspersed with rompings with her playmates
when school is out. A wonder child, indeed, but one who,
it is safe to say, will always remain lovable an unspoiled,
without any of the affectations of the precocious infant
protege.

nickel to you....") What a lyric! My mother was sitting in front of me, and
I suddenly thought of all the crap she had taken from my father, and how
mean he was to her. While I was singing, I started crying — which made it
only more dramatic. I was crying and loving my mother so much. The
tears ran down my face and wouldn't stop. I could have given Bernadette
Peters lessons.

Evidently it worked—not that it was exactly planned to turn out that
way. They decided I would be in this picture with W.C. Fields called *International House.* Get this: the picture was all about a new invention called
television! I had a cameo, along with Rudy Vallee and Bela Lugosi. The
film was to be directed by Brian Foy.

I thought, "Great, back to Hollywood." Unfortunately, it was a one-
day shoot on Long Island. The song I sang, "My Bluebird's Singing the
Blues," was written especially for me by Leo Robin and Ralph Ranger.

They used two pianos on the set (with the orchestra in back, of course). Herbie Steiner was on one piano and Ralph Ranger wanted to play the other piano. Ralph was thrilled with the way I sang. He said it was a hard song to sing, but he loved the way I sang it. I was so glad because I wasn't feeling too well that day, and I wasn't sure how I would sound. It must have been okay, because we did the scene in three takes and it was all over in about two and a half hours.

Between my movie debut and the start of my new NBC Radio job, I was kept busy doing shorts. Two with the bouncing ball (remember that?). I was the voice of Sally Swing in six Betty Boop cartoons. In the meantime, NBC was really going to make this new show a big hit. There was lots of publicity, new pictures, and guest shots. Mr. Schewing also decided that I should become a corporation. Not only because of the things associated with me like hair bows, dolls and dresses, but we now had a payroll. Herbie Steiner, Sam Ward, and a salary for my father. But not my mother: she was president of the corporation in name only; my father would give her a very small amount of money each week. NBC drew up the papers and, believe it or not, I signed the contract myself (my father had to sign it too, of course). So the Baby Rose Marie Corporation was formed. Big deal! I don't think we gained anything from it. Maybe my father did, but I don't remember my mother getting any of the windfall. By the way, I still have the logos!

My new radio show went on the air in May, as scheduled, and the mail started to pour in—more than ever before. The reviews were sensational. Everyone was happy, and we started to get the whole thing down to a routine. I even had time to make friends and play with the kids on the block. I began to wish for one special present for my birthday coming up in August. I wanted a big 26-inch red two-wheeler bike so I could ride up and down the street with the kids. Can you imagine how thrilled I was when Herbie, my piano player, gave me the exact bike I wanted for my birthday? Come to think of it, I don't think my father ever gave me a gift. I know my mother used to buy gifts out of the pittance she received from my father. She would have my father sign the gift cards. I saw him do it. I just don't remember him ever going out and actually buying me a gift.

I went to Atlantic City and appeared again at the Steel Pier with Milton Berle. I also went to Philadelphia and played the Earl Theater. I was able to play quite a few dates that were close to home and still manage to keep up the routine of school, the radio show, and time with my friends.

My grandmother kept harping on getting our own home. At least there would be some kind of equity in owning a house. She said to my mother, "She'll be getting a check every week. Try to save as much as you can, and let's go look for a house. The hell with what he says. Ask him for more money every week. I have a little money saved and I'll give it to you toward the house." My mother used to give my grandmother ten or twenty dollars every once in a while in case she wanted to buy something for herself—but she never did. If she wanted something, I would get it for her or my mother would.

They found the house in Palisades, New Jersey. It was about five minutes from where we were living, but in a grand section of Fort Lee. It was a Tudor two-story house. This time we lived on both floors! It was the second house from the corner on Claremont Road—the number was 63. It was truly beautiful and it was my mother's castle. We bought it from a man named Brenner. My mother also bought some of the drapes that were there and the dining room set, which was gorgeous. The house had Italian wrought-iron gates going from the living room into the dining room and going from the living room into the sun porch.

We later turned that room into a bar. Although we were never a drinking family—both my mother and father didn't drink, except for a glass of wine from time to time—we had a well-stocked bar for guests. I have the same thing now in my own home. I don't drink, but the bar is stocked for my friends.

My mother wanted a few other things that Mr. Brenner was selling: an eight-foot-tall mahogany grandfather clock from England and a three-piece mantel set with two urns and a clock, all in marble. The clock was said to be a gift that Flo Ziegfeld once gave to his longtime companion, the actress Anna Held. My mother *had* to have that.

All in all, it was a beautiful, solid house. My mother decorated it in the French period. Her taste has always been exquisite—remember the polka-dot coat? So we finally had our house. A small down payment and a *big* mortgage. It was worth it and it was ours. My mother felt like a queen in her castle, and my grandmother was the happiest she had been in years. If nothing else, we had a permanent roof over our heads.

The Tastyeast program lasted for three years, and again I did some tours in RKO theaters. By now I was eleven years old and had quit school. Little did I know that I would be going to school again in New Jersey at the Epiphany Parochial School. My brother had started school, and my mother wanted to have the two of us going to Catholic school. It was about eight blocks from our new home, so we walked to school every day. I was put into the seventh grade and Sister Alice Rita would be my teacher. She was also head of the choir, and I got to sing "Mother of Christ" every Sunday. She promised my mother my lessons would be sent to me if I ever went on the road so that I could keep up with the class. Sister Alice Rita discussed this at length with Father Banks, the head priest of the school, and he okayed the arrangement.

Every one of the kids looked at me like I was something odd. Sister Alice Rita made such a fuss over me. I guess she looked at me as a breath of fresh air in an otherwise dull routine. I had no idea of the discipline in a Catholic school. I was my usual clowning self. Most of the time, I would forget to raise my hand to answer questions. I would just speak out loud. She would smile, but always remind me I had to end my sentence with the word "Sister." ("Yes, Sister." "No, Sister.") I had learned how to print in Professional Children's School. These kids only knew the Palmer method of writing. Not only did I have to learn how to write; I was the only one who could *print* all of the homework assignments on the blackboard. This was my first clue to the difference in the teaching methods between both schools.

My first day was awful. I didn't know if I was ahead or behind my classmates. I was very quiet in catechism class that first day; mostly I listened. Then came our homework for that day. We had to learn the Divine Praises. It was cinch for me to memorize. I couldn't wait to get to school the next day to rattle them off. Sister Alice Rita was thrilled and told the class, "See, that's how you do your homework." The kids now hated me for the second day in a row.

A couple of months after I began school, Sister Alice Rita realized that my schooling at Professional Children's School was more advanced than she had originally thought, and that it would be more appropriate for me to be in the eighth grade. Of course, in time I got along with the other kids. There are still two or three with whom I correspond to this day. Sister Alice Rita and I remained dear friends until the day she died. Whenever I was on the road, in later years, and I traveled near New Jersey, I'd go and visit her.

I guess you could say I was quite a promoter—the kids loved my ideas. I became like the Pied Piper of Epiphany. I put on a play in the church hall. I got all the kids who were interested to help with the

Baby Rose Marie at the end of an era—about to
leave the "Baby" behind

playwriting, and whoever wanted to act got parts. I did the lighting, chore-
ography and directing. Not bad for a twelve-year-old! My next project was
a bazaar. The church needed money—don't they always?

Well, dear readers, this was a bazaar to end all bazaars. We raised
$506, a tidy sum in those days. When I first got the idea to do this, I told
Father Banks to announce the event at every Mass. I guess I must have
sounded very authoritative, because he agreed.

This bazaar didn't cost the church a single penny. I promoted everything. I went up to the attic in my house and took my mother's crystal and
sold it for ten cents each. You can just imagine my mother's reaction when
she found out. I told the kids to bring whatever they could from their
houses (with the approval of their parents, of course). I had a friend who
owned a candy store, and we got all the Coca-Cola we wanted. All of the

mothers were assigned tasks. One made lemonade, one made popcorn, and three or four made muffins and cookies. Mrs. Sheffield made several of her famous cakes. We set up booths and made up games to play. The prizes were plush toys. Sammy Ward gave me the money to buy these toys. Herbie Steiner supplied the dolls. Even the makers of the Baby Rose Marie dolls gave some of them to us for our event.

We then participated in a Catholic Youth Organization (CYO) radio competition, which I got my friend Norma Cuny to write. She didn't even go to my school. Once again, I was the director. We used about fifteen kids from my class as our actors. We did our show—a variety-type show with a serious playlet at the end—on a local station and won the competition. They have the trophy to this day in the church hall.

I graduated from Epiphany. My diploma is still there. I never picked it up. I decided to give up school again. I had no time for it. I was doing a fifteen-minute program on NBC three nights a week with a big orchestra. That too fell by the wayside after a few months. I was now at that awkward stage. Twelve years old. In between. Too young to be a grown-up, too old to be a child. We changed Baby Rose Marie to Miss Rose Marie and I started playing what were known as roadhouses in New England. It was the beginning of the lean years.

Chapter Seven

❧

From Baby to Miss Rose Marie

Don't misunderstand me, the roadhouses I worked were like country inns. They were geared toward families—with or without kids. They had a dining room, a bar, and a dance floor with a twelve-piece orchestra. Families could enjoy dinner and see a good, clean show with chorus girls in very pretty costumes, as well as a comic, a dance team, and a singer. Guess what? I was the singer. My wardrobe was a nice street dress and those damn Mary Jane shoes. I wore Mary Jane's until I was fifteen.

I couldn't find the right clothes for the stage that would be appropriate for me at my age. Thank God for Deanna Durbin. She was fifteen or sixteen and in the movies. The studio made some beautiful, youthful evening gowns for her. Lord and Taylor in New York had copies of those dresses. I opened a charge account there and got three of them. It is still my favorite place to shop. I wore those dresses until I was sixteen. So I was able to get clothes that were right for me.

Kids in those days had a rough time going from twelve to sixteen years old. There were no "in-between" clothes or shoes like kids have today. It was Mary Jane flats, Red Cross shoes, or high heels. The dresses were either too young-looking or too old-looking. Today, kids wear all kinds of nutty clothes. You don't know if they're twelve years old or thirty.

I worked in Fall River and New Bedford, Massachusetts, towns like that. It was a rough three years, but I worked wherever I could. It was the best experience I could get. It was a completely new and different way for me to work. I wasn't cute Baby Rose Marie anymore. I had to go out and develop a new style of working and singing, and I had to get used to a nightclub type of act. I have found, through the years, that you work differently in each medium. Each has its own style and rules. You work one way in TV, another way in the movies, another for legitimate theater, and still another (perhaps the hardest) way in nightclubs.

I remember one particular thing while working those roadhouse dates. I think it's the reason I don't drink. My father and I were sitting at a table in the back of the dining room—there's always one table in the back where you can sit in between shows. There was a big commotion going on by the bar, which was on the other side of the room. A drunken lady was making a lot of noise. Two men were with her. They were all over her, touching her here and there, laughing and making fools of themselves. My father said, "See that woman over there? She's drunk and the two guys are taking advantage of her. They'll probably ruin her for the rest of her life, all because she's drunk and doesn't know what she's doing." *My God*, I thought, *Ruin her for the rest of her life?* I thought about her not being able to have children....They could give her a disease and she would die....Oh, how terrible! I must say, I think that really did it for me. No drinking! I've got to know what I'm doing at all times. Besides, I didn't like the taste of booze.

Things were really getting rough. It was hard to get any theater dates. Vaudeville was dead, so I did club dates, one-nighters, and parties. I worked the Borscht Belt, which I truly hated, even though it paid pretty well. I played all the hotels in the circuit; Grossingers, the Concord, the Grand Hotel, Laurel in the Pines. You name the hotel, I played it.

I also worked in Newark at a theater where they put on a show every week. Jackie Gleason was the MC. We became very good friends and he's very special in my heart. More about Jackie later.

There were a few times when I didn't work for weeks at a time. The mortgage was overdue. One of the club date agents, Abby Greshler, would cancel an act and put me in, just so we'd have some money. I'll never forget his kindness to me.

Finally, it got desperate and my father went to "the boys" for help. We still lived in Palisades, New Jersey, about a mile away from the Palisades amusement park, which isn't there anymore. It's now all high-rise buildings. Across the street from the park was a pizza place and bar. It was a small place, but it was where all "the boys" from New York and New Jersey hung out. For some reason, Jersey was a great place for all that.

My father went to Tommy Brown (also known as "Three Fingers" Brown and "Tom Luchese") and asked him for a loan. He gave it to my father with the promise that we'd pay it back as soon as I started working. At least now the mortgage was paid up. I suddenly got a few good dates: Providence, New Haven, and a three-day date at a theater in Boston. Things were getting a little better, thank God. Of course, the first thing we did was pay off the loan. You just don't mess around with stuff like that. God bless those guys. They were very good to me and helped us out in more ways than one.

I was not yet fourteen. Richard Rodgers and Lorenz Hart were doing a new show called *Babes in Arms*. Richard Rodgers called the house and my brother answered.

The voice said, "Hello, is Rose Marie there? This is Richard Rodgers."

My brother Frank said, "Yeah, and I'm Napoleon," and hung up.

Frank started to laugh and told me, "Someone is playing a joke. He said he was Richard Rodgers.

I said, "Who would play a joke like that?"

With that, the phone rang again. This time I answered it. The voice said, "Listen, I'm not kidding. This is Richard Rodgers and I want to talk to Baby Rose Marie about a part in a new Broadway show."

I almost died. I said, "This is Rose Marie. Hello, Mr. Rodgers."

He said, "I guess whoever answered the phone thought this was a joke. You must have some strange friends."

He then went on to tell me about his new show and that they had written a part called Baby Rose Marie especially for me. I couldn't talk. I was so thrilled.

He said, "Can you meet us tomorrow for lunch and we'll tell you all about it?"

Well, being the shy girl that I am, I said, "I can make it today."

He replied, "No, tomorrow will be fine. 12:30 at Sardi's." Sardi's! Oh my God! The hangout of all the stars on Broadway!

I told my mother that I wanted to go alone. If any deals were to be made, my father could come later.

I couldn't sleep that night. Did they want me to sing for them? What? Sing at Sardi's? Nah. What should I wear? God! I was scared stiff. This could be the big, big break. Broadway! Wow!

Chapter Eight

❧

Sweet Sixteen...or Eighteen?

The next day I took the bus to New York. As I told you, we lived five minutes from the George Washington Bridge and the bus took me right into the city. I walked a few blocks to Sardi's and went inside. Naturally, they were at a front table, Mr. Rodgers and Mr. Hart. I tried to act cool. I said hello and sat down. They introduced themselves—as if I didn't know!

I said, "What can I do for you gentlemen?" Boy, that's really clever.

Mr. Rodgers did the talking. He told me about the show, my part and the songs I would sing. I couldn't believe what I was hearing. Special billing, everything.

I said, "I would love to do it!"

They said, "Fine."

I told them my father was my manager and they would have to talk to him about the money.

They said, "Fine."

We had lunch and I was dizzy with happiness. I couldn't believe it. A Rodgers and Hart show! A starring part on Broadway! This was it! I went home and told my mother. I started to cry. My father was not home. He never was during the day and sometimes he wasn't there at night either. I didn't care. Nothing could spoil my happiness.

The next day, my father came home around 4:00 P.M. I told him about the show. He showed no emotion at all. He just said, "Good, I'll talk to them." Mr. Rodgers called and I heard my father make an appointment to meet with them. He went into New York the next day and came home around 6:00 P.M.

Miss Rose Marie at sweet sixteen

He said, "It's all off. The Gerry Society won't let you do it. You're fourteen, ya gotta be sixteen to work in New York."

I said, "No, I can't lose that show because I'm fourteen! Damn, damn, damn!" But it was no use. They couldn't work anything out. The part went to another girl and they called her Baby Rosalie. Sounds close, but no cigar. They did the same in the movie too! Damn, damn, damn.

I hit fifteen and the people at the Roxy Theater called. They wanted me to do my act, plus work with a bunch of kids dancing the Big Apple—

the dance craze of the day. Okay...the Roxy Theater...not bad...four weeks...*almost* Broadway. (It was 7th Avenue—one street over.)

I had made up my mind not to lose it. I had signed with the theatrical agency Music Corporation of America (or MCA). Joe Sully and Bill Loeb were the agents taking care of me. I went up to see them and I told them that I didn't want to lose the Roxy gig, but that we might have trouble with the child labor law. I told them to say I was seventeen and push my birthday up two years. There was no way I was going to lose that date. So the contracts were signed and I played the date. It was wonderful. An honest-to-God theater again. We did four shows a day, five on Saturday and Sunday.

My real sixteenth birthday was coming up. My mother decided to have a big party for me at the Glen Island Casino in New Rochelle, New York. Glenn Miller was playing there. It was my favorite orchestra. My mother said I could have sixteen couples—formal. Well, my dears....It was to die!

I had made a lot of friends in Palisades, even though we didn't go to the same school. I had spent a great deal of time with them when I was home and I went to many of their school functions. It was hard to choose just sixteen people from my group of friends. For sure Dottie Schoenenbaum, who lived down the street and was my best friend. We still keep in touch. She just *had* to be there. We planned everything. The best part was that we got to invite the guys *we* wanted.

We went shopping for gowns....Deanna Durbin time again. Of course, it was a little more grown-up this time. We told the boys what kind of flowers to get us—wrist corsages, of course. I even called my friend Jean Okun (her nickname was "Petey"). I was really disappointed that she couldn't come to the party. I asked her if I could wear her white fox jacket. She said, "Sure." I'll never forget the feeling of that white fox jacket.

I was really excited about the party. It was going to be wonderful...until my father decided to make it a big publicity stunt. He notified all the newspapers and he sent me about thirty telegrams from different stars—to make it look like they had all remembered my birthday!

Earlier in the day, WMCA threw a big birthday party—on the air! They read all the telegrams and some local celebrities sang and said a few words.

After the show, I went home and got dressed for the big affair. I wore a pink off-the-shoulder dress with satin high heels dyed to match—and

Petey's white fox jacket. Growing up was kind of nice! Dottie came over with her date and they brought Frank Ciarleglio, my date. Nice boy. After the boys gave us our corsages, we got into the car and drove to the casino. They had set up a big table for us covered with flowers, right in front of the Glenn Miller Orchestra. One of the new, young, handsome, "hot" singers of the day was there; his name was Tony Martin. He came over to wish me a happy birthday and danced three dances with me! Glenn Miller announced my birthday and they all sang "Happy Birthday." It was thrilling for a sixteen-year-old.

Toward the end of the evening, a boy came over to me and introduced himself. His name was Chadwick Garoni, and he had come to the party with Helen Peterson.

He said, "You know my uncle, Al Pianodosi."

I said, "Oh yes."

He said, "My mother is his sister."

I said, "That's nice."

He asked, "May I call you?"

I said, "Sure."

I gave him my phone number. I didn't think anything about it, but the next day he called and asked for a date for Saturday night. I said, "Okay, we'll go to a movie and have pizza."

Saturday night arrived. When I let him in, he went to my mother and father (who was home that night) and asked them if he could take me out.

My mother said, "Fine, but she's to be home by twelve midnight."

My father said, "No later than twelve midnight, understand?"

So Chaddy and I went out on our first date (I always called him "Chaddy"). We had a delightful time and started going out together. We went out for about a year. He even taught me to drive a car. No, no sex! I guess it was sort of understood we would get married some day.

The war started, Chaddy was drafted and stationed in Chicago. We'd call one another from time to time. I saw a lot of his mother and father. They were wonderful to me. I was still doing gigs here and there. I went to Boston to play the Bradford Hotel roof. The owner, Ralph Snider, said he wanted me to meet his daughter. I said I would love to. I was thinking, *What do I want with that? A rich kid whose father owned the hotel I was working.* Then I met her. Her name was Ruth. I guess we were about the same age. We hit it off immediately and became so close that we were like sisters. I went to her wedding when she married Irving Shapiro. She had two little girls and is now a grandmother. We never lost the closeness. We would talk to one another almost every week, and whenever I play Boston, Ruthie is there with me. She loves showbiz and now handles a very talented comedienne, Bobbi Baker, who has also become a good friend.

I played the Bradford Hotel many times and during one of those times, I was awakened at 8:00 A.M. by a phone call. It was a shock to hear the phone ring at that hour since I am a late sleeper. It was Chaddy's mother…and she was crying. I thought, *My God, something has happened.* It had, all right.

His mother said, in between sobs, that Chaddy had met a girl and that they were going to get married. Talk about a shock.

I said, "What do you want me to do?"

She said, "Call him and talk some sense into him. Tell him to get an emergency furlough."

I called and tried to reach him in Chicago. He wasn't there, so I left a message. He called me about 7:00 P.M., just as I was getting ready to do the show.

I said, "Your mother called, what's going on?"

He said, "My wife just had an abortion."

I said, "Fine. The only good thing about it is she didn't bring another bastard like you into this world," and hung up.

I don't know how I did the shows that night, but I did. I cried for two days. Ruthie was with me the whole time, and she kept reminding me that "everything happens for the best."

I said, "Oh, sure."

Little did I know how right she was. Chaddy and his wife always come to see me whenever I'm playing in their vicinity. In fact, we still exchange Christmas cards. I'm glad we remained friends.

I was now seventeen years old. MCA got me my first real nightclub date. It was at the Versailles in New York City. Carl Brisson was the star. He sang—nice accent, but no act! I opened for him and was a smash… new nose, new pictures, new gowns, and good arrangements. It was a great date for me. MCA really kept me busy.

The Martinique, also in New York, with Zero Mostel followed. While I was there, Joey Jacobson, who ran the Chez Paree in Chicago, came to see the show. He came over to talk to me after the show to tell me he wanted me to play the Chez Paree. The Chez was one of the best places to play. If you played there, you were set as far as the nightclub circuit was concerned. He wanted me to play with Joe E. Lewis for sixteen weeks. He doubled the salary I was making at the Martinique. (I knew my salary, but I never saw the money. My father always got the check.) Great! Wonderful!

Except I was to open December 16th. I said, "I don't want to be away for Christmas. It's very important to me. Besides, sixteen weeks is a long time."

He offered, "Bring your mother with you. I'll pay for it."

I said, "My father travels with me."

He said, "Fine, bring him too."

"What about my dog, Snowball?"

"Him too," he said.

I knew it was the right thing to do as far as my career was concerned, but I hated the thought of being away for Christmas. That's where that famous piece of advice comes in handy: "You can always put a Christmas tree in the hotel room."

Ruthie Shapiro was in town and came down to see the midnight show. After the show, I told her how upset I was, but I knew it was the best thing to do.

She agreed with me and said, "The Bernard Brothers are playing at the Park Central Hotel, let's go see them."

I said, "Okay....I think I'll get drunk." She laughed and we walked up 57th Street to the Park Central. We saw the Bernard Brothers and said hello. I ordered a scotch and soda. Ruthie almost died.

I said, "I want four of 'em."

Ruthie said, "You don't drink.... You don't like the stuff."

I said, "Tonight is different."

I proceeded to get drunk.

Ruthie said, "We've got to get back to the Martinique. You have a 2:20 A.M. show. Oh my God, your father is going to kill me *and you*."

So we left and walked back to the Martinique, went into the dressing room. I started to throw up...in a champagne bucket, no less. I was never so sick in my life. Ruthie took her lynx jacket, rolled it into a ball behind my head, and I fell asleep. The show was about forty minutes away. Ruthie did everything she could do to sober me up. My father came around and knocked on the door.

I said, "I'm fine."

He went away. I did the show that night and Ruthie swears she doesn't know how I did it. Me neither! But I do know it's another reason for me not to drink.

I played the Chez Paree. It was a wonderful date and I played it many more times after that! "The boys" ran the Chez and they took very good care of me. I'd sit with them between shows, and always the same questions:

"Ya wanna drink?"

"Want something to eat?"

"Everything okay?"

"Got any problem?"

I'd always say, "I'm fine, thank you."

My next date was the Loews State Theater in New York and then the Ohio Villa in Cleveland, where we met the rest of "the boys": "Doc" Magine, Jerry Mallone, "Black Jack"—from the Cleveland Mob. How wonderful they were to me! Big parties in the club every night. I met their wives, ate in their homes. In fact, after this date, they came to our house in Jersey, bringing all kinds of wines, meat and butter, which were rationed at that time. We had steaks three inches thick!

Then I went to Detroit and played the Bowery. Another A-1 place. "The boys" all came down to Detroit and it was Cleveland all over again! They couldn't do enough for us. It was great to have them around because everybody knew not to mess with them.

Back to New York to play the Martinique again. Danny Thomas was the star and I opened for him. He was the hottest thing to come out of Chicago, from the 5100 Club. Everybody was raving about him and everyone was waiting to see the new hot comic out of Chicago. Danny was a smash. His style was different, something new. All the Mob guys were there—Frank Garbo, Tommy Brown, all "the boys" from Chicago.

My mother was sitting in front of Frankie Garbo, who was drunk and making lots of noise. My mother said, "Be quiet, there's a show going on." He laughed out loud and continued to be very boisterous. My mother started to say something again and Tommy Brown said to my mother, "Leave it to me, I'll quiet him down." He said something to him and Garbo never uttered another sound. God only knows what he told him!

Danny was the big hit of New York. His wife, Rosemarie (I call her the "other Rose Marie") and I sat at the back table in the club. One night Danny went out between shows. His wife and I had a cup of tea together. Danny came in all starry-eyed. I asked if he was all right.

He said, "I just did a benefit."

"Big deal, you did a benefit," I said.

"Yes, but it was at the Winter Garden Theater," he said. "Jolson sang on that stage. You know what I did? I bent down and kissed the stage. It was one of the biggest thrills of my life."

I said, "I hope you never lose that feeling."

We became good friends throughout the years and worked together quite a bit. We became like family. Danny went on to become one of the giants of our biz...and I don't think he ever did lose that wonderful feeling.

Life is funny. Little did I know I would be working for his corporation with *The Dick Van Dyke Show*!

Chapter Nine

❧

The Love of My Life

I always wondered who I would marry. Had I met him? Do I know him? Had I seen him? I found out I had seen him—many times—but I hadn't met him...*yet.*

My father and mother took me to openings and premieres quite often. One of the places we went was the Pennsylvania Hotel to see Kay Kyser. He had a radio show broadcast from there and he also played for the dancing. The radio show consisted of the Kollege of Musical Knowledge. They would ask musical questions and the winner would get a bottle of wine. Whenever there were celebrities in the room, he would call them up to play the game. It was fun to do and it went out coast-to-coast on the radio. It was good for Kyser because a lot of celebrities would come down to be seen and maybe get on the radio show. We would go down quite often and he always called me up to do the show.

I was to open at the Capitol Theater on Broadway and 51st Street for four weeks, with Mark Warnow and his Lucky Strike Orchestra and Ethel Smith, the organist from the MGM musicals. But first I needed some new gowns. After all, it *was* the Capitol Theater on Broadway. I found a great designer, Baron Max Von Waldeck. He had made some beautiful costumes for some of the acts and dance teams I worked with in Chicago. I got his name and number and went to see him. He was adorable, with the accent and all....about forty, bald, and sort of pudgy. I loved him. I ordered three gowns, a blue one, a white one, and a pink one. I must say they were the most beautiful gowns I have ever seen or owned. Goodbye, Deanna Durbin! I also had to have new arrangements because the

Mark Warnow Orchestra was big—it had thirty men. I wanted to be sure everything was right.

I'd been booked at Frank Daily's Terrace Room, in Newark, New Jersey, with Mal Hallet's Orchestra for two weeks right before the Capitol. It was sort of a break-in date. I opened on May 18. I remember the date because two years later, my daughter was born on May 18.

Frank Daily owned two nightclubs in New Jersey. The Terrace Room, where I was working, was the winter place. The Meadowbrook was world-famous—it was the summer place where the big bands played (Tommy and Jimmy Dorsey, Glenn Miller, and so on). Opening night at the Terrace Room went very well for me. Mal Hallet's Orchestra was okay. They were all kids because all the top musicians were in the army.

As I walked toward my dressing room to change, I had to pass the service bar, and the bartender Rudy said, "Great show, honey."

I thanked him.

"The gowns are too classy for this room," he laughed and said, "Get changed, I'll have your cup of tea waiting."

I went downstairs, changed, and went back up to Rudy. He had my tea. I sat on a stool at the end of the bar and started to drink, when this soldier came up to me and said, "You were great. My name is Bobby Guy and I'm from Trenton. You have relatives there, don't you?"

I said, "Yes, my father's cousin is the coroner, Joe Guiraro."

"May I sit down?" he asked.

"Sure. Would you like a drink?"

He said, "Fine."

He then proceeded to tell me he was in Kay Kyser's Orchestra before the war—that was how he knew Rudy, the bartender. The Kyser Band played the Meadowbrook many times. During the summer, Rudy worked at the Meadowbrook; during the winter, he was at the Terrace Room.

Kay Kyser! So I had seen him—every time I went to the Pennsylvania Hotel, he was there and I didn't know it! He was very nice, not too heavy—about 180 pounds, five feet eleven inches tall, adorable face, sparkling eyes that were a purplish color with a navy blue rim around the iris, a great smile, and a terrific laugh.

Rudy came over and said, "Did you meet one another?"

I said, "Yes, he's from Trenton and my father has a cousin there."

Rudy said, "Want another cup of tea? I know Bobby doesn't drink."

Well, I thought, *that's nice.* Bobby and I started talking. He'd been in the army about two and a half years and was stationed at Camp Shanks in upstate New York. He was in the band that played for the boys when they got shipped overseas, as well as for the groups returning home once their European duty was over. In addition to the band playing for the boys, Bobby said they would also do shows when there was a large group of guys being shipped out.

He asked me if I would come up and do a show sometime: "The band is the greatest, all top men from the Big Bands."

I said that I would love to, but I didn't know when. He told me that he had been best man at Mickey Rooney's second wedding (to Betty Jane Rase, Miss Alabama of 1944). He told me all about Mickey in the army when they were stationed together at Camp Siebert in Alabama, and how Mickey would think of wonderful things to do to keep up the spirits of the guys. We've all heard how much fun boot camp can be, right?

They were great buddies. As a matter of fact, Bobby got the marriage license, bought the rings and so on, so nobody would think it was Mickey who was getting married. Bobby spoke with real affection about Mickey and was very impressed with the fact that Mickey would call his mother every day from camp.

I asked Bobby what he was doing at the Terrace Room. He told me that Joe Schribman and Joe Gaukin had an apartment on 57th Street and that all the guys in the band from Camp Shanks hung out there. It was a place to meet or stay when they had days off. Schribman had booked Mal Hallet into the Terrace Room. They had two radio shows a night, and Schribman asked Bobby if he wanted to make seventy-five dollars for the week. Well, of course he said yes. So he came down to play the two radio shows as the first trumpet player. First trumpet is usually called the "sergeant" of the orchestra.

We continued talking, and I told him I was opening at the Capitol Theater in a few weeks and had new gowns and new arrangements. He told me that he had enjoyed my first show.

Just then Rudy came over and said to Bobby, "The band goes on the air in ten minutes."

Bobby said, "Thanks, Rudy." Then he turned to me and said, "I'll see you later."

I sat there and listened to the radio show. He played very well, had a great sound and played the ballads with a lot of heart. I thought to myself, he's good—Kay Kyser or not—he's very good.

He came back and sat next to me and I said, "That was great. Now I have to do my second show."

He said he would watch it again. "Maybe we can have another cup of tea before you go home."

I smiled and said, "Okay."

I went to my dressing room, changed my clothes, did the second show and changed into my street clothes. I ran upstairs to see if he had waited. He was there.

We had a cup of tea and he said, "I'll be here all week to do the radio shows."

"Wonderful," I said,

"I'll see you tomorrow."

With that I got up and left.

On the way home, all kinds of thoughts came into my mind. *He's awfully nice…a great smile and really great to talk to…and a very good musician. He's really adorable.* The next night, he did the radio shows and I did my two shows. In between shows, we talked and talked. He lived in California and was going back after he was discharged. His horns and clothes were in California. He told me about the movies he had made with Kyser. He had been with the band since he was seventeen. He was now twenty-eight, and he was sure that he would get his job back with Kay. I told him about being in showbiz since I was three, doing the theaters across the country and that I was looking forward to playing the Capitol Theater. We had our cup of tea and then I went home.

The next day, I got a telegram on the phone:

CAUGHT YOUR ACT AT THE TERRACE ROOM. NEW WARDROBE. NEW ARRANGEMENTS. AND CAN BOOK YOU ON THE GUS SUN TIME.
——CASPER FINITINBAUM.

I laughed so hard my mother thought I was throwing a fit. I hadn't told her about meeting Bobby, so she didn't understand the joke. She thought someone wanted to book me.

I couldn't wait to get to work the next day. My girlfriend Gerri Danna came down to the club with me. She was a wonderful hairdresser and had taken over her brother's famous beauty salon while he was in the army—and doing a damn good job of it. The minute I met her, she became my hairdresser, in addition to my very good friend. We went to

The love of my life, my husband, William Robert Guy, affection-
ately known as "Bobby"

the dressing room. I got dressed for the show. Gerri did my hair and we
went upstairs.

I saw Rudy at the bar and introduced him to Gerri. But Bobby wasn't
there. I said, "Where's Bobby?"

Rudy said, "Take it easy, he's in the john."

"Oh," I said, laughing.

Bobby came out and I introduced him to Gerri. She stayed with him
and Rudy while I did my show.

When I was through, Rudy said, "Tea for three?"

"Fine," I said.

I went and changed my clothes, went back upstairs and listened to the radio show. Bobby was really great—he pulled that orchestra together. By now, it was time for me to get dressed for my second show.

When I returned from the dressing room, Bobby said, "Did you get my telegram?"

I said, "Yes, and I knew it was from you and I laughed my head off."

He smiled and said, "Good, I gave you a laugh. I hope to give you many."

I just looked at him and smiled. This guy was really getting to me.

After my second show, I changed my clothes, went back upstairs again and said good night to Rudy and Bobby.

He smiled that great smile of his and said, "See you tomorrow."

On the way home, I said to Gerri, "Did you see that guy in the uniform?"

She said, "Yes...so?"

I said, "I'm gonna marry him."

She said, "That fat sergeant?"

I said, "Yes, and he's not fat. He's just solid all the way round."

She said, "You...who won't go on a blind date or double date....You've only known him three days."

I said, "I don't care. He's the man I'm gonna marry." She was dumbstruck!

Two more days and I would close at the Terrace Room. I saw Bobby every night. We had talked about everything under the sun, including some of the same people we knew. He also said I looked a lot like Margaret Whiting—I had never heard of her at the time. Little did I know then that we'd work together—for eleven years!—and that we'd become good, good friends.

He was wonderful to talk to, plus he had a great sense of humor. I found myself laughing a lot and really falling for this guy. But with all the talk, he said nothing about going out or seeing one another after the Terrace Room.

Finally he said, "You know Gene Krupa opens Wednesday?" (I was to close Tuesday.)

I said, "Yes."

He asked, "Do you want to go to the opening?"

I said, "I'd love to."

He said, "How are you coming into town?"

I told him, "I'll get my father's car and pick you up at Schribman's and we'll go to the Terrace Room. Then, when we leave, I'll drop you off at Schribman's and I'll go back home to Jersey."

He said, "That's great! Think your father will mind?"

I said, "I'll talk to my mother."

Of course, I was thrilled—I had a date with Bobby! My father drove me down closing night and picked up the check...as always. He saw me sitting with Bobby, but didn't say anything.

After the second show, I said good night to Rudy and told Bobby, "I'll see you tomorrow at seven."

He said, "Okay."

I said, "Give me your phone number at Schribman's, just in case something comes up."

He gave me the number—he already had my phone number, so that was that. Going home, my father didn't say anything about Bobby. I don't think he even noticed. The only time he said anything was if I went out with some guy three times. Then he'd say, "What's goin' on?"

I would say, "It's just a date, nothing serious," and that would calm him down.

That night when we got home, I told my mother about Bobby. I didn't say a word about how I felt, just told her about him, Kay Kyser and all that. I mentioned I had a date with him to go to the opening of Gene Krupa and that I needed the car tomorrow night.

She said, "Ask your father."

I said, "No, he won't give it to me. You just tell him I need the car tomorrow night, please mother."

She said, "All right."

I couldn't sleep at all. I really felt so funny and I said to myself, "I guess I'm in love. I never thought it would feel this way. It was like somebody hit me on the head and it hurt!"

The next day, I was all thumbs. I couldn't wait for six o'clock. I got ready, got in the car...with my father's words in my head, "Be careful with the *car*." Not "Have a good time," or anything like that. My mother always said, "Home by midnight." By the way, I never had a key to the house. "Only whores have keys," my father said, "Why would you be afraid to knock?" Therefore, no key.

I drove over the George Washington Bridge and went down to 57th Street, to his apartment. There was Bobby, waiting for me outside. I pulled up in front, he came around and I moved over to the passenger seat so he could drive. He smiled and got in. Years later he told me that really impressed him that I would let him drive. (I don't know why!)

Driving to the Terrace Room took about half an hour. During that half hour, he said, "I've got to talk to you. It's important."

I thought, *Oh my God, he's going to end this! He can't! I know he loves me. I just know it. He never said it, but I just know it.*

He went on to say that he didn't know when he would get discharged from the army. His life was in California, not New York, and he knew that all my work was in the East. He knew that he would get his job back, but not make the money he made before the war. Kay's band had broken up, but he had the same musicians doing the radio show only—he said he really didn't know too much about that, but he would find out when he got back to California. He planned to go back and asked if I would stick it out and wait. Would I go with him to California when he got out?

I looked at him, smiled and said, "Yes!"

That was my proposal of marriage!

Chapter Ten

✺

Spring in Brazil and Berle

Bobby and I went out quite a lot. We went to the opening of Harry James at the Astor Hotel. We'd see a Broadway show, go to movies, eat Chinese food. I met Joe Schribman and always saw four or five guys in uniform up at the apartment. It was a hangout for musicians in the army who were stationed close to New York. I learned another part of the biz: musicians and music. Who played in what band, who was good, who was all right, and so on. Another notch in my education.

One night we went to see the Claude Thornhill Orchestra (he was managed by Schrib) and I dropped Bobby off at the apartment on my way home. Before he got out of the car, he leaned over and kissed me...*finally.* He backed away and just looked at me.

I asked him, "What's the matter?"

He said, "Either you're giving me the greatest line, or you're the dumbest thing I've ever met."

I said, "What's wrong? Why did you say that?"

"Go home, it's late," he replied. "Call me when you get home."

I thought, *It's over. What did I do wrong? I just kissed him. Why did he say that? It took him two weeks to kiss me in the first place. Maybe I shouldn't have let him kiss me.*

I couldn't wait to get home. As soon as I got in the door, I called him and asked, "What's wrong?"

He said, "Nothing, sweetheart, I just love you very much."

Whew! I guess it wasn't that I wasn't a good kisser! Anyway, I was in heaven. He said he loved me! By now my father was getting suspicious, and I tried to avoid him as much as possible. I didn't want to start any-thing. I was to open at the Capitol Theater in three days and I wanted everything to stay calm.

The night before I was to open, we rehearsed in the basement of the theater. The full orchestra was there. I handed out the music. My father was with me, of course, and Mark Warnow seemed very annoyed with me, that he had to rehearse me. I only did three songs and the Durante number and "Chena Luna"—an Italian folk song—with a few little jokes in be-tween. I was done in an hour. We went home and I started to pack the new gowns and get my makeup and stuff ready for the theater the next day.

My first show was at 11:20 A.M. We were doing five shows a day. The first show Mark Warnow introduced me: "Here's a young lady I know you'll enjoy…Miss Rose Marie." I stopped the show, completely brought the house down. Warnow was staring at me with his mouth open. I guess he was surprised!

Second show. Introduction: "Here's a young lady who is a great singer. I know you'll love her. Miss Rose Marie." I stopped the show again.

By the fifth show, I got the longest introduction in the world: "Here's a young lady, a great performer, a great singer, one of the best in our biz. You'll thrill to her songs," on and on and on. God, I thought I'd never get on the stage! But I hold the record at the Capitol. I stopped every show—one hundred and forty of 'em!

Bobby came over to the theater a lot. We'd go out for lunch or just walk in between shows. One day, we were sitting at a little restaurant right across the street from the Capitol and I noticed three guys with a long ladder leaning up against the marquee. Mark Warnow's name was in big letters. Ethel Smith's name was in big letters. My name was half as big. We watched these guys as they took my little lettered name down and put it up in big letters—as big as the others. Wow! Talk about getting goose pimples!

My social life was at a standstill because I was doing five shows a day. Somehow, Bobby came to the theater. At least I got to see him every day.

One day, the phone rang in my dressing room and the voice said, "This is George Abbot's office. Mr. Abbot would like you to come to his office. He wants to talk to you."

I was as bad as my brother. I said, "Oh sure, and I'm the Queen of England," and hung up.

A few minutes later the phone rang again. I answered it and the voice said, "Listen, this is George Abbot and I want to talk to Rose Marie right now."

"Hello, Mr. Abbot," I said. "This is Rose Marie."

He said, "I know you're doing five shows a day, but could you come up to my office in between shows?"

I told him, "I can be there about three o'clock today."

"Fine," he said.

So after the second show, I went to George Abbot's office. It brought back memories of when I had been there when I was fourteen. I had gone to see Abbot about a part in *Best Foot Forward* –the road company, no less! The secretary hadn't let me get past the little gate between the office and the secretary's little cubicle. I did the old movie bit: "I'll be back one of these days, and you'll open the gate for me!" I had to laugh as I thought about it.

Sure enough, I walked in and the girl said, "Hello," and opened the gate for me. I never said a word, I just smiled.

I went into his office. He was sitting behind the desk and had two scripts, one in each hand.

I said, "Hello, Mr. Abbot."

He said, "Glad to meet you. I want to tell you something, young lady. I have been to the Capitol almost every day at different times. In the morning, in the afternoon and evening—and you stopped every show. I have never seen anything like that."

"Thank you," I said.

He then took the two scripts and said, "I'm doing two shows—which one do you want?"

I said, "That's very kind of you, Mr. Abbot, and thank you for your generous offer. You have no idea how much this means to me, But I'm going to do the new Milton Berle show, *Spring in Brazil.*

He said, "Oh! I'm too late. Well, if you change your mind, let me know. One show is called *Billion Dollar Baby* and the other is *Christopher Columbus* with Willie Howard."

Mitzi Green ended up doing *Billion Dollar Baby.* It was a two-year smash. The *Chris Columbus* show never saw the light of day.

When the Capitol run was over, I started rehearsals for *Spring in Brazil* with Milton Berle. Phil Rapp, who wrote most of the Danny Kaye movies, wrote the script, and Robert Wright and Chet Forrest wrote the lyrics and music. They had just won awards for *Song of Norway.* Lee Schubert and Monte Prosner were the producers. How could it go wrong? Milton did a show called *The Ziegfeld Follies.* It was just all right, but he kept it going for two years.

How could it go wrong? Easy. Milton and I got along great. He almost talked in shorthand to me because he knew I knew what he meant. He taught me so much! Things were going well. Bobby came to rehearsals a lot, he met Berle and the two of them hit it off.

By now my father knew something was up with Bobby. Our names were in the columns as a new couple. You know, "We hear wedding bells," and so on. I knew this was bothering my father.

One night Bobby picked me up after rehearsal. I called home and told my mother that Bobby and I were going to dinner and maybe a movie, so I would be a little late.

She asked, "Is Bobby going to bring you home?"

I said, "Yes, we'll take the Orange/Black bus and he will walk me to the house." (It was only about two blocks away from the bus stop.)

We had dinner, saw a movie; by the time we were finished, it was 11:30. I knew we'd never get home at midnight. Sure enough, by the time we got off the bus, it was 12:15. We raced up the block. I knocked on the door.

My father answered and I said good-bye to Bobby as I ran into the house. My father started in: "Is this the big romance? What the hell is going on? It's 12:20—only whores come home at that time. Where were you?" *Whack!* He slapped me right across the face.

I said, "I called mother and told her we'd be a little late."

"Who is this son of a bitch you're going out with? A musician who's all doped up?" *Whack!* I started screaming.

My brother came down the stairs and grabbed my father's hands. He said, "Cut it out, Dad, what's the matter with you?" I was running around the kitchen table and crying.

My father said, "You embarrassed me in front of the office. They made fun of the fact that you had a guy and what was I going to do when you leave. I'd have to get a job. What kind of shit is that?"

I tried talking to him, but it was impossible. My brother was holding on to him and I just ran up to my room. My mother was standing up there, scared stiff. I just looked at her and locked the door. Well, the yelling and screaming continued between my mother and father. My brother was trying to stop everything. It was quite a night.

The next day, I got up early and went into the city. I called Bobby and met him at Uncle Joe's. We went out for a bite to eat, and I told him everything that happened the night before.

He said, "I heard it all—from a block away. I started to walk up the hill to come back and beat the shit out of your father, but then everything got quiet. I didn't want to start anything again, so I took the bus and went back to Schrib's. I'm sorry, honey. I didn't know what to do."

I told Bobby, "It's better that you left, because he would have started all over again. I'm going to talk to my mother tonight and explain everything, that as soon as you get out of the army, we're going to get married and go to California. What can they do?"

He said, "I know your mother understands, but your father is another story."

I said, "Don't worry, I'll straighten it out."

Little did I know I could never convince my father. My mother did understand after I explained everything. Then she talked to my father and he told her, "I found out he's a drunkard, takes dope and is going to live off her."

My mother asked him, "Who told you?"

He said, "I talked to a few musicians and they know him."

This happened a lot. Mom would tell me, and I'd tell Bobby.

Bobby would reply, "Bring the guys in front of me and I'll prove they're wrong."

When my mother told my father that, he would brush it off and not mention it again. We were going around and around in circles.

I finally said, "Mother, I'll tell you everything from the beginning."

The next morning, everybody was home: my mother, my father, and my brother. I said, "I want to talk to all of you. His name is Bobby Guy. He's been with Kay Kyser since he was seventeen. He lives in California. His horns and clothes are in California and he wants to go back there. He knows he can get his job back. He has nothing here in New York. He wants to marry me the minute he gets out of the army and go to California. Those are my plans."

My father said, "What did he do, knock you up?"

I said, "No, we're just in love. I have never come home and said 'I'm in love with this guy or that guy and I want to get married,' have I?"

My brother said, "No, this is the first guy."

"Why don't you just meet him?" I asked my father.

My mother said, "Is he Catholic?"

I said, "I don't know, I didn't ask him."

My father said, "What about his family?"

I answered, "They live in Trenton. His mother, sister, and brother. His brother works at Bethlehem Steel and his sister is a schoolteacher. They are both married and have kids."

My father said, "I want to meet his mother."

I said, "Fine, I'll tell him and we'll arrange a meeting."

To make a long story short, we made the appointment. His mother came in from Trenton—my father never showed up!

His mother was *furious!* She said, "Who in the hell does he think he is?" I couldn't blame her. They never did get together.

I did a club date at Laurel in the Pines. They had a jeweler there who sold rings and bracelets to the rich folks. I saw a ring and fell in love with it.

I told the fellow who ran the store, "Could we come up to see you? Would you give us a break?"

He said, "You come see me."

His office was in New York City, so it was easy to go and see him. I told Bobby about the ring, and we decided to go and see this jeweler.

When we got there, I introduced Bobby and said, "We plan on getting married and that ring would be my engagement ring."

He brought out the ring—it had a cabochon ruby in the center, a half-carat diamond on each side, and four baguettes. There was one baguette on top of each jewel and one baguette on the bottom. It was truly lovely.

Bobby said, "Do you like that instead of one good-sized diamond?"

I said, "Where are you getting all this money?"

He said, "That's my problem, not yours. Do you really want it?"

I said, "Yes."

He then talked to the guy about payments. Bobby was making extra money doing radio shows for Joe Schribman's orchestras and he'd have it paid off in no time. I was thrilled, and the guy gave me the ring. Bobby put it on my finger and I was engaged! Of course, the papers found out and wrote about it, and my father went wild!

He cornered me one morning and said, "Let me see the ring."

I showed it to him and he said, "How much did *you* pay for it?"

I said, "I didn't buy it. *Bobby* did, and he is paying it off in payments whenever he does the radio shows for Joe Schribman's bands."

"How can he make any money? He's in the army," my father said.

I told him, "All the musicians at Camp Shanks are doing little dates on the side to make extra money."

My father said, "Who's this Joe Schribman?"

I told him about Uncle Joe (as we called him) and how the guys in the band from Camp Shanks hung out at the apartment. How he was getting them jobs playing the radio shows because all the good musicians were in the army. I said, "Everybody does it."

Well, he got mad and said, "I don't believe it! This Schribman guy could get into a lot of trouble." And then he stomped out of the house.

I was still in rehearsal with *Spring in Brazil*, and we were to open in Boston in two weeks. Everything was going smoothly, sort of, until one day Bobby called and said, "Could you come into town a little earlier? It's very important."

I asked, "What's wrong?"

He said, "I'll tell you when you get here."

Wow. I thought. *Something's very, very wrong.*

I went into New York and up to the apartment. Schribman was there, in a rage.

I said, "What's wrong?"

Schrib showed me a letter addressed to Special Services:

Dear Sirs:

I understand a Mr. Joseph Schribman has been using men who are in the Army to play in his orchestras all over town and in New Jersey. Don't you think it's a little unfair to the other musicians who need their livelihood, to give the jobs to the Army? I thought they were supposed to be IN the Army and not free-lancing around. One musician in particular, Robert William Guy, is making money on the side while he's supposed to be in service. This Joe Schribman should be told he's wrong in doing this. I, as a concerned citizen, object to this going on, and hope you will do something about it.

Sincerely, Joseph Hyman

Well, I almost died. Bobby was holding Schrib down in a chair. Schrib was fighting mad and he said, "That S.O.B. is causing nothing but trouble and he didn't even know Bobby's name." (Bobby's name was William Robert Guy, not Robert William Guy, but everyone called him Bobby.)

We all knew it was my father who had done this. I didn't know what to say.

Schribman said, "Don't say anything. Make him think he got away with it. I'll straighten it out. I know all the brass at Shanks, but I'm telling you, if he does anything else, I'll take him to court."

Things were quiet for a little while, and I left for Boston to open in *Spring in Brazil*. Ruthie was thrilled because we could spend a lot of time together. Bobby stayed at Shanks for about a week and then came up to Boston. I was staying at the Bradford—of course—which was next door to the Shubert Theater. When Bobby came up, he rented a room at the Bradford as well. Ruthie fixed it so that Bobby wouldn't pay for his room. He stayed until the opening. My father didn't come up.

It was a big opening and Ruthie threw a party after the show, while we waited for the reviews. They were awful! I must say that Milton stuck to the book—on opening night, anyway—but after the reviews he just did all his "shtick": talking to the audience, breaking out of character, and so on. We did planned "break-ups." He would do one, and if it got a big laugh, when we came off stage he'd slap me on the rear and say, "Leave that one in."

I'd say, "Okay."

One night Lee Shubert and Monte Prosner came to my dressing room and said, "We want to talk to you."

I thought, *Uh-oh! This is it.* But no! They asked me to do my Durante number.

I have to explain the Durante number. I was never an impressionist, but at some point I did a Durante number and it went over very well. Years before this, Jimmy and I were good friends. He always called me "Baby Rose Marie" and he showed me "how to do *him.*"

He'd say, "Raise your voice up here, swing your arm here," and so on, until I had a whole Durante number. It was always one of my big numbers. Every time I played the Capitol, I had to have a new Durante song.

So when Lee Schubert and Monte Prosner asked me to do my Durante number, I said, "Where?"

They said, "Before the second act finale."

I said, "That's the best spot in the show."

They said, "You'll do it 'in one' with just the curtain behind you."

I said, "It doesn't make sense. I'm in an airline stewardess uniform all ripped up because the jungle boy with the loincloth full of diamonds has dragged me through the jungle! And I break out in the Durante number? It doesn't make sense. It's stupid and asinine."

They said, "Do it!"

I said, "I have to send for my music."

They said they would special-messenger it, so that I could do it the next night. I almost died. But they sent for the music. I rehearsed with the band that afternoon and I was nervous as hell.

I called Ruthie and told her she had to come down to see this. She also thought that it was crazy. Bobby had gone back to New York after opening night, so I just called him and told him about it.

He said that I should call him later and let him know how it went. "Good luck," he said.

I laughed and told him, "Yeah, it will be the first time Durante dies!"

The time came for me to work it out in one and I started the verse of the Durante number. People were looking at their programs, turning pages, trying to find this Durante number. When I broke into the voice of Durante—which usually got a big hand—this time, *nothing!*

I kept going and, little by little, they started to warm up—I could feel it. When I did the two Durante jokes that Jimmy had taught me, the audience laughed and applauded. I finished the number with the Durante walk-off and the audience applauded and whistled. It was overwhelming—they kept applauding. I kept taking bows and they opened to full stage with the entire cast, which usually quiets the audience. But this time they kept applauding.

Monte Prosner said, "Take another bow." The whole cast onstage pointed toward the wings. I gulped, took another bow and we went into the finale. I had stopped the show.

While all this was going on, I could hear Milton backstage yelling: "Where the hell does the Durante number fit into a jungle scene? Who the hell okayed this? This is crap...it doesn't fit. God damn it," and so on. He went on and on until he had to make his appearance for the finale. When we took our single bows, I got the biggest hand, and then Milton came out. He too got a big hand. He looked at me with fire in his eyes, took my hand, kissed me, and then he and I took the last bow.

We stayed in Boston for four weeks trying to fix up the show. Next stop was Philadelphia for four weeks. We were always trying to improve it. The reviews in Philadelphia were a little better, but not very much.

One reviewer wrote: "For no rhyme or reason, Rose Marie does her famous Durante number, but thank God for no rhyme or reason." That didn't set too well with Milton. He never mentioned it again—except in *his* book.

We then went to Pittsburgh. The rumor was that the show wouldn't open in New York, so they would do a lot of towns to try to get some of the money back. I thought I'd rather leave the show and go back to New York. I could do better there.

Bobby came up to Pittsburgh and saw the show. He asked, "What are you going to do?"

I told him, "I'm leaving after two weeks." We were booked for four weeks.

On our day off, Milton called me and said, "Get Bobby, we're going to a burlesque show."

I said, "I've never seen one."

We went to dinner and the Ice Follies and then, at eleven o'clock or so, we went to the burlesque show. I never laughed so much in my whole life. Milton kept shouting "Put it on!" instead of "Take it off." We had one helluva time!

Back at the hotel, we sat in the lobby and talked for three hours about everything…showbiz, comics, and so on.

By four o'clock in the morning, I said, "I'm going to bed." I kissed Bobby and kissed Milton and went up to my room.

Milton kidded Bobby about going up to my room. He said, "I'll talk to you all night, so you can't go up." Big joke. Bobby was staying at another hotel! Milton couldn't believe it.

Bobby went back to New York, and I finished the two weeks. They got Mary Healy to replace me. She and her husband, Peter Lind Hayes, were very well known and had played all the top clubs, so Mary was very good. I went back home, and *Spring in Brazil* went on to Baltimore and God knows what other towns. It never opened on Broadway.

Chapter Eleven

Courtship in Hell

Bobby and I were able to spend a good deal of time together once I left *Spring in Brazil.* I had two weeks off before my next engagement. By this time, everyone was asking, "When are ya gonna get married?"

I kept saying, "As soon as Bobby gets out of the army."

I tried talking to my mother about inviting Bobby over for dinner. I couldn't budge her, because my father threatened to leave the house if Bobby were ever to visit. Christmas was only a few days away and I told my mother, "I want Bobby to come over for Christmas Eve."

She said, "Okay." Then she told my father. Sure enough, he did not come home for Christmas Eve. (I bet the "other" family was happy, anyway.) My mother liked Bobby from the minute she met him.

They talked and talked. She asked him, "Are you Catholic?"

"No," Bobby answered, "I'm nothing. When I was a kid, we used to go to all the different churches we knew were serving food."

I laughed, but my mother didn't think that was funny. Bobby said, "We have a priest at camp. I'll talk to him and maybe I can become Catholic."

I told him, "You don't have to do that."

"I want to," Bobby answered.

Then my mother said, "Why can't you stay here instead of going to California?"

Bobby said, "Because I don't know anyone in the East who could give me what I have in California."

My mother said, "I'm sure you could get work here, and Rose Marie can go on with her career; she doesn't have any contacts in California."

At this point, I spoke up: "With the way Daddy feels, he would make sure Bobby wouldn't get a job and would try in every way to make me think Bobby was no good."

Bobby spoke up. "Let me tell you something. Rose Marie doesn't have to work if she doesn't want to. I'm well known in California and am sure I will have a job shortly after we arrive there. I'll take care of her. I love her very much and I want to make her happy."

We finally sat down to dinner. My mother had really outdone herself—and she was one helluva cook. Bobby, my brother, my mother and I had a beautiful evening together. My brother and Bobby hit it off very well. Shortly after dinner, Bobby went back to Schrib's apartment.

My mother said, "He seems like a nice guy, I just don't want you to make a mistake."

I said, "Mother, I know he's a good man and we have a lot in common. We have so much fun together."

She got a funny look in her eyes, so I said, "No, mother, I have not gone to bed with him."

She smiled and said, "That's good."

I was so happy that mother seemed to like Bobby and that she believed the things I had told her about him. The next day, my father came home and my mother told him about meeting Bobby, that he seemed like a nice guy who truly loved me.

Always the one to say something unkind, my father said, "Oh, he fooled you too, eh?" I could see it was going to be necessary to keep quiet about our plans and my happiness for a while—or at least long enough to calm my father down…again.

I opened at the Copacabana in New York. Lee Schubert and Monte Prosner produced *Spring in Brazil.* Julie Podell, the boss, booked me to play there as soon as he learned I was leaving the show. It was one of the best places to play and it was a great date. I was booked for four weeks as the headline act. We did three shows a night, and in between shows, I was doing the Perry Como Chesterfield radio show, as well as a couple of Texaco shows with Berle. I think I did about eight of those shows with Milton back when he was "Mr. Television." I was the only one who would talk back to him. Everybody was afraid of him. I still say Milton was a genius—he just didn't know how to explain himself. I'm grateful for all his teachings…and there were many.

Bobby started sending me a rose every night at the Copa. Some nights

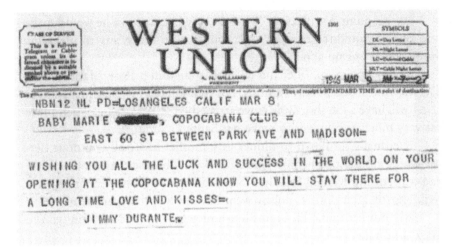

A cherished telegram from Jimmy Durante

I'd meet him between shows. I would do my first show at the Copa, go to NBC—a short distance from the club—and do the fifteen-minute Como radio show for the East Coast, go back to the Copa and do my second show, and return to NBC for the Como show for the West Coast. Then I would return to the Copa for the last show.

Many nights, Bobby would pick me up after the first show at the Copa and we'd walk down Madison Avenue and do some window shopping, go to NBC so I could do the Como show, and stop on our way back to the Copa to have a soda or something.

One night in February—it was 1946—he picked me up, we walked to NBC and he said, "You go on up and do the show. I'll wait down here for you."

I said, "Okay," and went to do the show, which took about 25 minutes. I came down to meet Bobby. He was up at the corner, with his arms around the signal light. I walked up to him and said, "What's wrong?" He was white around his mouth and he was sort of pale.

He said, "Your father was driving around the block and when you went up to do the show, he parked the car and started walking toward me and yelling, 'You S.O.B.....You stay away from my daughter. You no-good bum, stay away from her, or I'll kill you!' I was backing right up to the signal light and by now a crowd was forming. The crowd kept saying, "'Hit him, soldier. Don't let him talk to you that way....Hit him!'"

With Frank Sinatra and Rocky Graziano at the Copacabana, New York

Bobby said he put his arms around the signal light and kept saying to himself, *He's her father, I can't hit him.* What he did say out loud was, "I love her and want to marry her and make her happy."

He continued, "Your father kept raving and pointing his finger at me saying, 'Keep away from her, you whoremaster, or so help me God, I'll kill you.' With that, your father turned away, went back to the car and drove away."

What could I say? I started to cry and apologize to Bobby. I really didn't know what to do. I had to get back to the Copa and do my second show. I didn't know how I was going to do the show without crying. I wondered how much more poor Bobby could—or would—take. I guess I wouldn't have blamed him if he just called it quits. What the hell could I do? It just seemed so hopeless.

Bobby walked me back to the Copa and said, "I'll talk to you tomorrow." I knew it was over. What *was* I going to do? Somehow I managed to do my two shows and drive home. I went in to talk to my mother, but she was asleep, so I just cried and went to bed.

The next day, Bobby called about one o'clock and said he had to go to Shanks and at least make an appearance.

I said, "Will I see you tonight at the club?"

He said he was going to stay at Shanks for a few days. I just knew that was it. He said he'd call me from Shanks.

I said, "Okay, please, please call me. We'll work this out, honest we will."

He said, "I know, but it's rough to be called all those names, just because you love someone."

I said, "Please trust me, I'll make it work."

He said, "Okay, remember I love you," and hung up.

I went into my mother's bedroom and said, "I've got to talk to you, Mother, and you've got to help me." I told her what my father had done.

She couldn't believe it. She said, "He would never do anything like that."

I said, "He did, and I swear if he causes any more trouble and I lose Bobby, I'll leave this house and never come back."

She hugged me and said, "Don't say things like that, we'll work it out."

I said, "I hope so, because he and I can't take any more of this and I think I'm old enough to know what I want."

Bobby didn't call the next day. I left a message at Schrib's and asked him to please call me. Schrib said he was at Camp Shanks. I didn't see Bobby for three days, and it was driving me crazy. He finally called the next day and said he wanted to see me. He sounded okay, but I was scared stiff. I knew he was going to call it quits. I told him to come to the Copa for a bite to eat between shows (there was no Perry Como show that night).

I did my first show and Bobby was waiting out front. We kissed and hugged and I said, "I've missed you so."

He said, "I missed you too. Come on, let's get something to eat. I've got some news for you." *Uh-oh!* I thought, *Here it comes.*

We went to Schrafft's on Fifth Avenue. It was near the Copa. We ordered and Bobby started talking. He said, "I've got a lot to tell you. First of all, I love you with all my heart and I would never let you go. Second, I think I'm getting out of the army in June, and we're gonna get married, go to California and leave all this crap behind us. We'll elope and that's it! Are you with me?"

I said, "Oh yes, yes, yes! I love you too and I want to be with you. I'll leave the gowns and the music here, so they don't think you're going to live off of me...like my father has done all these years."

It was only February, and June was three months away, so we had time to make all of our plans carefully. I would get my clothes together. I would bring my gowns to Max. He would hold them for me. I would leave my music at the house. I called my friend Scotty Murphy and asked if she and her husband would stand up for us. They said they'd love to. Scotty and I had been friends for years, and she knew what we had been going through.

The next few days went fine. Bobby came to the Copa and brought me my single rose. We were so happy, but still careful. I was to close at the Copa in two days. The night we closed, I drove into the city alone. My father was playing cat and mouse. Some nights he would come down to the Copa, and some nights he wouldn't. He was trying to catch Bobby and me so he could start something.

I packed up my gowns and did the three shows. While I was packing, Julie Podell, the boss, knocked on the door. He said, "Here's your check, and thanks for doing such a good job." He hugged me and left.

I called Bobby to help me put all the stuff in the car. We had a bite to eat and I looked at the check. It was $1,750. Wow! I didn't know I was making that kind of money.

I told Bobby, "The boss gave me the check. He usually gives it to my father."

Bobby said, "So what?"

I said, "This is going to be trouble. I have never gotten my check before."

Bobby said, "Oh, don't worry, it can't be all that bad."

I hope so, I thought. I drove Bobby to Schrib's and took the George Washington Bridge home.

My father was waiting for me—I had no key, remember? The minute I walked in, he started in: "Did you get the check?"

I said, "Yes, Julie gave it to me because you weren't there." *Whack!* Across the face.

I said, "What could I do? I had to take the check."

"Embarrass me, will ya?" *Whack!* "How dare you do that to me, you tramp."

I said, "I'm not a tramp."

Whack! "Don't answer me back."

I started screaming. My brother—my hero—came down and held my father as he had done before and said, "Cut it out, Dad. Are you crazy, or what?"

My father tried to break free, but my brother held on tight and said to me, "Go upstairs."

I ran out of there like a bat out of hell and locked my door.

The next day my father said to my mother, "She's a tramp. She's been sleeping with him."

My mother said, "No, she's not. She told me."

"And you believe her?" my father asked.

My mother said she did. I came downstairs at that moment—leave it to me to make an entrance—and my father started in again: "You stay away from that bum. He takes dope and he's a drunk."

I said, "No, he's not."

He said, "I found out from Tony Pastor. He's worked for Tony Pastor." (Pastor was a well-known bandleader at the time.)

I said, "No, he hasn't. He's been with Kay Kyser and nobody else."

My father said, "He lied to you. He's a liar too."

I thought to myself, *What's the use?* So I went upstairs again. And he and my mother had it out again. My poor mother was trying to hold up. He wore her down and then left for the day.

I came downstairs and told my mother, "Thanks, but it's useless. He'll never come around, no matter what." I never told her that Bobby was getting out of the army in June. I thought I'd better leave well enough alone.

My next date was in Hollywood, Florida, at the Colonial Inn for two weeks. They had gambling there! Joe Adonis was running the place, which meant that "the boys" owned it. My father and I stayed at the Roney Plaza and rented a car. It was a twenty-five-minute drive to Hollywood from Miami Beach.

During the day, I never saw my father. He'd give me a few bucks and say, "I'll see you tonight." Thank God for Ruthie. She and her husband Irving were in Florida for the winter season. She and I spent a lot of time together. One day we went window-shopping and I saw a pair of cuff links, ruby and gold.

I said, "Oh! I've got to get those for Bobby's birthday."

Ruthie asked, "Where ya gonna get the money?" They cost eighty dollars.

"I'll find a way," I told her.

That night I went up to Joe A.—Joe Adonis—and said, "I gotta talk to you, I need help."

"What's the matter?" he asked. "Somebody bothering you?"

I said, "No, but I gotta talk to you."

"What is it?" he asked.

"I need eighty dollars to buy my boyfriend some cuff links for his birthday. Can you give me a horse that can't lose?"

Joe said, "What do you mean, a horse that can't lose?"

I said, "You know, a race where the horse can't lose."

"Does your father know about this?" he asked.

I said, "No, Joe dear, please don't say anything about this to my father, please! We're having enough trouble as it is."

Joe looked at me and said, "Get out of here. I'll talk to you later."

After the show, I was in the lounge, having a cup of tea. Joe A. came in looking for me. He sat down beside me and said, "Can you place the bet?"

I said, "Easy, we've got a lot of bookies hanging around the hotel. How much should I bet?"

"Six bucks across the board. Don't tell anyone about this, understand? No one."

I nodded my head.

He said, "The name of the horse is Santa Claus. At Gulfstream. Fifth race."

I hugged him and gave him a kiss.

He said, "Remember, don't tell anyone. And I want to see the cuff links."

He got up and went into the other room. Oh God, I was happy. Joe A. was so wonderful to me. I couldn't wait for the next day. Of course, I called Ruthie. She couldn't believe it.

She said, "I'll tell Irving."

"No! No. Don't tell anyone—not anyone. I promised."

Ruthie said, "Can I bet him?"

"Yes, but only as much as I'm going to bet."

"How much is that?" she asked.

"Six bucks across the board. By the way, can you loan me six bucks?"

Ruthie started to laugh and said, "Sure, I'll be right over, and we'll place the bets."

She was there in fifteen minutes! We went over to one of the bookies I knew. Everybody called him "Choocha Cholar" because he couldn't say "Coca-Cola."

I said, "I want to place a bet, Chooch."

He said, "Does your father know about this?"

I said, "No. Please don't tell him. Please. It's very important that he not know about this, please!"

He said, "Okay."

I placed the bet and Ruthie placed her bet. We were so excited. The next day we went to Collins Avenue and window-shopped again. We came back to the hotel about five o'clock, looked for the bookie and couldn't find him.

I told Ruthie, "I guess we gotta wait till tomorrow. I gotta get dressed to go to the club."

She said, "I'll call you in the morning."

She left. I went up to the room, showered and got ready to leave for the club. My father knocked on the door and said, "We're leaving in ten minutes."

"Okay, I'll be ready. Meet you in the lobby."

We got to the club and I tried to find Joe A. He wasn't around, so I went backstage to get ready for the show. Joe A. was backstage with Harry Richman and Xavier Cugat. They were fighting about who should get top billing. Harry Richman said he should. Cugat kept yelling in Spanish (I'm sure he was cursing) that he always got top billing.

Joe stepped in and said, "If you two don't stop this, I'll put her name on top. It's her show anyway." I almost died. He walked out and everything got quiet. I ran into my dressing room. I didn't want to get into anything with Richman and Cugat!

I did my first show, then went into the lounge for a bite to eat. Joe came in and sat down.

"Did you place the bet?"

I said, "Yes, but I don't know what happened. I couldn't find the bookie and I had to get ready for the show."

He said, "Okay. I'll talk to you later."

Well, "later" came and went. I didn't see Joe. A. I couldn't tell my father that I wanted to see Joe A., so we went back to the hotel. Ruthie had left three messages for me to call her.

When I got up to the room, I called her. She said, "We won—guess how much we won?"

I said, "How much?"

She said, "Eighty-six dollars."

I was stunned. Six bucks for the bet and eighty bucks net. I couldn't believe it. I was thrilled and planned to get the cuff links the next day. Ruthie came over around noon. We had breakfast and looked for Choocha. He was in the lobby. I called to him and he came over, gave Ruthie her eighty-six bucks and handed me my eighty-six bucks.

"Where'd ya get the tip?" he asked.

I said, "No tip....I just liked the name of Santa Claus."

He looked at me, smiled, and said, "Okay, but no more bets."

Ruthie and I went to the jewelry store and I bought the cuff links. I was so happy! Bobby would flip over them.

Ruthie went back to her hotel and I went back to mine. For some reason, I bought the paper. Sure enough, the ad for the club had my name on top and Harry Richman and Cugat's names were under mine. I couldn't believe it. Joe A. had done that. He was too much!

On closing night, I went up to Joe A. and said, "I don't know how to thank you."

He said, "Lemme see the cuff links."

I showed him the box. He opened it, looked at the cuff links and said, "Yeah, they're okay. I hope he likes 'em."

"He will, I know he will," I said.

The date was finished and my father and I went back home. By now it was March and Bobby's birthday was March 28. I wanted to throw some kind of party, but it was impossible to get it together, so we just went out to dinner together. I gave him the cuff links.

He looked at me and said, "They're beautiful, but they don't go well with khaki."

I said, "Don't worry, from now on we'll make your birthday a big event, and we'll have a spectacular party every year, I promise. Then you can wear your ruby cuff links." That promise I kept!

April and May came around, and Bobby and I were busy getting the license and matching wedding bands. We figured we needed a car, so we went to some used car dealer in Jersey.

The guy knew who I was, so he said, "Does your father know about this?"

Again I had to say, "No, no, please don't say anything to him about this....*Please!*" I had saved about $1,400, and we asked him to give us a break because that was all we had and we had to get to California. We picked out a '41 black Mercury two-door. Not bad! Cars were hard to buy at that time. We told him we'd buy it and pick it up around June 1. His last words to me were, "Don't tell your father where you got the car."

I had no work in sight and things were getting tight around the house. My father still kept telling me, "He's no good. Stay away from him or so help me, I'll ruin him. I'll report him to the army, that he's working on the side and taking money, instead of doing his job in the army."

I said, "You already did that and it didn't work." He looked at me with a stare that could kill.

"I'll tell the newspapers he's a drunk and that he takes dope."

I said, "Please stop. I just can't take it anymore," and ran upstairs.

My mother was in her room and said, "I hope you're satisfied. Your father is going to tell all the newspapers. It will be a disgrace for you and for him." I looked at her and couldn't believe what I was hearing. He had turned her against me again. *Oh, what's the use?* I thought. *This will never work out.*

I had a date with Bobby the next night at seven o'clock. I was afraid to tell him that it had started all over again. I was so disgusted; I went into the bathroom and took my father's sleeping pills.

I woke up with my mother shaking me and crying, "Get up, get up. Rose Marie, please get up." It was nine o'clock the next night. Bobby had started calling at 7:30 and kept calling every fifteen minutes. Finally he said, "Put her on the phone. Get her up, call the doctor. Don't you know what she's done? Put her on the phone."

My mother tried to get me up. I was so groggy I almost fell down the stairs. I got to the phone and said, "Halloo...."

Bobby said, "Are you all right?"

I said, "Yeah, I guess so....I'm so sleepy."

He said, "Make your mother call Dr. Verdon right away and try to stay awake. Please, darling, stay awake."

I hung up the phone and passed out again. The next thing I knew, Doc Verdon was talking to me and saying, "Come on now, Rose Marie, open your eyes. You're okay now."

I looked at him and smiled.

He said, "Come on, honey, have a cup of tea."

I sat up in my bed and I was feeling a little better.

He told my mother, "She'll be all right now, but for God's sake, whatever the reason is she did this for, tell her everything is fine…and keep telling her."

My mother said, "All right."

He went downstairs, where my father, who couldn't have cared less, was reading the paper.

He looked up and said, "How is she, Doc?"

Dr. Verdon said, "She's fine now. There's no telling if she will try this again. Whatever it is, stop torturing her. Give her a chance to overcome this. I'm warning you…she had to be very desperate to do this. I'll call tomorrow and see how she is…and by the way, she's still a virgin!"

I didn't know what was going on in New York. Schrib told me he had had to hold Bobby down and sit on him. He was fighting mad, crying, and had a big kitchen knife in his hand, saying, "I'll kill that son of a bitch.…I'll kill him, so help me God." Buddy Moreno, a band singer in the army with Bobby, was with Schrib and said the two of them sat on Bobby until he calmed down.

Schrib kept saying, "She's all right.…Everything will be fine.…Take it easy." You have to know that Bobby was Irish-English, but more Irish than "Paddy's Pig." When he got mad, he was a tiger. He once told me that he had hit a kid in school with a baseball bat. The poor kid almost died. When he heard that the kid was going to be all right, Bobby swore he would never lose his temper again. I guess he forgot in this case. I can't say as I blame him.

Things got a little quiet after this episode. In two days, I was fine. I spoke to Bobby on the phone every day and neither he, nor I, nor anyone else ever mentioned the incident. It was peaceful for a change. My father said as little as possible to me.

When I was feeling better, I brought my gowns over to Max's to be repaired and cleaned. I told him I would let him know when I would pick them up.

I had another set of three Perry Como shows to do. It seemed that whenever I was scheduled to do Perry's show, something tragic or dramatic usually happened. I wondered if it would be the same this time. The last time I was to do his show was in April 1945. I went to the studio and nobody was there. It seemed like everybody had left town. I couldn't find a soul. Something had happened—something bad. I finally found a woman in one of the offices and she was crying.

I asked, "What's going on? Where's the Como show?"

She said, "President Roosevelt has died."

Oh! My god.... The President is dead! I thought of the time I sang for him. I think I was about six years old. After the show we went into his office and I spied some poker chips.

He said, "Do you like to play with those?"

I said, "Oh yes," and sat down on the floor with the chips.

He pulled up his wheelchair and picked me up and said, "You're a very lovely child and you sing very well."

I remember I said, "Thank you," and went back to playing with the chips.

Poor President Roosevelt...he was very kind to me.

This time everything went well. I did the three Como shows with no disaster.

Bobby found out he would be discharged on June 19, so it was getting close. I called Gerry Danna, who couldn't believe I was going to marry "that fat sergeant."

I told her, "I'm packing my clothes and on the night of June 18, give me the secret whistle. I'll open my window and throw the bags out." My window overlooked the driveway, and we had arranged a secret melody to whistle as a signal.

She said, "I'm gonna get killed for this."

I said, "No, you won't. Just promise me you'll do it."

She said, "All right."

We then called Scotty and Murph and asked them to help us. The four of us went down to pick up the car. Scotty and Murph said they'd keep the car and we'd meet them on June 19.

Here's how it went: I got up early, around 7:00 A.M., walked in to my mother's bedroom and kissed my mother, who was still sound asleep. Then I left the house to walk to the bus stop. I waited there for Bobby to come in from New York. Scotty and Murph were there, with our car and theirs. We drove to Gerry's house and picked up my suitcases.

Gerry said, "Your mother called and wanted to know what was going on."

I lied and said, "I don't know."

"She sounded real mad."

We packed the car with my clothes. Poor Bobby had only one pair of pants, a sport shirt, and a jacket. We then drove the two cars to city hall in New York City. Scotty bought me a bouquet of flowers and a flower for

Bobby's lapel. When the judge said, "If anyone here knows why these two should not be joined in holy matrimony, let him now speak or forever hold his peace," I held Bobby's hand so tight, I almost drew blood. I expected my father to burst in and say, "No!" But nothing happened—and we were married at 3:45 P.M., June 19, 1946.

Chapter Twelve

Heavenly Honeymoon

After we got married, we went outside to say thanks to Scotty and Murph for standing up for us.

Murph said, "You better get going and get out of here fast."

Bobby said, "You're right. We're gonna stop in Trenton to see my mother and sister. We'll probably stay in Philly overnight."

Hugs and kisses and off they went. I called my friend Judy Applebaum in Philadelphia and told her I had gotten married. She almost jumped through the phone.

I said, "Please make a reservation for us at the Sylvania Hotel—we're staying overnight."

Judy said, "Sure thing, but I am going to throw you a wedding party."

I laughed and said, "Okay. I'll call you when we arrive."

We got into the car and we were off. I couldn't believe we were really doing this…but I was happy. We stopped at Bobby's sister's house—my new mother-in-law lived with her daughter and son-in-law. Everyone was around the radio listening to the Joe Louis–Billy Conn fight.

Bobby said, "Hi, Mother. We're here and we're married."

They looked at us and said, "Great," and went back to the radio.

I said, "Aren't you going to wish us luck?"

They said, "Oh sure…yes…congratulations," and so on, and back to the radio.

I said to Bobby, "Let's go."

His mother came over, gave me a kiss on the cheek and said, "Make him happy and I'm sure he'll make you happy. He's a good man."

I said, "I know. I'll do my best," and we were out of there.

We drove to Philly and went to the Sylvania Hotel. Judy and her parents were in the lobby waiting for us.

Hugs and kisses. "We're so happy for you," Judy said. "Get changed, we're going out for dinner and a party."

So we went upstairs and changed. We had a lovely room. Every time I worked Philly, I stayed at the Sylvania, so they knew me. They all said, "Congratulations." It was nice…it sort of made it special. After changing, we came downstairs, met Judy and her folks, and went to Bookbinder's for lobster. We had a ball. We ate lobster until it was coming out our ears. The owner had a cake made with wedding bells and doves. It was so sweet. They ordered champagne, but since Bobby and I both don't drink, we just had to sip to be polite.

Joe, Judy's father, asked "What are your plans?"

Bobby told him, "We're driving out to the coast. We bought a car and we're leaving tomorrow."

Joe owned some garages, and he said, "Stay another day. I want to go over the car and make sure it's all right to drive for such a long trip."

We said, "Okay, sure." We had nothing in view and no time limit as to when we had to arrive in California. After our little wedding dinner party, we all went back to the hotel, said our good-nights and went to our room.

To tell you about my wedding night…well, it's too much to describe. But I was so dumb. I knew nothing of sex! Bobby was so wonderful. He was very gentle and kind and only worried about how I felt, if I was all right.

I kissed him and said, "I do love you so much."

He said, "I'm with you, Mommy" (his nickname for me…and I always called him "Pap"). "I love you with all my heart and always will."

The next day we had breakfast in the room. I said to Bobby, "I think we better do a little shopping. You need some clothes." We went out and bought a couple of shirts, two pairs of pants and a pair of shoes. I had all the clothes I would need, so we came back to the hotel.

Judy called and said, "We'll have dinner."

I said, "Okay," and told Bobby the plans.

We met Judy and her parents and went out to dinner.

Joe said, "Your car will be ready tomorrow morning. I put four new tires on and went over everything. The car is now in ship-shape order!" The tires were hard to get at that time, so we were grateful.

Bobby said, "That's wonderful. Thank you, Joe."

Before Bobby could say anything else, Joe said, "That's my wedding present to you both."

Judy's mom, Annie, said, "You don't need a piece of silver at this time, so here's my wedding present." And she gave us a check for $350.

Judy said, "And here's my wedding present." She gave me a check for $250 and said, "Use it as best you can for what you want."

Bobby and I were dumbfounded. We couldn't thank them enough. God, I have such wonderful friends. We took off the next morning after all the good-byes—and we didn't get a bill from the hotel. They said that was *their* wedding gift.

Bobby had gotten a map from the auto club, and it laid out where we should stop and the names of the hotels where we should stay. We were going to drive about 350 to 400 miles a day until we got to the coast. We'd make reservations a day ahead to be sure we had a room, since it could be very difficult in those days to get a room.

Next stop: Pittsburgh. Bobby said, "Kay's band used to play here a lot. Let me go in and see what I can do." It was the William Penn Hotel. Bobby came out in fifteen minutes and said, "We're all set. We got the bridal suite!"

I said, "How come?"

Bobby said, "I was waiting in line when this man came over to me and said, 'Are you Bobby Guy?' I said, 'Yes, why?' The guy said, 'Don't you remember me? When Kay Kyser played here, I used to bring the instruments to the stage so you guys could set up. After the show, I would put them away.' 'You were the band boy!' The man nodded and smiled. 'What are you doing here?' 'I just got married.' He pulled me out of the waiting line and snapped his fingers to the guy behind the desk and said, 'The bridal suite for Mr. and Mrs. Bobby Guy.' Well, the band boy is now the manager of the hotel." Of course, we didn't get a hotel bill. So far, we were batting a thousand!

We left the next morning on our way to Cincinnati. We made good time. We were not rushing. We took it day by day, with not a care in the world—until we were outside of Chicago.

I called my girlfriend, Marty Dawson. She and I had worked together at the Chez Paree and kept up our friendship. She sounded very frightened when she said, "Bypass Chicago. Your father has called everybody here. They're just waiting for you to come to town."

I said, "All right, we'll go on to St. Louis. How did you find out about him calling everybody? Who did he call?"

She said, "All the guys at the Chez Paree. One of them called me and told me because he knew we were friends. So, get going! I'm really happy for you, honey. Have a wonderful life."

I told Bobby and he looked a little frightened. We drove to St. Louis. On the way there, we stopped for gas and I called Jim Scarpelli, the "Big Boss" of St. Louis. His wife, Kay, answered.

I said, "Hi, Kay, it's Rose Marie. I just got married."

She said, "We know, your father called, but Jim wants to talk to you."

Jim got on the phone, "Where are you?"

I told him, "Outside of St. Louis, about twenty-five miles. Should we keep going and not stop in St. Louis?"

He said, "No, I want to see you…and I want to meet him. Are you all right?"

I said, "I'm very happy and we love each other very much."

Jim said, "Where are you gonna stay?"

I told him, "The Chase Hotel. I worked there and I thought maybe we could get a room there."

Jim said, "I'll make the reservation. We'll have dinner. We'll meet you in the lobby about seven o'clock, okay?"

I said, "Fine."

Bobby looked at me and said, "Are you kidding? Why do they want to have dinner with us?"

I told him that they wanted to meet him.

He said, "Fine. We'll eat, and then he'll kill me!"

I said, "Don't be silly," and away we went to the Chase Hotel.

We arrived about five o'clock. Everyone was so kind—the desk clerk, the bellhops, everyone. It felt good to be fussed over. The room was nice, nothing special, just a nice double room. We got dressed and went to the lobby at seven. Kay and Jim were waiting for us. I introduced Bobby. Kay— bless her—hugged Bobby and kissed me and we went upstairs to the roof for dinner. We had a beautiful table and each of us had our own waiter! Talk about *class!* Jim was a big man…about 250 pounds. Kay was about a size 14, petite, very warm and loving. During dinner, we had the usual conversation: "You look good," "Are you happy?" "How did you get here?" "Where are you going?" and so on. It was very friendly and enjoyable.

The show went on. Romo Vincent, the star, announced that I was there and I had all the stale marriage jokes thrown at me. It was really great fun. When the show was over, I said I wanted to go to the ladies room. Kay said she would go with me. In the ladies room, Kay said, "He's nice and he's very much in love with you. You two look so happy together. I'm glad for you."

I said, "What about Jim?"

She said, "Don't worry, he's on your side."

That made me feel a hell of a lot better! We went back to our table. Bobby had a white line around his mouth and looked kind of pale. I knew something was up.

We finished our dinner and Jim said, "I wanna see the room they gave you." We went to see our room and Jim looked around and said, "It's okay."

We said, "Thanks for a lovely dinner, so good to see you," and so on.

Jim looked at me and said, "Take good care of him. He's an all right guy."

Bobby and I both breathed a sigh of relief and then they left. Bobby fell on the bed and said, "Whew! I have never been through anything like that in my life." I asked him, "What happened?"

He said that when we went to the ladies room, Jim looked at him and said, "Her father called and wanted me to send her back home—alone. But we don't butt into any *poisenal* stuff. She's old enough to know what she wants and if you're it, fine. As I say, we don't butt into any *poisenal*." He then leaned over the table and looked Bobby in the eyes and said, "But if you hurt one hair on her head," and snapped his fingers and his arm made the whole table shake. His hands were as big as hams, Again he said, "You kids look like you're in love and as I told you, we don't like to butt in on family problems…business is another story. You harm her in any way," and again he snapped his fingers and the whole table shook again.

Bobby kept telling him, "I love her. I just want to make her happy. I can take care of her if she doesn't want to work. It's about time she had a life after all she's done for everybody."

Jim just looked at him and smiled. "You're all right, kid."

That's when Kay and I came back to the table.

We left the next morning—and again, no hotel bill. I guess Jim paid for it. Like I said before, those guys were so wonderful to me!

On to Route 66, through Amarillo and Albuquerque. We averaged about four hundred miles a day, nice and easy, stopping where we wanted to, not a care in the world. I don't think I could make a trip like that today; it seems like I'm always racing against time. I'm always trying to get here and there and get back.

We stopped in Las Vegas. There were only two hotels, the Last Frontier and the El Rancho. Nothing around but sand and desert. The Bernard Brothers were playing at the Last Frontier, so we went to see them. I had worked with them many times. We saw the show and had a cup of tea afterwards. We didn't gamble. We were afraid to lose a buck! We stayed at a motel—my first glimpse of a motel. They were not as common as they are now.

The next day, on to Los Angeles. We went to Bert and Bob Zaccho's Kennels in the San Fernando Valley. They were friends of Bobby's from before he went into the army. Bobby owned the first boxer dog in America. A doctor friend of his was getting a divorce and was so mad at his wife that he took this boxer, worth about $7,500, and gave it to Bobby. Bobby showed the dog in many dog shows and won a lot of prizes. All boxers today stem from this one. Ingo Von Hager was his name. Bobby knew a lot about the show world of dogs. Bob Zaccho was a handler and Bert, his wife, ran the kennels. They were wonderful to us. They said, "Stay with us until you get settled." Bert was an excellent cook, so I learned a few tricks about cooking. After all, I was now a housewife—living in a kennel!

Chapter Thirteen

❧

Hollywood—Love, Home, and Work

We arrived on a Sunday, and Bobby went down to see Kay Kyser at NBC on Monday to see what was going on. They were all so happy to see him. Kay had most of the original band together. However, it was a different deal. Instead of $450 a week, which Bobby was making before he went into the army, it was now scale—$75 for the radio show only. What a comedown!

One of the trumpet players, Pokey Carrier, came over to Bobby and said, "Sure glad you showed up. I have an offer from Glen Gray and didn't know how I could leave *this* show. Now you can take over. We rehearse Monday and Wednesday and do the radio show on Wednesday."

They talked to Kay and he said, "Fine. Come in Wednesday, we'll rehearse and you'll do the radio show."

Bobby said, "Fine." He called Tommy Jones, another trumpet player and good friend; he had Bobby's horns and clothes. Bobby said he would pick them up. He was going back to work. Then he came back to the kennel and told me what had happened. He was worried because he hadn't touched a horn in two months, so he immediately started to practice.

He said, "I'll be through at nine o'clock, pick me up at NBC in Hollywood."

I drove him to work and came back and listened to the show. He was great! He did impressions of Harry James and Clyde McCoy, and of course he played the entire show. He really sounded good. He came out from the studio and he looked like a whipped dog.

He got in the car, put his head back and said, "I'm tired."

I said, "But you did a great show. I'm proud of you, sweetheart."

When we got back to the kennel, Bert made him something to eat and Bobby told me all the news about doing the show for scale. He said, "I've always been with Kay, I've never had another job. Now I have to start looking for other work. Oh, by the way, Pokey is going with Glen Gray and his wife is visiting her folks in Louisiana. They asked me if we wanted to rent their house in Culver City."

I said, "Fine. It's easy to move. We have no furniture, nothing, and we can buy things we need little by little."

So it was set: as soon as they moved out, we would move in. At least we would have a place of our own for a couple of months. Pokey's wife called me and said, "Everything is there to use. Use it—sheets, pillow cases, dishes, silverware, pots and pans."

I thought, *Great!* We'd start getting our own things, little by little. Until then, we'll use her things. It was really a blessing.

Bobby was worried about work. He said he'd have to try to make some contacts.

I said, "Don't worry, once they find out you're in town, they'll call you. You have to refer to your book."

He said, "What book?"

"Look, when they call and ask you if you're available, you say, I have to check my book." I said. "They will think you're all booked up and busy! Then you say, 'What day?' Wait awhile and say, 'Oh yes, I'm available.' It always works!"

And it did!

Perry Botkin, Bing Crosby's guitar player and contractor, called Bobby and asked if he was available. Bobby did exactly as I told him to.

He said, "I have to check my book." I smiled at him. He looked at me and I gave him the okay sign.

He then said, "What day?"

Perry said, "Thursday. It's for the Crosby show."

Bobby said, "Oh yeah, I can make it on Thursday." I died laughing. He was learning fast.

He got off the phone and said, "My God! First trumpet for Bing Crosby!"

I said, "There'll be more."

Bobby also took a job at Ciro's, which meant he had to work every night, but it meant more money and we could start buying our own furnishings.

I've always handled the money. I don't know why, but Bobby used to come home and give me his checks. I'd give him about thirty dollars to have in his pocket and would try to pay the bills with the rest—rent, groceries, cleaners, telephone, all that.

He said, "You take care of things. I don't like to do things like that."

I said, "Okay." Little did I know, he was training me to make decisions on my own, bless him.

Berle Adams found me somehow. He was head of Mercury Records. I had owed them two sides on a record deal.

He said, "I'd like to clear this up. We'll pick the songs and Earl Hagen will make the arrangements." The wheel goes round and round: Earl Hagen later wrote the theme song and all the music needed for *The Dick Van Dyke Show*, and we became the best of friends.

I asked Berle, "Big band?"

He said, "Yes."

I then said, "I have a list of the musicians I want in the band, and Bobby plays first trumpet. I want Dave Klein to contract it."

He said, "All right. Get your list ready and I'll call you tomorrow."

I hung up and said to Bobby, "Give me the names of all the top musicians in town."

He said, "Why?"

I told him I wanted everybody to know he was in town and working. I wanted Dave Klein to set up the date and I wanted his brother, Manny Klein, one of the great trumpet players of all time, to be in the band. "You will play first trumpet," I said. Talk about guts—but it worked!

Bobby and I walked into the studio together. We both greeted Dave Klein, who said, "Your father gave me a cigar when you were born."

I said, "This is my husband, Bobby Guy. We just got married and I want you to take care of him as far as dates are concerned." That was a little pushy, I know, but I had to do my part to help.

Dave said, "He's a good musician. He'll work, don't worry."

Bobby went up to the brass section. Manny Klein was there, and Conrad Gozzo. The first chair was open for Bobby. He told me later, he almost died, but he sat down. Manny introduced himself, as did Gozzo. Manny leaned over to Bobby and said, "We have an unwritten club here for first trumpet player. You get double time on all your dates. If I find out you took less, you won't work in this town."

Bobby gulped and said, "You got it, Manny."

As for me, I had never heard of the songs I was going to sing. I told Earl, "Please play them through for me so I can get an idea."

They played the arrangement, I had the sheet music with the lyrics—I can't read music—and Earl showed me where to come in.

They played it again and I said, "Okay, let's make one!" It turned out to be pretty good, so we went on to the next song. They played it twice and we made the second side. I thanked Earl and the band. They were amazed. We did both songs in an hour, on a three-hour session. The guys in the band were impressed, and my Bobby just smiled and winked at me.

Things were going pretty good. Now we had a little money and the house we rented was cute and small. I was cooking every night and learning a lot of new recipes. My girlfriend Dottie, from Jersey, gave me *The Joy of Cooking*—it was a godsend.

One day Bobby said, "Why don't you make some beef stew?" I was cooking mostly Italian food, which I knew how to make.

I said, "Okay, tonight we'll have beef stew."

I went to the store and the butcher was very nice and understanding. I said, "I've never made beef stew, but I have a recipe I can follow."

He said, "I'll give you the best meat for stew," and he did. It was beautiful to look at. I went home, got the book out and started to make beef stew. It's an old joke, folks, but it happened to me, honest to God. The stew was doing beautifully, and it smelled great. As I turned my back, the page in the cookbook flipped over to the next page! I looked at the recipe and it said "1/2 cup parsley." So I dumped a half cup of parsley in the stew. It turned a muddy green, but I thought, what the hell, maybe that's the way it should look. It smelled good and tasted great—it just looked muddy green.

Bobby came home and we sat down to eat. By now I had noticed what had happened with the cookbook, but I didn't say anything. I served the stew. God, it looked awful. Bobby looked at it...didn't say a word...took a bite and said, "This is delicious, but I've never seen beef stew with such a funny color."

I said, "It's Irish Stew!"

Honestly, I said that—and he bought it. At least I think he did.

We were very happy and doing all right. Bobby was doing the Kyser show, Bing's show, "Take It or Leave It," and doubling at Ciro's. Pretty soon he had to quit Ciro's because he was getting a lot of other shows, including the old Danny Thomas radio show. (Again, the wheel goes round and round.)

Bill Loeb from MCA called me and said he wanted to talk to Bobby and me. I thought, *Now what?* I told Bobby and we made an appointment to meet with him. We went to Beverly Hills and met Bill at the MCA offices. Bill was now working in California and had moved his family out here.

He started to talk to us. "Okay, you've proven your point. You're married, and Bobby is doing well, but *you* are turning down thousands of dollars—for what? I've had a lot of offers for you. You still owe a few dates, like the Capitol Theater in New York, Mounds Club in Cleveland, and Lowe's State. Why are you doing this?"

I said, "I have no gowns or music. I would have to start from scratch, plus I'm showing my father I don't have to work."

Bill said, "Big deal. Listen, you're old enough to be on your own. You proved that by getting married. I'm telling you, you take some of these dates and in five years you and Bobby can stick your five fingers to your nose to *everybody!* Don't be a fool. Bobby, talk to her."

Bobby said, "That's her business. If she wants to do it, fine; if not, fine. It's not my decision. Me? I'm a trumpet player. Ask me how to hit high C, I can tell you. It's her business, talk to her!" This was Bobby's answer whenever people tried to get to me through him with regard to work.

Bill continued, "Abbott and Costello are doing a hospital tour, and they want you—$2,750 a week for two weeks. I'm sure you can use it. Think about it. Call me."

I said again, "Bill, I have no gowns or music. I can't do the hospital tour, so tell them I can't make it."

Bill said, "Okay, but think about this, honey, I think you're making a big mistake if you don't start taking some of these dates. Slapsie Maxies [a big nightclub in Hollywood] called. Sammy Lewis wants you for two weeks, $2,750 a week. This date is in October, so you can get your gowns, and if needed, have new arrangements made."

I said, "I'll call you. Bobby and I have to talk. It's not as easy as you think."

So we left and drove home. Neither one of us said anything going home, but once we were inside, I sat him down and said, "Listen, Pap. He's right. I could be making good money. We can get all the things we need sooner and we *can* stick our five fingers to our nose in five years. But I'm also telling you: They're gonna call you 'Mr. Rose Marie,' because I'll be making more money than you, even though you're working and doing as much as you can. If you know what we're doing and I know what we're doing, then we can make it. What do you say? It's up to you."

During my first club date at Slapsie Maxie's nightclub, Los Angeles

As always, his answer was, "I'm with you, Mommy. And nobody will ever call me 'Mr. Rose Marie,' but you'll always be Mrs. Guy." He was so right. Nobody ever did call him "Mr. Rose Marie." He knew how to handle it. He was always the man of the house, and everybody knew it. It was a wonderful combination, and it worked for twenty years.

I told him I would call Max and find out about my gowns. When I got Max on the phone, he said, "Your father was here and wanted your gowns. I wouldn't give them to him. They're *your* gowns. *You* paid for them. So what do you want me to do?" Bless dear Max.

I said, "Send them out to me. I might be doing some dates."

He said, "Good. Don't let your father stop you. Are you happy?"

I said, "Oh, Max, it's heaven on earth—Bobby's so good and wonderful and he's doing great." I told him about all the shows Bobby was doing.

Max said, "Good, and if you need anything, let me know. I have your dress form here and I can still make your gowns."

"Oh, Max, that's wonderful. I probably will need a couple of new ones as soon as I start making some money. Meanwhile, I'll use the three you made. Just ship them out to me." I gave him the address, told him I loved him, and hung up.

Bobby said, "What about your music?"

I said, "I don't know. What do you think?"

Bobby thought for a minute and said, "Bill Fontaine has been making arrangements for the Kyser band. I think he could do it. You know your music by heart and you can sing them to him."

I said, "Great! Call him."

So that was arranged and that's how everything worked out. Bobby took care of the music department. He got the books for the music and got me the best arrangers. It was a perfect combination.

Of course, I couldn't do the hospital tour with Abbott and Costello, but I did take the Slapsie Maxies date. It was good money, and my first real chance to show Hollywood Miss Rose Marie, rather than Baby Rose Marie. Jerry Lester was the star, but somehow the reviews all raved about me. One headline read, "Rose Marie, We Love You." I was thrilled.

On opening night Durante was there. After I did the Durante number, he jumped up and said, "I don't know which one of us is me!" The place went wild, and I got a standing ovation. Standing ovations were not as common then as they are today. It was truly a great night. Lots of stars were there—Danny Thomas, Phil Silvers, George Burns and Gracie Allen, and so many more. It was wonderful. I had finally made my mark in Hollywood.

The next day everybody called and gushed about the reviews and congratulated me. Bill Loeb was there, of course, and he called me the next day to tell me that he had been right—I was great. I felt marvelous. Bobby was so proud—he always was. He was my greatest booster. So I began the two-week gig. Bobby came down almost every night he didn't have to work. I, of course, started buying linens, dishes, pots and pans. I started my own trousseau.

Pokey and his wife came back into town and wanted their house back. So Bobby and I had to find a place to live. We found a little house in

Burbank at 1114 North Evergreen. It was already furnished, but it was a start. Bobby used his G.I. Bill loan. I think the price was $12,500. So little by little, I'd throw out the sofa and get a new one; throw out the table and get a new one. I decided that my house was going to be done in the Early American style.

We were so excited and happy. Little by little we did the house. Bobby painted—he was no painter, but at least he tried. I met some of the wives of the Kyser band: Mickey Gunkler, who was also a new bride, and her husband, Hynie; Gus Bivona and his wife, Ruthie; Perry Botkin and his wife, Ginny. We all became very close. Bobby looked at Perry as a father figure. They looked at us as kids. We had a ball. We had dinner parties, played bridge, went bowling, and so on. It was wonderful.

One night at the club, I noticed that my dress was a little tight. I couldn't imagine why. I wasn't eating that much. I told Bobby and he said, "Why don't you go to the doctor? I'll call Janet, Ish Kabibble's wife. I know she's probably got a good doctor." I didn't tell Bobby that my period had stopped. Before I was married, it would stop for two or three months, but I wasn't doing anything, so I didn't worry about it. I went to see Dr. Verdon in Jersey before I was married. He told me once I got married it would straighten out. It did, for two months, but then it stopped again. I didn't think anything about it, but I went to see Janet's doctor. He examined me, my first internal examination. It was awful.

I asked him if I was pregnant.

He said, "No. Do you get bad cramps?"

I said, "Yes."

"Then come into my office."

I went in. He took a book from the shelf and underlined a sentence in the book, which evidently had many pencil markings on it as it was ripped through. He said, "You have to have your uterus stretched." He got on the phone and started to make an appointment.

I said, "Whoa! Wait a minute, I have to talk to my husband about this."

He said, "My dear child, it's not a matter of choice, it's a necessity."

"Thank you, doctor," I said, "but I can't do anything without my husband knowing about it."

I ran like hell out of that office and told Bobby what he had said. I also told him that I didn't like the doctor and that I was *not* pregnant.

My gowns were getting tighter, and it had me worried. My mother wrote me a nice letter and told me that my father's heart doctor, Dr. Edelstein, was now in Los Angeles, and that if I needed a doctor I should go see him. At least I knew him, so I called and made the appointment. What a different examination—it was like night and day. Dr. Edelstein was gentle and kind—not like that other rotten doctor.

Dr. Edelstein said, "You find yourself gaining weight?"

"Yeah, but I eat a lot of junk food…potato chips, popcorn."

"Do you feel dizzy in the morning?"

"Yeah, but it goes away."

He said, "My dear child, you are two and a half months pregnant!"

"Are you sure?"

"Oh yes, dear, but we'll do a test to be very sure." I found out that I could have lost the baby if I had followed that other doctor's advice! I couldn't wait to tell Bobby.

He was working at NBC, doing Bing's show. Frank Sinatra was the guest. I drove up and parked right in front! Frank came out first.

I ran up to him and said, "Frank, you're the first to know. I'm pregnant!"

Frank said, "Does Bobby know?"

I said, "No, not yet."

Frank said, "I'm gonna wait and see how he reacts when you tell him."

So we waited about three or four minutes and Bobby came out, gave me a kiss and said, "What did the doctor say?"

I said, "The rabbit died."

Bobby said, "What?"

"You're gonna be a father. I'm two and a half months pregnant!"

Bobby said, "I'll be a son-of-a-bitch!"

Frank said, "Is that all you're gonna say?"

Bobby said again, "I'll be a son-of-a-bitch!"

Frank said, "Come on, Bobby. Wake up, say something nice. Your girl's gonna have a baby."

Bobby: "I'll be a son-of-a-bitch." Then he grabbed me and kissed me.

Frank started laughing and said, "Congratulations, honey." He hugged me and kissed me on the cheek. Then he hugged Bobby.

Chapter Fourteen

The Flamingo Opening

My pregnancy was the happiest time of my life. I only gained about eleven and a half pounds, wore most of my own clothes, and went everywhere and did almost everything. We got involved with dog shows and Bobby judged a lot of them. He became an expert on boxers, so in time, we were breeding boxers. We had sixteen boxers at one time. It was a whole new world, but it was fun. However, I wasn't used to large dogs. I wanted a small dog. Bobby got me a purebred Scottie from Carnation Farms. He was adorable. His full name was Carnation Vindicated—we called him Sam. I even showed him in a big dog show and *he won!*

November rolled around, and I got a call from Bill Loeb about playing Las Vegas. A new hotel called the Flamingo was opening. Xavier Cugat and Jimmy Durante. I certainly didn't want to turn *that* down—to work with Jimmy. I was thinking we could even do a little finale at the end. Of course, I had played with Cugat at the Colonial Inn in Florida. I had it all figured out in my mind. The money was great: $2,500 a week. I okayed the date and found out that "Bugsy" Siegel owned the Flamingo. "The boys" again. I had never met Mr. Siegel, so that would be interesting. I could get away with my gowns, even though they were getting tighter. They wanted to open December 24.

I said, "I can't make it on the 24th."

"Why?"

"I just can't make it until Christmas is over."

Somehow they agreed and we opened December 28. I was to leave the day before, but there was a rainstorm and the only plane to Vegas was

Jimmy Durante   Rose Marie   Tommy Wonder   Xavier Cugat's Orchestra
ip 91   Las Vegas, Nevada   Telephone 4000 for reservations.

Flamingo Hotel table card, Las Vegas

canceled. Bobby said he didn't want me to drive, and he couldn't drive me because he had all his shows to do. I could go the next day, which was the opening night. I waited until the next day and took the morning flight. Durante was on the plane; Cugat was on the plane. So I thought, *We're all here. They can't open without us.*

We stayed at the El Rancho because the Flamingo's rooms weren't finished. They only had a dining room, the casino and lounge, and a coffee shop. We rehearsed, and Jimmy and I planned the finale.

Here was what we decided the finale would be. While Jimmy was doing his act, I would come out and say in a Durante voice imitation, "Wait a minute, wait a minute. Stop the music!" Jimmy would say, "There's an imposter here and I don't know which one it is." Jimmy would then play the piano and he and I would sing, "Who Will Be with You When I'm Far Away?" Jackson would do his strut and we would all walk off using the "Durante walk-off." It would be a smash.

After rehearsal, we went to our hotel to get dressed. The show was at eight o'clock. When we got to the Flamingo, it was the most beautiful hotel I had ever seen. It looked like Broadway. The other two hotels on the strip looked so drab compared with the Flamingo. Tommy Wonder,

On stage at the Flamingo Hotel

who was the opening act, and I went into the coffee shop for a bite to eat, just to hold us until after the opening. Well, they started coming in: two plane loads of stars, and I mean *stars*: Cary Grant, Lana Turner, Caesar Romero, Joan Crawford…to name just a few. It was so exciting. Billy Wilkerson from the *Hollywood Reporter* had an interest in the hotel; he had promised Mr. Siegel that he would get the stars for the opening…and that he did!

The place was "Glitter Gulch!" The show went on. Cugat's band played two or three numbers. Abby Lane was the band singer. Then Tommy Wonder came on and did his dance act. I followed Tommy and really did a great show. Then Durante and then, of course, *our* big finale. We really broke it up. Everyone was standing and yelling. It was one helluva night. Bobby

Flamingo Resort Hotel Jammed at Opening

Five-Million-Dollar Hostelry Resembles Fancy Hollywood Setting; Durante Wows Audience

By WALLY WILLIAMS

The Flamingo resort opens its doors last night. Guys and dolls from Las Vegas and suburbs, such as Los Angeles and Hollywood, jam the joint until it appears the proprietors will have to disjoint the walls to take care of the mob.

The hostelry itself looks like somebody visited the lot on which Cecil B. DeMille is operating from, steals the swankiest set of the super-colossal production, transports it to Las Vegas and sets it down in the sand and sagebrush.

The guys who attended the opening say they never see anything like it, and the dollars wander around like they are in a delicious dream. There are few of the patrons present who realize they are awake, for that matter, for once you get inside the place it's another world.

The dining room is packed all evening. Cugat and his orchestra are presiding on the podium and when he starts his rhythms there are more people on the dance floor than you can shake a sacroiliac at. The terpsichorean department is so well taken care of that the dancers have to be careful where they quiver. Some of them are and some aren't, with the result that the dance floor looks like a mass of jello already for serving in its six delicious flavors — mostly South American.

In the epicurean department, the chef serves a plate on which you don't even know it's spinach you're eating and the rest of the dinner is of a like stature. We eat Chateaubriand bon viveur and don't know it is a filet mignon until the head waiter tells us. We don't know, you see, that we have to know French to be able to eat our fill of the good stuff.

It takes the Nevada Projects, Inc., five million bucks and eight months to build the establishment, but after Jimmy Durante is on five minutes in the floor show the management is about ready to junk the whole idea and sell the remains to Moe Judnik, the old clothes man.

Durante, the star of the floor show, wows the audience, which is kept ducking old hats, pieces of piano and other bric-a-brac which sail over the establishment during the show.

Durante is sharper than a GI bayonet during the evening and while he is on the stage he rips apart a $1,600 piano and scatters Cugat's music all over the dance floor. It's funny to everybody except the management and Cugat.

Eddie Jackson, Durante's partner, gives the folks plenty to applaud about when he sings. Especially when he comes out with "Bill Bailey Won't You Please Come Home."

Rose Marie, who is featured in a previous act, comes on to join the routine. She almost out-Durantes Durante with her impression of "The Schnoz." Finally Durante, Jackson and Rose Marie wind up the uproar with a trio.

This Rose Marie is a glamorous blonde doll, all dressed up in a pink evening gown, and gives forth with warbles which seldom are heard in these desert parts. She sings "I'm a Big Girl Now," "Remember Me," and a couple of compositions of her own, the one which is dedicated to a sergeant wowing the audience which calls her back for plenty more artistry in the Rose Marie manner. She's tops and the audience likes her immensely.

The show is opened by Tommy Wonder who gives the ringsiders a sophisticated routine of splits and whirls, to the music of "St. Louis Blues," and then comes on later to provide a ballroom dance with a mannequin as a partner.

All in all the show, including Cugat's band which performs in solos and in chorus, is rated by the patrons as among the best seen in Las Vegas since t having floor shows in th hotels.

It's a great opening, bar and the casino gett share of the play from and the dolls who attend nothing like the Flami where in the nation mustn't miss it if you

From the *Las Vegas Review*, December 27, 1946

came up the next night and said he never saw anything like this show. It was such a smash—but only for two nights!

The two planeloads of stars went back to Hollywood, and the third night we had ten people in the audience! The locals were afraid to come in. I really think Vegas's slogan "Come as you are" started because of the Flamingo. It was so high-class. Not like the Last Frontier or the El Rancho. They looked like country inns by comparison. So that's how the two weeks went—ten to twelve people a night. It was such a shame, because the show was so great.

The end of the first week, Tommy and I were in the coffee shop between shows when this man came around and started to hand out our checks. I looked at mine and there was eleven dollars missing.

I called out to him. "Hey! I gotta talk to you. There's eleven dollars missing from my check."

He said, "Did you draw any money?"

I said, "Are you kidding? Eleven dollars? Who's gonna draw eleven dollars? No, I didn't draw any money. Look, if you need eleven dollars, I'll give it to you, but don't take it out of my check."

He said, "Let me find out about this. I'll get back to you."

I went back to sit with Tommy. He said, "Do you know who that is?"

I said, "I don't care, they took eleven dollars out of my check and I want to know why."

Tommy said, "Forget it. Please forget it. That was Bugsy Siegel!" After I heard that, I figured I would be picked up in an envelope.

I got my eleven dollars. It seems that Siegel found out what had happened. They had to guarantee the room at the El Rancho for the night I didn't come in. The Flamingo paid for it and then took it out of my check. Imagine, eleven dollars for a room! Mr. Siegel was very nice about it. When he handed me the eleven dollars, he said, "I'm sorry about this."

I said, "Oh, forget it. I just wanted to know what happened."

He said, "I'm glad you did and I'm glad you brought it to my attention. You're all right, kid!"

"Whew," I said—to myself.

We got very friendly after that. I met Virginia Hill. She was in the lounge one night and called me over. I sat down and she said, "I think you're great. You do a helluva show. Too bad the locals don't come in. I hope you don't mind me telling you this—your gowns are just beautiful and you look great, but it would be so much better if you lost about ten pounds."

I said, "I intend to…as soon as I give birth to this baby. I'm pregnant."

She almost died. She said, "I'm so sorry, I didn't know."

I said, "Nobody knows except my husband and my doctor."

She laughed and said, "I'm going to Paris tomorrow. What would you want me to bring the baby from Paris?"

I said, "I would love a christening dress and bonnet."

She said, "Okay. I'll get the nicest one I can find."

I said, "I'll pay you for it. I really want something special."

She said, "Don't be silly—it will be a gift from me and Benny." Benny was Bugsy's real name. She came back in a week and gave me the christening dress and bonnet. It was white lace and organdy, with white satin bows. It was truly beautiful.

One night, while we were sitting around between shows, Mr. Siegel came over to me and said, "Do you know how to play 'Shimmy'?" (Meaning chemin de fer, a card game.)

I said, "Of course, I know all the gambling games."

"Good." Then he handed me $10,000 and said, "Go over there and play. Maybe you can bring a little excitement to the game."

"Mr. Siegel, I am a performer, not a shill!" I said.

He said, "Go ahead and play. You're not doing anything else but sitting here."

Well, he was right about that. I took the money and went over to play. I won $25,000! Soon it was 11:45 P.M., and I had a show to do at midnight. I asked the dealer, "Is Mr. Siegel around? I've got to do the show." No one could find Mr. Siegel, so I went backstage, got dressed and put the $25,000 in my girdle. I went on and did the show. The gown was even tighter with $25,000 on my stomach!

After the show, I got dressed and went into the casino looking for Mr. Siegel. He was in the lounge having a cup of coffee.

I walked over to him and said, "May I sit down?"

He said, "Sure, would you like some coffee?"

I said, "I'd love a cup of tea."

He called the waiter over and ordered. I sat next to him and, once the waiter had gone away, said to him, "Here's your money. I won $25,000 but couldn't find you when I had to do the show."

He said, "I know. I know everything that's going on. I wasn't worried about you."

I said, "Thanks, but please don't ask me to do anything like that again. I was never so scared in my life."

He said, "You don't have to worry about anything here. I'll look out for you, and I won't ask you again, I promise." And that was that. I finished the two weeks and closing night I was called into Mr. Siegel's office.

He gave me my check and said, "You're all right. I like you and you do a great show. I hope to have you back here soon. Thanks for everything." We shook hands and I left. The next day, I flew home. A month later, I was saddened to read in the paper that Benny "Bugsy" Siegel had been killed in his house!

Chapter Fifteen

Presenting Georgiana Marie Guy

It was good to be home and just like a normal person again. My baby was due on April 23, but it was now May 17 and nothing had happened. I had planned a dinner party for Sunday, May 18. Alice Faye and Phil Harris were invited, as well as Perry and Ginny Botkin. It was to be an Italian dinner—what else?

Saturday night Bobby was doing a record date with Phil. I was home making sauce and setting the table, when suddenly I felt these little feet all across my stomach—no pain, just a little flutter. I sat down, got a clock out and timed the flutters. They were coming every fifteen minutes. Bobby came home around midnight. I told him about the little flutters and that they were coming every thirteen minutes now.

He said, "Call the doctor."

I said, "What for? This isn't *it*—wouldn't I know?" (As if I had given birth forty times before!)

He insisted I call the doctor.

I said, "Okay, but it's stupid. It's not pains, it's little flutters."

Again he said, "Call!"

I did call Dr. Krahulik, one of the best obstetricians in the world. We had met him through Kermit Ryan, a pediatrician friend of Bobby's who had said to use Dr. Krahulik. He was so right. I called and told him about the flutters.

He said, "Did your water break?"

I said, "No."

He said, "Get to the hospital, I'll see you there." I hung up and thought the whole thing was dumb. I had no pains. I was feeling fine. We'll go to the hospital and then come home—stupid!

Bobby's mother Nan had come to California to help me with the baby. I knew nothing about babies. I even asked, "What do you do when they cry?" Nan loved brand-new babies and she was wonderful. I had a great mother-in-law, and I grew to love her. She was a very beautiful woman, and she must have been a real cut-up when she was younger.

We got ready to go to the hospital. Woke up Nan, got my suitcase, walked to the car, got in and drove to the hospital very carefully. No rush, nothing. We got to the hospital and I was put in a wheelchair and scooted up to some room. After all the preparations were done, I was lying in the bed on my side.

The nurse came in and said, "Would you like to see your husband?"

I said, "Sure," and in he came, wide-eyed and a bit confused

He asked, "Any pains?"

I said, "No. Now listen to me....Call up everybody and cancel the dinner. Tell your mother to put the meatballs and sausage in the refrigerator. Put the sauce..." and just then my right knee started to shake. I put my hand on my knee to stop it and said, "Oh, I've got a little pain...not much, just a little." My knee started to shake again. Again I put my hand on my knee to stop it and said to Bobby, "You'd better go now," and he left.

I had some more pains, and the doctor came in and they wheeled me someplace. I guess it was the delivery room. They put a mask on my face and I thought, *Great. Gas....I'll be knocked out.* I started to sniff like crazy—nothing.

I said to the nurse, "You'd better check this out, I don't smell anything."

She said, "It's just oxygen dear, breathe easy." The next thing I knew, I heard the little slap and cry. They wheeled me over to the side, I opened my eyes and Bobby said, "Well, you got your girl."

I said, "What time is it?"

He said, "10:10 A.M."

"Is she all right?"

The nurse said, "She's got five fingers on each hand and five toes on each foot, and she's beautiful."

They wheeled me out to my room. Nan was beside me and said, "She's going to be beautiful, her eyes are wide apart."

I was so groggy, I said, "Fine."

The next thing I knew, I was in my room and Bobby was at my bedside looking at me. "Are you all right?" he asked.

Georgiana Marie Guy, nine months old

I said, "Fine. Go home and I'll see you later."

He came back that night and I was feeling great. He told me he had called everyone and cancelled the dinner. Everyone was thrilled about the baby. He said he sent telegrams to my mother and father, his sister, and Joe Schribman. We were listening to Walter Winchell on the radio and heard him say, "Rose Marie and Bobby Guy—she, who was Baby Rose Marie—now have a baby of their own, a little girl born this morning in Hollywood." We were thrilled and wondered how he knew.

We decided on the name Georgiana Marie. Georgiana because it was different and because it was the name of my mother's best friend. Marie because she was born in May. Like my mother, I didn't like the name of Mary either. Bobby liked Vicky—I didn't. I thought about Roberta, after Bobby—he didn't like that. So it was Georgiana Marie Guy.

Dr. Krahulik sent me home after five days and ordered me to stay in bed at least five weeks. There was nothing wrong…that was just his S.O.P. (Standard Operating Procedure).

Nan was taking care of the baby, and I was doing fine. Nan was teaching me how to take care of our little girl. Everybody sent flowers and gifts.

We got a letter from my parents, enclosing the telegrams we sent with "We're not interested" written across them. I knew it was my father and not my mother. She wouldn't do anything like that. I found out later she never saw the telegram. She read about the baby's birth in the newspaper!

Bill Loeb called and said the Capitol Theater wanted me to play off the date I owed them, so did the Mounds Club in Cleveland and the Loews State.

I told him, "Give me a break, I don't want to do anything for at least six months."

He said, "Okay, but keep these dates in mind."

So for six months I was with my baby and my Bobby having the greatest time of my life. The doctor had asked me how much I wanted to weigh after the baby was born. I told him 125 pounds.

He said, "You're gonna have to work for it."

I began to exercise and watch my diet and in six months, I weighed 125 pounds—ready to go back to work.

During all this time, Bobby and I looked at different houses. He loved to do that, and he *loved* cars. He was doing *The Ozzie and Harriet Show* on TV, and one of the musicians in the band was doing some real estate on the side. He told us about a new development called Cameron Woods, a nice section in Van Nuys. So we went over one day. It was a lovely area. A lot of well-known people had built houses there: Audie Murphy; Bob Russell, the songwriter; John Raitt, who had done "Oklahoma" and "Carousel"; and Jack Benny's head writer, Sam Perrin. We didn't see a house we wanted, but we looked at the remaining lots.

To make a long story short, the builder of the entire street, Bill Bucher, came over and we wound up buying a particular lot and having him build our house for $25,000. That was the total for the lot *and* the house. I told Bill not to put up one piece of wood until we had paid him $12,500—half of the price. He said that we didn't have to do that. I told him we wanted to because in the back of my mind, I knew these dates had to be played and I would have the money for the down payment.

It was now getting close to the time for me to return to work and start building our house. My cousin Marie called me. She and her husband had moved out to California. She was wonderful. She was the one who told me the *complete* story about "the other family."

I was shocked. God bless my Bobby. He said, "So what? Who cares? We're a family now, and nothing can change that." He made me feel wonderful—about the biggest shock of my life. I asked Marie to go on the dates with me. I didn't want to travel alone. It was only for five weeks. So, we left and went to New York, to the Capitol Theater.

What I didn't know was that my father had threatened MCA and the Capitol Theater that something would happen if I appeared there. The manager, Mr. Mann, told me about it and said, "Don't worry, we'll take care of things at the theater, and we'll have a guard outside your dressing room. Please don't worry."

I said, "All right."

But I was thinking, *What could my father do?* Knowing him, almost anything. When I walked on stage for that first show, there were policemen lined up on each side of the wall of the theater. You would have thought we were being invaded! Nothing happened, and I went on to finish the two weeks. Then the Mounds Club, in Cleveland. "The boys" again.

The minute I got into town, I called Doc Maginie and told him, "I'm going to play the Mounds Club for two weeks and I'm inviting all of you, with your wives, to the opening."

He said, "We'll see," which didn't sound much like Doc. He told me he had a little bar/restaurant called the Wagon Wheel. It was on the way to the Mounds. We could stop there. I didn't understand that—and I didn't ask.

Every night it was the same thing. We'd stop at the Wagon Wheel before I had to go to work, have a bite to eat, and I'd try to talk them into coming to the club. They would always have excuses. Finally, one night Doc said, "Make a reservation for eight people for tomorrow night, and let me know what they say."

I said, "Okay." So I went to the club that night and spoke to Moe Dalitz, the boss. I told him I wanted to make a reservation for eight people for the next night. He said, "Who's coming?" Which knocked me for a loop—they never ask that!

"Doc Maginie, Jerry Maloney, and all the Italians I know." I said, laughing.

He said, "We're all booked up. There aren't any tables open."

Well, I almost died. I was right—something was wrong. I said, "How about the following night?"

He said, "No, we're all booked up."

I knew then and there not to ask any more questions. I said, "Okay, Moe, thanks."

I couldn't wait to get to the Wagon Wheel to tell Doc and the rest of "the boys." I did my two shows and we drove to the Wagon Wheel. I told Doc what had happened and that I was so sorry. Then I said, "What's up?"

He said, "Never mind. I knew they wouldn't let us in."

I said, "Why?"

He said, "There's a little something goin' on between the Italian and Jewish mobs...and that's all you need to know."

I said, "Fine with me, Doc. I just wanted you to come and see my show."

He said, "I know. Next time. Meanwhile, we'll have a party here on your closing night."

It was a very strange feeling—all the guys mumbling and talking to each other. Finally one of them came over to me and said, "When you go to the club tomorrow night, look at the check stand. There are three bulletholes there. I put 'em there." So *that's* what must be wrong! I knew that the Mounds Club had had a robbery about a month before, while Peter Lind Hayes and Mary Healy were appearing there. It had been in all the papers.

I went to work the next night, and sure enough, I looked at the check stand and there were the three bulletholes. So that's why they're not talking to one another. Evidently it was a big feud—even bigger than the papers reported. That night at the Wagon Wheel, I didn't say anything about the club, except that the shows had been good and that we had had a good crowd.

Closing night we went to the club. I did my shows, got my check and thanked Moe Dalitz. He said, "Thanks for doing a good job and tell your friends we'll see them soon." I almost died! I couldn't wait to get out of there. We drove to the Wagon Wheel and I told Doc what happened. He just smiled and said, "Oh, I'm *sure* we'll see them again."

They put on a very nice closing night party for me. All of "the boys" were there with their wives. It was fun to be with all of them. The food was delicious—but you could feel the tension in the air!

Chapter Sixteen

Florida and the Ski School

They were building our house and we were going through all kinds of traumatic emotions. Did we forget to put in closets? Should we add another bathroom? Anyone who has built his or her first house goes through this, I'm sure of that. I had been shopping for materials and wallpaper all over the country—New York, Cleveland, even Vegas. I found imported French wallpaper for the hall. I found two little antique French chairs in Lord and Taylor. It was going to be beautiful. The builder, Bill Bucher, even put in some extra things, like a trellis in the kitchen. All the cabinets were hand-finished. It was our dream house. We planted Rose Marie roses on the fence in the front, and also an orange tree. We owed $12,500 on it, which seemed like twelve million dollars, but we were happy and both of us were working. I worked when I wanted to, and Bobby was one of the top hornmen in California. We moved in March of '49.

I was home quite a bit and loving every minute of it. I did some guest shots—*The Rudy Vallee Show*, Bing's show. I wanted to do some dramatic TV. I got a call about *Gunsmoke*. It was the top TV show at the time.

I went into the offices and the girl said, "Have you seen a script?"

I said, "No."

She handed me one and said, "The part is Mrs. Monger."

Here I was, cute figure, little black and white cotton dress, and short white gloves—just adorable. I read the part. It was a sixty-year-old woman sawing wood on a ranch! At first I thought it was a mistake, but no, the girl insisted that the part was Mrs. Monger. I figured, *What the hell, I'm not gonna get this part, but I'll go in and read for it anyway.*

I met Lynn Stalmaster, the casting man and producer. I also met the director John Rich (the wheel goes round—I would work with him later on *The Dick Van Dyke Show*). I sat down and Lynn Stalmaster read with me. I put my voice even lower and I was going to clown my way through it, thinking of every Western I had ever seen. We read from the script:

Lynn: "Howdy, Mrs. Monger."

Me: "Howdee, Sheriff."

Lynn: "How ya feeling today?"

Me: "Poorly, thank *ye*." (The script had said "Thank you.")

When I said "ye," they all started to get up, which meant that the reading was over. I said, "Thank you, gentlemen," and started to walk out, knowing I hadn't gotten the job before they said anything to me.

John Rich came to the door with me and said, "Would you mind cutting your nails?"

I said, "Why?"

John said, "I don't think a woman sawing wood would have nails that long."

I said, "You want *me* for this part?"

John said, "Yes, I think you'll be great."

I almost died. The shoot was wonderful and I enjoyed every minute of it. One day we were shooting a scene with these guys sitting around a table. I was supposed to ladle them some stew from a pot I was holding. We did a take—they were delivering their lines, and I began putting stew on their plates.

John said, "Cut," and called me over. He said, "If you're going to spoon that stew like you are, nobody will even look at the guys! You're giving me comedy timing and nobody will even know what they're saying."

I said, "I'm sorry. I was just trying to do my best and not interfere with their lines. I didn't know I was doing comedy timing. Sorry, I'll try it again. I was just trying to pad my part." We both laughed and we finished the show. My first dramatic show—*Gunsmoke* with James Arness. Not bad!

Bill Loeb called and told me about a date in Florida, at the Clover Club in Miami. All the big stars played Miami Beach, but this was Miami. I wasn't too thrilled about it. The Vagabonds and Jan Murray were on the bill, and the money was lousy for four weeks. But I wasn't getting any calls for my dramatic work—ha ha—so I figured, *What the hell*. They wanted me to open in December. I told them that I didn't work on Christmas, so the date was set for January.

Bobby and me at waterskiing school in Florida

What started out as four weeks turned into eleven weeks. We were breaking all of the records—we were the hottest act in town. Martha Raye was at the 500 Club, Sophie Tucker and Joe E. Lewis were at another club, as was Jerry Lester—all in Miami Beach. We were the only hot spot in Miami itself. We did three shows a night: 8:00 P.M., midnight, and 2:30 A.M. They would line up outside an hour before each show—it was amazing. The Vagabonds, with whom I had worked before, were a great act, and we had a lot of fun together. I've known Jan Murray since I was a kid. It was a happy group and we were doing great business. Woody Woodbury was the lounge act and he became my big brother. He was so much fun to be with. We have remained good friends to this day.

We all worked until 3:30 A.M., and then we'd get up at 10:00 A.M. and go to waterskiing school. The Vagabonds started it—and soon enough, every star in Miami Beach was showing up at 10 o'clock in the morning: Martha Raye, Jerry Lester, Jack E. Leonard, and Woody Woodbury. Of course, some of "the boys" were there—Joe Frechetti; his brother, Charlie;

Jack Goldman, from the Clover Club—all of us acting like kids, waterskiing. If you didn't know how, they taught you. You *had* to water ski! The laughs and the jokes were going all the time. I have home movies of this.

I would call home and tell Bobby what was going on and say to him, "Come on down. You can take your vacation now. We'll have a ball and just wait till you see the show and the business we're doing."

So he came down. All the people from the waterskiing school, the chorus girls from our club, everyone went to the airport to meet his plane. Everybody thought a big celebrity was on the plane. Bobby got a big kick out of it, and he joined the waterskiing school set. He didn't know how to water ski, so everybody taught him. God, what fun we had.

Bobby went back home, and after the eleventh week, I went home. The so-called act—the Vagabonds, Jan Murray, and I—went to Vegas, where we broke all records. Following that, we went to the Riviera in Jersey, and all the Jersey mob and the Frechetti boys came down for our opening—Tommy Brown, Frank Costello, Willie Morretti…just about everybody. We were the "pets" of "the boys." After all, we had all been water skiing together! It was a helluva date. I stayed at my mother's house because it was so close. When I arrived there, I found out that when my brother was out of the service, that he had gotten married to Marion, his high-school sweetheart, and that they had moved to Florida. They had the big wedding!

My mother cooked up a big Italian dinner and the Vagabonds came over: Dom, Al, Tillio, and Pete. We were like family; we had worked together for so long. My father was there and he was pleasant, but that's about it. I was still sending money home, but I wondered if my father had done anything about making money on his own. From what I could tell, he hadn't, and I was still supporting them. However, I gave the money to my mother this time!

Chapter Seventeen

Our Social Life—California Style

Back home, Bobby and I had become part of the Hollywood crowd. I had played Ciro's for six weeks. Everybody and his brother came to see the show. The reviews were great. Bobby was doing the Alice Faye-Phil Harris Show and we all became good friends. We spent some wonderful times over at their house. One Easter "Noop" went with us.

"Noop" was Georgiana. Bobby had a nickname for everyone. Once he was feeding our daughter some prunes and she got them all over her face. Bobby said, "Oh, look what you did to your noop [nose]. Poor Noopy." It's been "Noopy" from that minute on. Of course she was and is an exact replica of Bobby.

She was all dressed up for Easter, and she looked like a doll. Alice fell in love with her and gave her a beautiful Easter bunny. Walter Scharf and his wife Betty were there. Walter was the musical director at 20th Century Fox. He and Betty were close friends of Alice and Phil. We were having a wonderful Easter brunch. I was fooling around and started to imitate Sheldon Leonard, who played "The Tout" on Phil's show. Phil laughed and thought it would be a good idea if I played the Tout's sister, who talked like Sheldon. I wound up doing a few of the shows and Bobby became Walter's first trumpet. Everything Walter did, Bobby was on the date, including movies like *Guys and Dolls, Funny Girl, Top Banana,* and many more.

While we were at Ciro's, we met Desi Arnaz and Lucille Ball. They came backstage after the show, and they were both so wonderful.

Lucy said, "We want to do a TV show for you."

I couldn't talk, I was so excited. We became very good friends. We did a

Noopy and Daddy

pilot called *2 Girls on Broadway*. Peggy Ryan played my sister and Ray McDonald played the boyfriend. Desi and Lucy were making another pilot at the same time called *Those Whiting Girls*, with Margaret and her sister Barbara. They sold *Those Whiting Girls*, and our little pilot got lost in the shuffle.

However, our friendship with Lucy and Desi was getting stronger. We'd go over to one another's house for dinner. Lucy loved our house and said, "Don't ever sell it, I love it here." One night they came over for dinner after working all day on *The Long, Long Trailer*. I thought they would cancel because they had worked all day, but they didn't. They came over, we had dinner and Lucy said, "Do you want to see the scene we did today? Desi was just wonderful." So there we were, in the living room: Lucy and Desi on the couch, Bobby, Noopy, my mother-in-law, and me. Just like we were at the movies. They went through this scene, just like they did it in the movie. What a night! To think we had America's top couple in our living room doing a scene from the movie they were just shooting.

We went to all of the New Year's Eve parties that Lucy and Desi threw. Lucy never forgot my birthday, and she would always address the card, "To Baby Rose Marie." I never forgot her birthday either. We are both Leos and we remember!

I played Ciro's again, for six weeks this time. The owner, Herman Hover gave me a silver tea set in appreciation.

Bobby's birthday was March 28, and I always had a big birthday party for him every year. One year it was a circus party. The theme was "come as your favorite circus performer." I had a cotton-candy machine on the lawn. We served hot dogs, popcorn, soda, Cracker Jacks, and hamburgers. Everyone came in costume.

Another year we had a "Hobo party"—come as a hobo. We served mulligan stew on tin plates, loaves of bread, no forks or knives, tin cups for coffee, and—as always—a huge cake. We gave out prizes for the best costume. Nothing big, just little things to remind them of the party.

We had a "Come as your favorite song title" party. That was a beaut. Andy Devine came in a Chinese outfit—his song title was "Slow Boat to China." Sheila MacRae came in a gypsy costume—her song was "Golden Earrings." I had three sets of falsies in my sweater and came as "She's Funny That Way." Bobby just tied a pepperoni to his pants and came as "Lover." Ginny Botkin came with a pillow under her dress and a sign saying, "You Made Me Love You," and on her back another sign saying, "I Didn't Wanna Do It." But Gordon MacRae won the prize that night. He came dressed in an old terry cloth robe with a set of false teeth in one pocket; toothbrush and toothpaste pinned to the robe and a douche bag for a hat. The song he had come as was "These Little Things Remind Me of You." We served shrimp boats—a half loaf of bread with shrimp in an Italian sauce.

What wonderful memories. Bobby was always so proud. We had such good friends and in our social life we were batting a thousand. Whenever I played Vegas, everyone would come up to see the show. I also played Tahoe and Reno. Many of our friends would come to see me in those places as well.

While I was in Reno, playing the Riverside Hotel ("the boys" again—Wurtheimers), I got a call from Bobby. I had been out shopping all day and when I came back to the hotel, around five o'clock, there were many calls from Bobby. I thought something was wrong with the baby.

I called him and he sounded very nervous. He said, "No, the baby is fine, but your father died today."

I said, "Oh!"

Bobby said, "I've made all the arrangements. I told them at the hotel what happened and they said you could leave tonight. I have your flight number and your brother will meet you at the airport."

I said, "Okay. I'll call you when I arrive in Jersey."

I hung up. Didn't cry—couldn't even try to cry. I felt nothing! I packed and left on the eight o'clock plane. My brother met me at the airport and we went home to my mother. She was a wreck. She did manage to tell me he died at "*the other house!*" What a mess. He humiliated her even at the very end.

My father's cousin arranged everything for the funeral. My mother didn't want to go to the funeral parlor—she cried a lot. "I don't want to see him," she said.

I said, "We gotta go, but I promise you there will be no more embarrassing moments."

We went, and my mother just fell apart at first, but she wound up being okay. I was in the side room with my girlfriends. My brother Frank and his wife Marion were taking care of things in the front and I went to my father's cousin and said, "I don't want the other family here, understand? No matter what they say, they are not allowed here...and I leave that up to you." I don't think I shed one tear. That sounds cruel, I know, but that was the way I felt.

I talked to my mother about what she wanted to do. She didn't know yet. She wanted to keep the house, which I knew I would have to support.

Chapter Eighteen

Phil Silvers and Broadway...Again

Bobby insisted that my mother come to California just to get away from everything. I was playing in San Francisco, at the Bal Tavern, and my mother came out with me for the four-week engagement. After the date, we came home to southern California. My mother and my mother-in-law got along like two peas in a pod. It was wonderful. Bobby used to take them out to the movies, and of course we'd all go sightseeing together. It was good feeling and we were really a family.

My mother left for New Jersey in late May. I worried about her being alone in that big house. She was happy in her castle and had her girlfriends over a lot. I was paying the bills, but I didn't mind because I knew she was happy and that *she* was getting the money.

I had to play the Roxy again, so I went to New York and stayed at my mother's house. At least I didn't have to pay a hotel bill. While I was at the Roxy doing five shows a day, I got a call out of the blue from Phil Silvers. He was doing a new Broadway show and wanted me to be in it.

I said, "No, it means being away too long from Bobby and the baby."

He said, "Bobby can come in from time to time and you can bring the baby with you."

I thought, *Hmm, Broadway again...I wonder if the show will make it?* I knew the Broadway legit crowd loved Phil, so I told him to send me a script. He sent about fifteen pages with pages saying, "Phil does funny bit here....Phil does funny elopement scene here." I never saw a script like that in my life. It was written—if you can even use that word—by Hy Kraft, who I think had some credibility in legit theater.

Noopy, Bobby, my mother, Stella, and Bobby's mother, Nan

I told Phil, "This is stupid, there's no script."

He said, "I know. We'll do it as it comes. It's all about burlesque and we can all add things to it."

I said, "You gotta be kidding."

The only good thing was that Johnny Mercer had written the music and lyrics. Paula Stone and her husband, Mike Sloane, were the producers. They got Jack Donahue for the director—thank God for him. Donahue had done all the Esther Williams movies and had been in the biz for years. He was like a teddy bear and kidded Phil all the time. We practically wrote the show. The rest of the cast were burlesque comics. They were the best! Joey Faye, Herbie Faye, Eddie Hanley and Jack Albertson. Herbie Faye later played the guy with the cart full of goodies on *The Dick Van Dyke Show*.

When I say that they were the best, I mean that they knew all the old burlesque bits. If we ran into a snag in a scene, one of the guys would say, "Hey, how about the bit about…?" Donahue took Hy Kraft to see a TV show so that he'd know what we were doing. Actually the show we were

With Phil Silvers in *Top Banana*

putting on was about Berle and his Texaco show, and how crazy he was when he did his TV show. The only difference was that Phil played a comic from burlesque who had a big hit TV show.

The rehearsals were the most fun I have ever had. All of these great comics…I was in my glory. Phil and I did a duet that became a classic. Johnny Mercer wrote a song for me called, "I Fought Every Step of the Way." It was a double entendre combining boxing with getting a guy. The lyrics were unbelievable. Each chorus was a round of boxing. Round One: I knew that he outweighed me, but "I fought every step of the way," and so on.

He wrote six rounds and said, "I know you'll be doing encores."

"Oh, sure," I said.

We opened in Boston, so Ruthie was with me all the time, which was great. I could blow off steam with her. I got so many flowers and telegrams on opening night. One from Jackie Gleason said, "Watch Silvers, he's pretty

With Audrey Meadows in *Top Banana*

sneaky," signed "The Great One." Phil was a dream to work with. As with Berle, we both knew what the other wanted. We had a shorthand language of our own. The elopement scene hadn't been written yet, and Jack Donahue called a great act to come to Boston...Walter Dare Whal and Johnny. Walter was a big man and Johnny was the little guy. They would get all tangled up holding hands and would try to get out of the tangles. Donahue thought it would make a great elopement scene. How right he was. It was one of the highlights of the show. The opening was a smash...standing ovations and all. We knew we were in a hit show, and Ruthie threw a big *Top Banana* party.

Bobby came to Philly for the opening and gave me a big charm with the masks of comedy and tragedy engraved, "To my mommy, the greatest star I know." I wear it all the time. Bobby, Phil, and I had a great time in Philly. The reviews were raves. Judy Applebaum and her parents came to see the show. It was a nice reunion. They were so happy for us.

Bobby went home, and we went to New York. He couldn't come to

New York because of his work, but at least he saw one opening. He would come to New York every two or three weeks, so it all worked out fine. Opening night in New York was *sensational!* My "I Fought Every Step of the Way" number stopped the show. Again, it was before the first act finale. Usually when the curtain opens up to full stage and the star—in this case, Phil—is in the scene, that really kills a hand, but they kept applauding and the entire cast turned to me. Phil took off his hat and put his arm out to me. Talk about thrills! This was at the Winter Garden Theater on Broadway—and I stopped the show with my first number.

I must say, Johnny Mercer and I worked hard on that number. Every night in Boston, he would come in with new lyrics for my song—*every night!* Change Round 2 to Round 3, take lyrics from Round 1 and put in Round 3, like that. Me? I would try to learn them while I was making up and do them that night to see if they worked. Johnny was amazed that I could learn them that fast—but hell, it was *my* song and I wanted it to be the best I could make it. It proved itself opening night on Broadway. Phil was nervous.

I said to him, "Stop it, we've done this for eight weeks. What are you nervous about?"

He just said, "Shut up—if I wanna be nervous, I'll be nervous!"

I laughed and walked away. Everybody was on edge, and I was feeling fine. I was starting to get worried because I *wasn't* nervous. I always think of Ethel Merman when it comes to nerves. She once told me, "I never get nervous. I know what I'm going to do. The audience should be nervous, they don't know what they're gonna get!" I've never forgotten that.

The rest of the show was a smash. Phil's elopement scene got such big laughs, I saw people taking out hankies to wipe their eyes. Truly, it was a gem. The duet stopped the show. It was called "A Word a Day." You've heard of fractured French? This was fractured English. It's one of the most brilliant lyrics ever written.

The show was over: standing ovation, whistles, and bravos—it was delicious! We went to Sardi's to wait for the reviews. Marlon Brando was there, and he became a part of the group. He sat down with us and was just wonderful.

After reading the reviews, Brando said, "You must be very proud stopping the show twice in one night."

I said, "I've worked all my life for that!" He gave me a kiss on the cheek and got up and left.

We were running into a rather comfortable routine. I stayed at my mother's and drove into work every night. Bobby would come in every second or third week. My mother always had a little something to eat for me when I returned after the show. One night I went home and was setting the table when I heard, "Hello, Mommy." It was Noopy in the doorway, with Bobby standing behind her. I was so surprised. He said, "I think she should be with you." So she stayed with me.

The first time I took Noop to see the show was a matinee. I told her to sit still on the high stool and not to say anything. She was wonderful, and she loved the show. Phil fell in love with her. She was always in his dressing room. He told me, "I can't walk around in my dressing room. She comes in and says, 'Pheeel.'" Then they'd hug and I'd have to go and get her. By the time she'd attended her fourth matinee, she was an old hand. Knew every song, every scene. She was unbelievable.

When we took our final bows, the cast would come out in sets of two or three. I was next to last and then Phil. One day I took my bow and we waited for Phil. When he came out, the whole audience went "Ahhhh." I looked around—he had Noop by the hand. We all took our first bow. The curtain came down and up again for the second bow. Phil said to Noop, "Hold on to my hand" and he did the bit he did in the elopement scene— Noop holding on and doing what we used to call the "hand bit." The audience went wild, applauding even louder and laughing.

When the curtain finally came down, Phil picked up Noopy in his arms and said to me, "Remember: I was the first one to put her on a stage."

I said, "At the Winter Garden yet!"

We settled into a routine. I was home all day with Noop and my mother until I had to go to the theater. On matinee days, I took Noop with me and she always wound up in Phil's dressing room, telling him, "Pheeel, today we'll do the hand bit *after* I take my bow, okay?"

Phil would laugh and say, "Okay, Noop."

What I didn't know was that my mother was teaching her to sing "Top Banana"! I only found out when *The Sam Levinson Show* called and wanted Noop for his show. Sam Levinson was a schoolteacher who had become a stand-up comic and had gotten his own TV show. It dealt with celebrity kids who had problems with their parents.

I called and asked someone at the show, "What do you want her to do?"

"She'll have a problem with you."

"Oh really?" said I, "And what kind of problem is that?"

"Oh, she'll say she likes to take a bow."

I said, "Well, that's true. Is that all?"

"Yes. Sam will talk to her and ask her what her problem is and she'll say, 'I like to take a bow.' Sam will make some comments and that's it."

I said, "I'll have to ask her if she wants to do it."

"You're going to ask a four-year-old if she wants to go on TV?"

I said, "Yes, if she doesn't want to do it, she won't do it, so I'll call you back."

I asked Noop if she wanted to do the show and she said, "Oh yes, and I'm gonna sing 'Top Banana' too!"

I told her, "You have to learn some script lines."

She said, "I can do it, and I'll sing 'Top Banana.'"

Well, I was floored. I looked at my mother and said, "Did you teach her 'Top Banana'?"

My mother said, "Of course, and she'll do the Durante walk-off!"

Well, need I say more? My mother had her second chance at showbiz with her granddaughter!

The script arrived, and it was very short—thank God. Sam would say, "What's your problem?"

And Noop would say, "My mommy thinks I'm a big ham!"

Sam: "Why does your mommy think you're a big ham?"

Noop: "Because I like to take a bow."

Sam: "You mean after you sing or dance?"

Noop: "No—I just like to take a bow!"

Then he'd have her take a bow and that was it. So I rehearsed her on the lines, not really knowing if she would do them.

On the day of the show, my friend Gerri Danna did her hair. I bought Noop a cornflower blue organdy dress with yards and yards of skirt. It was adorable. My brother and Marion were in Jersey for a visit, so my brother Frank, Gerri, Noop and I went into New York for the rehearsal. Sam Levinson was a warm, friendly kind of guy. He immediately fell in love with Noop and took her into his dressing room to talk to her.

He asked simple questions like "What did you have for lunch?" She would answer him. Then he'd throw in a script question and she would say, "What?" She'd take a breath and then she'd answer by the script. He thought that was great. I wasn't so sure. So we went in to rehearse and she did the same thing. He'd ask her a question, she would say, "What?" take a breath, and answer. So we went through that all right.

Then she said, "I wanna sing 'Top Banana.'" I almost died.

Sam said, "Go ahead."

So she started, and the band—not knowing the song—just added the bass, drums and piano for a vamp kind of thing. Then at the end, she went into a 4/4 tempo and did the Durante walk-off. The band died, so did Sam and everybody in the studio.

The band leader said, "We'll give her a keynote."

I said, "Fine," and we left to get a bite to eat.

My brother was so nervous, he kept going to the bathroom. I said, "What's the matter with you?"

He said, "They're gonna give her a keynote for the song. What if she starts in the wrong key?"

God, I never thought of that! Gerri was fussing with her hair. I said, "Leave her alone, she'll get nervous." Of course, I was a wreck. I knew she had a good ear, so I just prayed.

The time came for the show. Sam introduced her and she walked onto the stage like Phil Silvers—hands swinging and straight up. Phil had taught her to walk like that on stage.

Sam said, "Who's your mommy?"

And she said, "Rose Marie," and out I came.

He went on to the script and said, "What's your problem?"

She said, "What?" took a breath and said, "My mommy thinks I'm a big ham."

Sam: "Why?"

Noop: "Because I like to take a bow."

Sam: "You mean after you sing or dance?"

Noop: "No—I just take a bow."

The place went wild. Me? I was crying. I knew Bobby and his mom were watching it in California, as well as my mother in Jersey. I'm sure everyone was crying. Then she said, "I wanna sing 'Top Banana,'" and the trombone player gave her a keynote and she hit it right on the nose and went into her song. At the end she slowed down to a 4/4 beat.

"Ya gotta start from the bottom up," and did the Durante walk-off. It was terrific. Sam thanked us, we went off stage and my brother drove me to the theater and drove Noop and Gerri home to Jersey. Phil Silvers and the whole cast had seen the show in the theater and Phil said, "She was a sensation." I said, "Yeah, but *I'm* a wreck!"

In 1955, I was working at the Chez Paree in Chicago. I got a call

With Zero Mostel

from Harry Zevin, who had been the stage manager when I did *Top Banana.* He asked me if I wanted to do a play called *Lunatics and Lovers,* by Sidney Kingsley, with Zero Mostel and a cast of great actors: Neville Cooper, Marjorie Lord, Casey Adams, Pamela Britton, and John Golden. I told him to send me a script. He said it was to play in Los Angeles at the Carthay Circle Theatre for four weeks.

I read the script. It was a straight comedy. I had never done a straight play.

Bobby said, "I don't think you can do it. You have no song to fall back on. It's just a straight comedy, and you would be playing a femme fatale. No, I don't think you can do it."

He certainly knew how to push my buttons. I said, "Oh, I think I *can* do it," and I accepted the show.

Zero Mostel was considered the toast of Broadway, having appeared in *Fiddler on the Roof, A Funny Thing Happened on the Way to the Forum,* and *Rhinoceros.* He received a Tony Award for each of those shows. He was a brilliant actor, as well as a great comic. He also did Shakespeare!

I met him before he became such a big star. He was doing a stand-up nightclub act. He was booked into the La Martinique Club in New York and again I was called to open for him. I guess I opened for every comic in the business. Maybe that's why I became a comic—so somebody could open for me!

We met at rehearsal. He was kind, funny, and very nice to me. He suggested we do some kind of finale at the end of the show. I said, "Fine, I love finales." We decided to do a jitterbug dance. It was fun and the people loved it. I think we played four weeks there.

Even though I was quite young, I had heard lots of rumors accusing him of being a Communist. He never mentioned anyone who was rumored to have Communist leanings when we would talk or have a cup of coffee together between shows. He was a very intelligent man, and I enjoyed listening to him talk.

We got great reviews for the four weeks we played the Carthay Circle, so much so that they decided to make a small tour of it. We went to Tacoma, Portland, and Seattle. Pamela Britton, Marjorie Lord and I stuck together. We shared a dressing room at each of the theatres in which we appeared and got adjoining hotel rooms in each town. The guys in the play were wonderful. Zero called us "the three broads." Zero was sensational in the play and such a pleasure to work with.

We played San Francisco on the last leg of the tour and that was that. Zero went back to New York and continued being the toast of Broadway. It was a great experience working with him.

Chapter Nineteen

The Singer's Curse—Nodes

While I was doing *Top Banana* eight times a week, my throat began getting very sore and I could hardly talk, much less sing. I couldn't take a day off to rest my throat because my understudy didn't know the part. It finally got so bad that I went to a doctor in New York. He was known as a good throat man.

The doctor said that I had nodes on my vocal chords. Nodes are like warts on the vocal chords for ill use of them. Every time you say or sing anything, your vocal chords rub together. If there are nodes on them they can't meet, and air passes through and it sounds like you have sore throat.

I told the producers that I had to be operated on and would have to be quiet for four weeks. They got Audrey Meadows to work the show for four weeks. She watched the show a few times and I showed her as much as I could for the part, like the movements and so on. She did a great job and we became good friends. When Audrey was ready, I went home for Christmas—and a node operation.

It's scary to know that they're going to cut into your throat, but of course I was knocked out the whole time. I woke up in the hospital room. My Bobby was there and said, "Say something."

The doctor was there and said, "Say something."

I couldn't—I was afraid to say anything. They assured me that everything was fine and I should be as good as new in a month. No talking, not even whispering. I had to write everything down. As long as I was home, I didn't mind. Being home for Christmas made me very happy.

The month flew by. I went to the doctor to make sure everything was fine and I finally spoke a word or two. It was so clear, it didn't even sound like me. Phil had been calling every week to see how I was and when I could come back. He said the duet hadn't stopped the show since I left. I loved him for saying that.

So in five weeks, I went back to New York and the show. The first night we did the duet, it stopped the show and Phil hit me on the rear and said as we were going into the wings, "Welcome home, baby. I missed you."

So we were back to visits from Bobby every other week and again he brought Noop, which made me happy and my mother was in her glory again. Of course, Phil had to keep his boxer shorts on because Noop would just walk into his dressing room—unannounced!

The show was going great. Everything was running smoothly until Mike Sloan, the producer, came in one day and said they were closing in a couple of months and going on the road. Did I want to go on the road?

I said, "How much more in salary?"

He said, "Fifty bucks."

I said, "Are you kidding? Fifty bucks more for the road? Hotels, eating out all the time....No way! I'd rather go home."

He said, "Will you do the show until we find someone?"

I said, "Okay, but it will cost you! I want two first-class fares to California."

He said, "Okay."

So I went on with the show. They had Gale Robbins, a Hollywood actress, come in and watch the show. After watching three performances, she said she couldn't do it and went back to California. They again asked me to stay on. I think I stayed an extra three months (with bonus money every two weeks) until they found Kaye Ballard, who took the part on the road.

One day I got a call from Warner Bros. A Mr. Lou Edelman said they were casting *The Jazz Singer* with Danny Thomas and that they wanted to see me. Could I come down that afternoon?

It was about twenty minutes from the house, but I said, "I could be there in an hour." (Let 'em wait!) Mr. Edelman met me at the gate to Warner's. They parked my car. I thought, *Wow! That's service.* I thought Doris Day was set to play the lead and they wanted me for the girlfriend, but *no*—they wanted me for the lead! I couldn't believe it. I went into Michael Curtiz's office. He was going to direct.

We shook hands and he said, "I understand you're very good."

I said, "I just finished a Broadway show called *Top Banana,* and I've been in show business since I was three, so maybe I know a little."

He said, "We'll make a test."

I said, "*Fine,* wonderful."

He gave me a script about forty pages long.

He said, "We'll do a song, a comedy scene and a dramatic scene."

I said, "Great."

After I finished, he said, "We'll call you." I'm *still* waiting for that call. I never knew what happened or why, but Peggy Lee got the part.

Meanwhile, I got a new TV agent and started from the beginning all over again. Nobody had heard of Rose Marie, the actress. They wanted me to add a last name—and I had a good one, Rose Marie Guy.

I said "No, I've used just Rose Marie and I don't intend to change it."

Well, this TV agent named Jim Maloney was getting me a lot of shows. I did *The Virginian,* with Joan Collins. She's a helluva gal and we got along great.

We did this scene with a horse and buggy. She was scared stiff.

I said, "What's the matter?"

She said, "I'm deathly afraid of horses and they know it." We had a great crew who held on to the horses until we needed to use them, but every time they let go, she would jump a mile and we couldn't get the scene.

I said, "For God's sake, why are you doing this show? You know it's a Western and it's all horses."

She looked at me and said honestly, "It's such a good part."

Jim Maloney called me one day and said, "I'm sending over a script for *Heinz Playhouse.* You can do a Southern accent, can't you?"

I said, "Sure." That's what I liked about Jim—he'd get the part then ask if I could do it. Ride horses, accents—I said yes to everything. He told me that this was a comedy. The script arrived and it was anything but funny. It was all about a woman who has eight kids, one of them living in the stable because she's blind. "Oh," I said, "Very funny. I can hear the laughs now." Her sister loses her son in an accident and she can't have anymore children, so she wants to take the blind kid and pay for it! To help me out, I said to myself, *Ah, the people will die laughing with this show.*

I called Jim and said, "You sent me the wrong script."

He said, "Is it called *A Little Care?*

I said, "Yes, but it's not a comedy, it's a heartbreaker."

He said, "The director wants it played for comedy."

"Oh great! The director must be a little nuts too!"

An appointment was made to meet the director, Boris Segal. In I walked the next day to meet Mr. Segal.

I threw down the script and said, "You want to play this for comedy? I think you're out of your mind."

He said, "If you play it straight, the audience will hate you. If you play it as a comedy, they have to feel sorry for you because you think you're doing the best thing for the little blind girl."

My mouth fell open. He was right. I said, "I'm sorry. I didn't see it that way, but you're right."

He said, "Always look at a part from a dramatic view and from a comedy view. If you can give it a comedic reading, always go for the comedy. It's harder, but it always works."

I have never forgotten that. A few years later, I saw him at a party at Lorne Green's house and he said, "I understand you do comedy and very well, I hear."

I said, "Ah, yes." (I was doing *The Dick Van Dyke Show* by then.)

He said, "It's funny, I only know you as a fine dramatic actress."

I was doing a lot of guest shots: *Jim Bowie, D.A.'s Man,* and *Adam-12,* thanks to Jack Webb. I did an *M Squad* with Lee Marvin, who taught me about my "light" on the set: "Always look for your light and don't let anyone stay in the way of that light!" He was a dream to work with, and he taught me a lot of tricks. You can never learn enough!

One day I saw Dick Wesson in a grocery store. He and his brother did a comedy act and we had worked together in theaters and clubs. I knew he was on *The Bob Cummings Show* and also writing it.

I said, "Write me a part. I'd love to do the show."

He said, "Okay," and in about three weeks I got a call for *The Bob Cummings Show.* I played Martha, one of the office girls who was always looking for a guy. I did that show for three years. Dear Paul Henning was the producer and head writer. What a brilliant man. It was a very happy set to work on. My part grew bigger each week and then I'd be off for two weeks. But it was a recurring part, so I was thrilled.

And talk about learning—Bob Cummings was the ultimate teacher. He used to say to me, "Too much Mickey Mouse," and I knew what he meant: I was being too broad with my expression. After all, I was used to the stage, where you have to really project—even doing my act in clubs, you overdo every action. So when I did that, Bob would say, "Mickey Mouse," meaning cut down the reaction, don't make it so broad. He showed me how to fake a fall, how to keep my face toward camera, how to cut down on actions. He was just wonderful to me and I loved the three years I worked on the show. I worked with some great people during those years: Paul Henning and his wife; Rosemary DeCamp; and Ann B. Davis, to name a few.

When *The Bob Cummings Show* went off the air, I did a year of *My Sister Eileen,* which was written by Dick Wesson, bless his heart. In between these shows, I did my club act. I got a call from Jack Goldman from Florida. He was now connected with the Riviera in Vegas and wanted me to play the hotel with Jeff Chandler. The Riviera had opened with Liberace, and Jeff Chandler was the second star to play there. I told Jack I would have to let him know. I called the Flamingo and talked to Moe Sedgeway. I had always played the Flamingo, and I didn't want them to think I would just go over to some other hotel without their permission. I had no contract with them, but they had kept me busy working Reno and Tahoe. I didn't want to get in bad with "the boys"!

I told Mr. Sedgeway that I had been offered the Riviera for four weeks.

He said, "How much are they paying you?"

I said, "Twenty-seven hundred and fifty dollars."

He said, "Okay, take it."

I said, "Are you sure? Is it all right? I still want to play the Flamingo."

He said, "It's all right, but I'm glad you called. Play the date and thanks for calling." *Whew!*

I had played Vegas a lot, and since this was another hotel, I got some new gowns made by Lloyd Lambert. He made most of the costumes for the other hotels, and he was a genius. He made my gowns until he passed away in 1992. I needed a new piano player, and Bobby found one for me. He called Dave Klein, who said that a new guy from Florida was looking for work, and that he seemed to be pretty good. His name? Buddy Freed.

Buddy and I stayed together for about eight years and he became one of our closest friends. I had some new comedy material written for me by Morey Amsterdam. He knew just what to write for me, and of course, I had George Wyle make my new arrangements. George and I had been together for many years. I had met him through Phil Silvers. He wrote a lot of material for me as well as doing my arrangements. Buddy came over to rehearse and we were ready to go to Vegas.

With Bobby, showing off our matching suits

Jeff Chandler was a great guy, but he was no singer. He put together an act and we opened at the Riviera. He came with a conductor, piano player, light man, press agent, and manager. None of it helped. He had subbed for Sammy Davis Jr. when Sammy was in a serious car accident which caused the loss of his eye. Sammy was working at the Macombo and they asked Jeff to sub for him. Anyone who goes on for an ailing fellow performer is always a hit. Jeff was a good friend of Sammy's, and he loved to sing. Everybody raved about Jeff's singing, but let's face it: He really didn't sing very well. He definitely had the guts to open in Vegas. I love to dance, but I can't do *Swan Lake,* and certainly wouldn't try it in Vegas. Jeff did the soliloquy from *Carousel* and a parody on Davy Crockett. It was okay, but it didn't get a standing ovation.

I was billed as "Extra Added Attraction," and I did very well. Danny Thomas and his wife came to see the show, as did Sheldon Leonard and his wife.

After the show, I sat with them and Sheldon said, "Don't you ever bomb?"

I said, "Not if I can help it."

Jeff left after three and a half weeks. He had to get back and finish a picture, so I was in the headline spot for a week. Imagine headlining in Vegas! It was a great feeling, and to top it off, when I was done with the gig, all of the waiters and waitresses chipped in and threw a party for me. They gave me a menu with all of their names on it that said I was their favorite star.

That's rare, but to me it was a big moment in my career!

Chapter Twenty

My Illustrious Movie Career

Bill Loeb had left MCA and went on his own with Gabbe, Lutz, Hiller and Loeb. I signed with William Morris, but Bill was still my manager.

I was busy doing TV episodes and playing Tahoe, Reno, and Vegas—the Flamingo again. Sammy Lewis called and wanted me to play Billy Gray's Bandbox, a little club on Fairfax Avenue. Lenny Kent, a comic, was to be on the bill. It was home and the money was good, so I said, "Okay." During rehearsal, Lenny and I decided to do a little finale—nothing great, just something together. The reviews came out with raves and called us a "Great New *Team*." Hell, I didn't want that. It was a date for four weeks and that's that, but then Abe Lastfogel, head of William Morris, called and wanted to talk to me. He asked for Lenny too.

Now, Lenny Kent had been in the biz for years and was also signed to William Morris for eleven years. He had never met Lastfogel. This tickled me, because I would just walk into his office à la Noopy with "Pheeel." I went to see him and he said, "I want you both to follow through with this team idea. It's not a marriage, but I think you two could get some mileage out of it." I didn't like the idea, but I said to myself, *What the hell!*

So we played Reno, Boston, Florida, Vegas, and Ciro's and La Vie en Rose in New York City. We were a smash. The hottest new team—but I hated it. I was on the road again too much and now I was saddled with a partner, so I broke it up after New York. Things were happening in California and I wanted to be home.

I had heard that I was up for a movie called *Two Tickets to Broadway* at RKO with Durante, Tony Martin, Smith & Dale, and Janet Leigh. I called the office and they said, "Yes, you are up for the part." *Well!* It was at RKO and Jimmy Kern was the director. He was one of the Yacht Club Boys—a great nightclub act. When the act broke up, Jimmy became a director. Hal Kanter, the great comedy writer, was one of the writers. Sid Silvers was another writer. I was home free. I *knew* all of them.

I went to the studio, where they had called a meeting. As far as they were concerned, the part was mine. Howard Hughes had just bought RKO, and he wanted a test. So here we go again. The others all said they didn't need a test, they knew my work, but Hughes insisted. I told them I didn't mind. Hal Kanter said it would be one of the most expensive tests ever made. It was to be made in color. I did *five* songs—and five little scenes to go with each song. Jean Louis made a dress for me; Bobby knew the makeup man, whose nickname was "Shotgun," and most of the crew, because he had made about five Kay Kyser movies at RKO before he went into the army. What more could I ask? I made the test...and waited...and waited...for them to call.

Finally, Jerry Wald called and said that the test had been wonderful, but they couldn't give me the part because I wasn't a movie name. If I did the Durante bit with Jimmy, as we had planned, they would have had trouble with the other girls in the movie complaining that I was getting equal money and billing. I won't name the girls, but it was quite a blow to me, to say the least!

Then, while I was playing Vegas, I heard that Mike Curtiz was scouting for the girlfriend role in *The Helen Morgan Story* with Ann Blyth, and was seeing all the shows on the strip. I called Steve Trilling, head of Warner Bros. at that time—I knew his brother Al from the song plugger in New York. I really took a chance calling Steve, but I did get him on the phone.

I told him, "Curtiz is in town scouting for *The Helen Morgan Story*. He's testing everybody and his brother. All I want is a crack at it, a test. I'll get him to see the show, but please, Steve, all I want is to test for the part."

Steve was very nice and said, "Okay. I'll see him when he comes back from Vegas."

I hung up and made arrangements to make sure Curtiz would come in to see the show. I told everybody I knew to tell him to see the show. I told Dennis, our maître d' to let me know when he came in. One night he came in. I did a helluva show. Dennis told me he loved the show and was applauding like crazy—so that was done. I finished the date, went home, and about two weeks later I got a call from Warner Bros. to come in to see Mr. Curtiz!

I went with Jim Maloney, who didn't know I had arranged all this. We went to Mr. Curtiz's office and Curtiz said to me, "Hello, I saw your show in Vegas. You were terrific."

I said, "Thank you."

He said, "It's the part of the girlfriend."

I said, "Fine."

He said, "We make a test."

I said, "Again?"

"What do you mean?" he said.

I said, "You wanted to test me for *The Jazz Singer* and you never called me."

Curtiz said, "Who did I use for that? Oh, Peggy Lee—big trouble."

So I said, "Do you really want to test me for this?"

He said, "Oh, yes. Do you mind dying your hair?"

I said, "For the picture or the test?"

He said, "For the picture."

I said, "Okay, sure. Thank you, Mr. Curtiz."

Jim and I walked out. I'm still waiting for *that* phone call too!

I got a call from the office to do a benefit for the 20th Century Fox annual Christmas Party. They told me I should do it because everybody from the gateman all the way up to the president of the company would be there. So I said I would do it. I think Buddy Freed was out of town for some reason, so I called Sammy Prager, who was Danny Kaye's piano player. The Pragers were friends and we'd play bridge together every so often, so I felt free to call Sammy to play for me. He said he'd love to and knew everybody at 20th because Danny Kaye had just finished a picture there. So I was set.

It was strange going into the Ambassador Hotel at Coconut Grove. The place was packed. I sat at a front table with Debra Paget, Mitzi Gaynor...all the starlets at that time. Nobody knew me—and I was going to Chicago in a week to *headline* at the Chicago Theater! Jack Paar was the MC and everybody he introduced had just finished a picture at 20th—even the damn dance team had just finished a picture. Everybody knew everybody—except me.

My introduction from Paar: "Here's a young lady I understand is very good....Ladies and gentlemen, Rose Marie." I went out and did one helluva show and came back to the table. They whistled and applauded—and I milked it for all it was worth. I stood up from the table and bowed and sat down, got up and then sat down. They were still applauding and I finally had to get up and do a thank-you speech. (I had nothing rehearsed!) The mumbling and whispering was all over the room. Jack Paar didn't know what to say. I teased him about this later—every time I did his show.

Frankie Laine followed me and did his first number. Everybody was still talking, and Frankie said, "I don't blame you, ladies and gentlemen, wasn't she just great? Baby, take another bow." They put the spotlight on me and I got up from the table to take my bow. I never will be able to thank Frankie enough for what he did; it just made it all the better. He then said, "I'm going to do my two hit records and get off." Wow! That really made it great for me.

About two weeks later, I got a call from 20th Century Fox for a picture called *The Marriage Broker* with Thelma Ritter, and George Cukor directing. I went to see Mr. Cukor. The minute I walked in, he said, "That's the way I want her dressed, just like that, little two-piece suit." He gave me some pages of a script and said it was the part of the telephone operator.

I said, "How do you want her? Brooklyn accent, straight, hard/soft voice?"

He looked at me for a minute and said, "Play it straight," which is what I did.

He said, "Wonderful. Pick up a full script and be here tomorrow morning at ten."

I thanked him and went home. I was so excited. Finally, to do a big picture, with Cukor directing! I got home and read the script. The telephone operator was throughout the picture and it was a good comedic part.

I went there the next day at ten and had to read for three other men. Mr. Cukor said, "Okay, Rose Marie, do it like you did yesterday." I did and they laughed and said, "Great. Be here tomorrow at 10:00 A.M. I thanked them and went home.

The next day I was there at 10:00 A.M. Mr. Cukor said, "Okay, honey, one more time!" So I read the part and they all said, "Wonderful."

Mr. Cukor said, "We'll call you. We start in a week." I thanked them and couldn't wait to tell Bobby about the picture. I'm still waiting for that call!

Don't think I didn't make any movies. I did *The Big Beat* at Universal for Will Cowen. I did *Dead Heat on a Merry-Go-Round* with James Coburn, as well as *Man from Clover Grove* and *Fun with Dick and Jane*

With Milton Berle

with Jane Fonda and George Segal. None of which was ever nominated by the Academy.

Bobby was doing *The George Gobel Show, The Milton Berle Show, The Dean Martin and Jerry Lewis Show,* as well as *The Tennessee Ernie Ford Show* and *The Dinah Shore Show.* He was doing just fine and finally wound up on staff at NBC, where he did *The Tonight Show.* So things were going beautifully.

One day, out of the blue, Bobby decided we should move. I said, "Why?"

"They're going to build a drive-in theater in back of us and it will be annoying—the noise and everything."

I said, "I don't care, I know every nail in this house."

He said that the house would go down in value and that, in time, I would come to hate the drive-in theater. I knew he was right, but I hated the idea of selling our little dream house.

One day, Ginny Botkin called and said there was a house for sale in *Variety*. She said it must be sold by now, because it sounded too good to be true. She read me the ad and said, "Let's go see it—call the real estate agent." I did and we made an appointment for the next day.

We met, and the location was beautiful—all very pretty houses and a lot of land. It was three-quarters of an acre, with six gorgeous walnut trees. The house was pretty from the outside: lots of used brick, which I love. Then we walked inside and everything was beige, the walls and the furniture.

There were three bedrooms, all done in wild flowers. There was a maid's room and three baths. Quite a large house, but I really didn't like it. However, it had *some* possibilities. It had a lot of shutters and high-beamed ceilings, and all of the woodwork was done in a natural stain. It truly had an Early American look. There were three fireplaces, including one in the master bedroom, and also a built-in barbecue.

But still—I wasn't thrilled. Ginny said, "Once you get your furniture in here, it will be beautiful. Let the boys see it," meaning Bobby and Perry Botkin, and we left. I told Bobby about it and the four of us went the next day. Bobby loved it from the minute he walked in, and Perry said, "This house should be in Beverly Hills. Once you get your furniture in here, it will be terrific."

I said, "What do you see that I don't see?"

Bobby said, "I love this house. I want it, and you can do whatever you want to do fixing it up your way. You have carte blanche."

I said, "It needs a lot of changing!"

We found out that the builder of the house had built all the houses on the street and had built this one for himself and his wife, but it got too big. Everything was oversized. The plumbing was all copper. It was very well built. In fact, they told us we had the foundation of an apartment house, which comes in real handy during an earthquake!

We sold the "dream house" and moved into the new house. I changed everything! Wallpaper, light fixtures, paint, everything. It actually was a brand new house because the builder had never lived in it. We worked day and night, sleeping on the floor in the maid's room.

Of course, we had to get more furniture, so I called George Montgomery. He was married to Dinah Shore. He was a master at making Early American furniture. I met him during *The Bob Cummings Show*. He was charming and said he would love to do the furniture. He made our four-poster, Early American pine, king-sized bed, our large "lazy Susan" dining table and six chairs, the TV cabinet, and three milking stools. They were and are truly beautiful to this day—and all signed underneath by George! All of the other work, like woodwork, painting, taking off doors, putting in louver doors in the bedroom, was done by Lofty Smearer, a bass player from 20th Century Fox. Bobby knew all these musicians who would do things on the side for extra money.

Poor Bobby tried to do as much as he could. In fact, we found two Tiffany lamps that had to be wired. The guy where we bought them told Bobby how to wire them. Bobby did it and when he said, "Turn the switch on," I thought the whole thing would explode. It didn't. Our house was really getting to look beautiful. It was a lot of work, but it was well worth it. I still live in this house today!

Chapter Twenty-One

☙

The Dick Van Dyke Show

Bobby was now doing *The Danny Thomas Show* along with all the other shows. He called me one day from the studio and said Danny Thomas wanted me to do a benefit for an Italian church in San Diego. "I told him to call you, because it's up to you," Bobby said. "Me? I'm a trumpet player." Danny thought that was wonderful. Everybody knew they couldn't get to me through Bobby. I know that's another reason why they respected him so much.

Danny called and wanted me to do this benefit for the Italian fishermen who were losing their jobs because the Japanese fishermen were coming and taking over.

He said, "We do benefits for everybody. This is for our people...the Italians."

So I said, "Okay." What else could I say?

We went down to San Diego, and I met Harry Bianconi, the San Diego end of the mob. He was a great guy and doing as much as he could for Monsignor Travasoni, who was the head of that church.

We put on a great show. Afterward Danny said to me, "There are five people who can dictate to an audience...laugh now, cry now, and hold them in the palm of their hands...and you're one of them."

"Well," said I, "does that mean I will finally do your show?"

Danny laughed and said, "Your time will come."

"Great," said I.

The whole day was really wonderful. The benefit went well and it was for a good cause. I could, I hoped, look forward to being on Danny's show someday.

With Dick Van Dyke

I had the pleasure of meeting and talking to Monsignor Travasoni, who arranged for me to get into the Vatican and meet the Pope on a later trip I took to Rome. By the way, it was a wonderful feeling to have Harry Bianconi on my side. Anything I needed, he took care of...not only on this trip. Each time I went to San Diego and did a show for the church, Harry was right there. (More about Harry later, in connection with my daughter.)

About two weeks later, I got a call from Ruth Birch, the casting lady for Danny. She said, "Go to Desilu Studios at 2:00 P.M. tomorrow. Sheldon Leonard wants to see you."

I said, "Finally, I'm going to do *The Danny Thomas Show!*"

With Morey Amsterdam and Dick Van Dyke

She said, "No! This is for a new show called *The Dick Van Dyke Show.*"

I said, "What's a Dick Van Dyke?"

"You'll see," she told me.

So I went to Desilu Studios the next day, saw Sheldon and met Carl Reiner. Carl said to me, "Sheldon told me if I wanted the best, I should get Rose Marie."

I said, "Thank you. What's this all about?"

They told me about the story for the pilot. I asked, "Who have you got for the third writer?"

They hadn't picked anybody yet. I was the first one cast after Dick. So I said, "How about Morey Amsterdam? He is a writer and a comic and he knows every joke ever written."

They said, "Do you know where we can reach him?"

"Yes, he lives in Yonkers, New York," I told them and gave them his number.

Then we started to talk about my contract...five years starting at twelve hundred and fifty dollars a week and going up every year until it

Sally and Buddy

reached twenty-five hundred. There were no residuals at that time, but they gave me six reruns, which meant that if I was getting twelve hundred and fifty dollars that year and they ran a particular show (in which I appeared) six times during the year, I would get another twelve hundred and fifty dollars. It was a good deal at that time. I was to costar with Dick…good billing. They gave me everything I asked for. When I left, I said to myself, "Self, you should have asked for more money!"

By the way, for all of you who think I still get residuals, forget it! I haven't gotten a dime for the past thirty years from that show. In the meanwhile, every time the series is sold to a station such as Nick at Nite or a station in some other state or town, it is sold for over a million dollars. The millions continue pouring in to the owners of the show…Dick Van Dyke, Carl Reiner, the Sheldon Leonard estate, and the Danny Thomas estate. None of the cast has ever gotten a bonus or cut of any of the residuals!

When I went home after signing the contract, I called Morey and told him they were going to call him about *The Dick Van Dyke Show*.

He said, "What's a Dick Van Dyke?"

I said, "It's a new show and they're going to call you."

He called back in a half hour and said, "I'll be out there Monday."

Morey and I have been friends since I was about ten years old. I did *The Al Pierce Show* on which Morey was a regular. We used to visit his nightclub in New York. He wrote a lot of material for my act. He called me and said he got the part.

I said, "Great, now you have to move out here!"

I understand Mary was the last one to be signed. Danny Thomas remembered her as the girl with three names. Richard Deacon was already signed, as well as Larry Mathews.

Now, the true story of *The Van Dyke Show* and how it came about is this: Carl had written thirteen scripts, and he called the show "Head of the Family." He made a pilot with himself in the lead. Barbara Britton was his wife, and Sylvia Miles played my part. I think Morty Gunty played Morey's part. (We all saw the pilot about a year after we started the show…our way was better.)

Carl went to Sheldon Leonard to try and sell his show. Sheldon loved the idea and the scripts. But he told Carl, "Why don't you become the producer of the show? I don't think you're right for the lead."

Poor Carl, he was so upset and thought it was all over. He told us he felt awful. Sheldon told him not to worry, that they would *do* the show. When Sheldon went to New York, he saw *Bye Bye Birdie,* the musical Dick was starring in. He went backstage and asked Dick if he wanted to do a series. I'm sure Dick said yes and came out to California. So, in a sense, *The Dick Van Dyke Show* was all due to Sheldon. Carl wrote it, but Sheldon put it together and held it together.

From the first day of rehearsal, everyone seemed to get along beautifully. Dick is a dream to work with. In the five years we were on the show, I never heard him say, "No, I won't do that." I never saw him lose his temper or get angry. Every so often, before a taping of the show, he would say to me, "Is this show funny?"

I would always say, "Are you serious? It's great."

He would smile and we'd do the show.

Dick is so talented; even he doesn't know how much talent he has. He can do everything…dance, sing, and move…but my favorite is when

Morey and I dance it up for *TV Guide*

he "phumfed." He's the best at "phumfing," which means deliberately trying to get the words out correctly when you've already stumbled over the
past fourteen words! There's nobody like him. He was a joy to work with.

So was Morey, who was the easiest guy to get along with. He was
always happy. In all the years I knew him, I never heard him say a bad word
about anybody. Richard Deacon was like an older brother to me. I could
talk to him about anything. Larry Mathews, who played Richie, was adorable. His mother was always on the set and we got along fine. Larry's birthday is August 15…same as mine!

Mary and I never became very close. I don't know why. We liked each
other, worked well together, but never really got close or became what you
might call "bosom buddies." Mary used to say, "I'm going to have my own

production company called MTM, and I'm going to use a lil pussycat as a logo like the MGM lion." She was very ambitious about her career and knew what she wanted. She got her comedic timing from all of us. She learned fast. But I always felt badly that we didn't become better friends. I really think I was jealous! She was younger than I was; she was prettier; and she had a better figure, so I was jealous....Do you blame me?

All the guys had a crush on her, including Dick, which he admits to. Carl's son, Rob, once went over and patted Mary on the butt. Mary laughed about it and told Carl, and it wound up becoming a big joke. But no one ever patted me on the butt! Maybe I was getting upset because they seemed to be paying more attention to her and worrying about her all the time. Me? I think they took me for granted, knowing I was the "old school," so to speak. Mary was very much the novice. Whenever Sheldon would give notes, he'd tell Mary about a line and tell her to do this and that. He'd do the same to Dick. He would even tell Morey about a move on a line, but he NEVER said a word to me.

I finally went up to him and said, "Have you got any notes for me?"

"You don't need any," he told me. "You know what to do." I really sorta felt left out. I know it was a very big compliment, but I felt stupid. I should have been pleased he felt like that, but at the time, I felt awful.

Mary had a lot of problems, which I didn't realize at the time. Her sister died of an overdose, she was getting a divorce from her first husband, she had a son to bring up, and she was going out with Grant Tinker, who lived in New York. He was with the advertising agency that had our show. Mary started doing commercials for Kent cigarettes with Dick. Morey and I never did any commericals. Little by little, Mary was becoming very well known and getting closer to her goal of becoming a major star and having her MTM production company.

I'm so sorry we never became close. I sometimes feel we missed some good times through the years, but I'm happy to say we are good friends today. We see each other when we can. She lives in New York, and I live in California. When she comes to California, we do try to see each other.

As I said, Sheldon Leonard, Carl Reiner, Dick Van Dyke, and Danny Thomas owned the show. The company was named CALVADA. CA for Carl, L for Leonard, VA for Van Dyke and DA for Danny Thomas.

We would rehearse from 1:00 to 5:00 P.M. on tape day, then get made up. Our hair was done earlier, about 11:30 or noon. We'd go to dinner (on the lot) from 5:15 to 6:45, then come back to the stage, have our makeup touched up, get dressed, and then our hair would be combed out last. At 7:00 P.M. the audience came in, and Carl would introduce each of us. The three cameras would come out, and we would start the first scene. After the scene was over, Morey and I would talk to the audience and keep them "up" with jokes and kidding around. Carl told stories and was very funny.

Morey was known as the "human joke machine." He would tell the audience, "Give me a subject." Someone would yell "tree" or "umbrella," and he would do a joke on that subject or whatever they called out. After about ten or fifteen minutes, we'd be ready for the second scene. We would do this audience participation between scenes. That is, if the cameras needed reloading or we had a change of clothes, somebody was always out in the audience keeping them up and ready for the rest of the show. We would tape from 7:30 till 9:30 P.M. We did it *one* time, not three or four like they do it today. We did it once, and that was it! And they all turned out to be classics.

Sometimes the whole gang of us would go out for a bite to eat. We'd go to Trader Vic's or some other nice restaurant. We'd talk about the show we just filmed and rehash everything about the show. What laughs, what fun. It was a wonderful way to end the night.

Sheldon directed the first three or four shows. Then, John Rich came in. It was like old home week for me! John directed for a year, I think, maybe two. All I know is he is the best comedy director I have ever worked with. He knew what all of us were thinking. We would come in on Wednesday, read next week's script through, and make comments. Sheldon and Carl would be there…and then all of a sudden, Sheldon would be gone. He would make his comments and leave. We nicknamed him "The Shadow." We gave him a floor mat with the name Lamont Cranston— The Shadow. We would then read *this* week's script, which we had commented on the week before. We were always a week ahead. After reading the scripts, we would get up on our feet and feel our way around the scene. John would then say, "Move over here on that line. Make it a two shot on that line," etc., then we'd do the scene again and go on to the next scene.

One time we were doing a scene in the office. There were five of us in the scene. I got stuck on a move, and I didn't know if I should sit down or walk on the line or what. I looked at John, and he looked at me, shook his head with his hand, said, "Wait." When we were finished with the scene, he walked over to me and said, "I know you were stuck. I think you should walk on that line." I was floored. Five people in the scene, and he knew *I* was stuck.

John taught me so much. He'd show me camera angles, what lens they were using, and during our lunch breaks he would bring me into the editing room and make me edit a scene or two on the Movieola. A Movieola is three machines with each machine a camera filming the same scene. You cut from one, two, or three into the final edit. Believe me, I learned a lot, and I'm grateful to John and always will be for what he taught me. Most of all, I treasure his friendship.

Carl was brilliant when it came to changing a scene…or writing something to fill in. When he decided I should do the Aunt Agnes lines, he would come up with the damnedest lines and throw them around like bullets. Even Morey would come up with lines. Our wonderful script girl, Marge Mullen, was a gem. She would write down all the Aunt Agnes lines and, finally, when Carl decided which one we would use, she'd put the others in the back of her book and label it "SOS"—meaning "Some Other Show."

When we did the Twizzle episode, the first scene wasn't working right. Our routine, on tape day was: We'd do the whole show with all the cameras, in case we made any changes. Then, as I told you, dinner, makeup, hair, audience. This time we were all trying to make the first scene work. When we finished with cameras, Carl said, "We'll go at it in the commissary. We'll see if we can fix this thing." So we all went in and sat at one table and started from the top.

Morey said, "Why don't I say…"

Carl said, "Great. Then Roe will say this and Deac will say…."

And Deac said, "How about if I say…"

"Great," said Carl and we went through the whole scene like that.

When we finished we yelled and screamed, "That's it! That's it!" Carl said, "Did anybody write it down?" We all looked at one another…nobody had written it down. Marge Mullen yelled from another table, "I got it on a napkin. I'll type it up and have it in your dressing rooms before the show." What a gem. A great gal to boot! The whole cast and crew were like that. It was a loving, hard-working company…at least for me. I couldn't wait to go to work every day.

We started shooting the first show on June 19, my wedding anniversary. The pilot had us doing comedy bits and me doing my Durante routine. Morey did his cello bit and Dick did his drunken uncle bit with me. It was a great show, and it was sold that night for thirteen weeks to CBS. Our sponsor was Proctor and Gamble.

We did the thirteen shows...then we were canceled. We were up against Perry Como, who went on at 9:00 P.M. for an hour. We were on at 9:30 P.M. on another network. Nobody gave up Perry for us. Sheldon went back to New York and talked to the sponsors and said, "I know this show will make it. It's too good to go off." In those days, the sponsors had their say, not like today where the networks control everything. He kept saying, "There's so much talent in this show, you gotta go with it. Keep it on during the summer. I know it will catch on." They finally agreed because they had faith in Sheldon...and we stayed on for five years. The rest is history.

Each summer Dick would do a movie. He did *Bye Bye Birdie* the first year and told us when we came back to work, "If you're a friend of mine, don't go to see the picture." The second year he did *Mary Poppins*. I don't have to tell you what a classic and wonderful film that is. Then one year he did *Lt. Robin Caruso, U.S.N.* which he didn't like.

All of us kept busy during the summer. Mary and Grant were happily married by this time. I think they spent their summers just enjoying being together. Morey did his act all over the country. I played Reno, Vegas, and Tahoe and did *The Tonight Show* many times. Dick was always doing a picture.

As for me, it was the happiest and saddest time of my life!—1961 to 1966!

Chapter Twenty-Two

My Dear Friends—My Angels

Things were going along pretty well. Bobby was playing a lot of golf, so our pediatrician, Kermit Ryan, suggested that I get Bobby a membership at Lakeside Golf Club, the golf club that Bing Crosby and Bob Hope started. We had to wait until another party sold its membership. I think it went for $2,000 at that time. I think it's worth about $250,000 now! I gave Bobby the membership for his birthday and they gave him an application, which had to be signed by two members. Dr. Ryan signed it, and when Bobby went to work on the Crosby show, he asked Bing to sign it. Bing said, "Proud to do it, ol' Rob. So the girl bought you a membership for your birthday. We have to play a few rounds sometime."

Bobby handed in the application, and we didn't hear anything for about two months. I said, "Something is wrong. Call the club and ask them." So he did and they said they had never gotten Bing's signature, so they were trying to get ahold of him and ask him. When they finally reached him he said, "Yes, I signed it....That's for Bobby Guy, right?" So they let him in the club.

Bobby played golf with Gordon MacRae, James Garner, and George Gobel. Bobby and Gobel became such good friends, they were like two teenagers, calling one another on the phone and talking for hours. It was a wonderful friendship. Bobby called him "Little Bit" and Gobel would say, "Gobel and Guy, that's the cry." When Bobby made his hole in one, it was like New Year's Eve. We threw a party at the club. Gobel always said, "I've never trusted a guy who didn't drink, but I would trust you with my life." They were such good buddies.

It was the same with Gordon MacRae. When our daughter had to start school, Gordie told us about Egremont Private School. His kids were there, and he said it was great because they pick up the kids in the morning and drop them off after school at the house. They never drop them off unless the mother, father or another relative is there. We both thought that was great because my hours at work were different all the time and Bobby's were different too. But "Grammy," Bobby's mother, was there all the time, so that worked out fine. Noop stayed there until the 6th grade and then she attended Robert Fulton Middle School and, after that, Van Nuys High School. Thanks to Gordie, Egremont School really gave her the best start in Noop's education.

Gordie also recorded a song I wrote with Ruthie Bivona. She was Leo Robin's sister and Leo was a great lyric writer. I guess Ruthie got the talent from the same place that Leo did. We were having dinner at our house with Gordon and Sheila MacRae, George and Alice Gobel, and Perry and Ginny Botkin.

Gordie said, "We're going to record next week. Did Van Alexander call you?" Alexander was the arranger and conductor.

Bobby said, "Yes, Gordie."

"We're having trouble finding another song for the fourth side."

Bobby said, "What kind of song are you looking for?"

Gordie said, "A nice ballad."

Bobby said, "Well, Roe wrote a beautiful song called 'One Misty Morning.'"

Gordie said, "Can you sing it or play it?"

I said, "Yes, I can do both."

I sat at the piano and sang the song. He loved it and said he'd record it. What a wonderful thing to do. I just had to go down to the recording session of course, where I heard the beautiful arrangement of my song by Van Alexander. What a weird feeling to hear twenty-eight men play a song you wrote! And Gordon sang it—and I mean, he *sang* it. He had such a great voice and really sang the hell out of it. It didn't sell very well, but I was ever so grateful to Gordon for doing that—he was one of my angels!

I told you about Gleason and how we both did club dates for five dollars a night. He turned out to be another one of my angels and a dear, dear friend. I was working at the Band Box in Los Angeles. He came in quite a bit, because it was a club where all the comics would meet, talk, and tell jokes. Among the regulars were Joe Frisco, Eddie Foy Jr., and whoever else was in town.

One night Gleason came over to me and said, "I want you to do my new television show."

I said, "Fine."

He said, "I'm not kidding—and I'll pay you more money than you've ever gotten for a TV show."

I said, "Oh sure. I've had so many promises and nothing happens."

"Well, this time you're wrong, honey," he said, "because we go back a long time and I think you're one of the greats of our biz and I'm gonna make sure you do my show."

I said, "That's wonderful, Jackie, thanks."

He said, "What's the highest salary you've ever gotten on a TV show?"

I said, "Twenty-five hundred dollars."

Jackie said, "Okay, I'll pay you five thousand dollars."

We both laughed and I forgot about it. Sure enough, he started *The Colgate Comedy Hour* in New York and I got a call for the show. And yup! He paid me $5,000! I wound up doing his first and last show of every season. Then he got his own show in Florida, and I did his first and last show of every season on that show, plus we would do numbers together. I did sketches with him. He was great to work with. He hated to rehearse, so we'd do it once and that was it. And it was always great. We did "Razz-A-Ma-Tazz"—a song and dance. We did three Durantes—Gleason, Art Carney, and me! What a great bunch of shows they were. Through the years, I would drop him a line and he would always answer me. I really loved that guy. He was a very special friend and an angel to me!

Another angel and friend was Johnny Carson. There was a PTA picnic at Egremont one year, but nobody knew Carson—this was before he got *The Tonight Show.* Somehow we wound up together at a picnic table—Johnny, his first wife, Bobby, and I. He had his boys enrolled at Egremont, so we talked kids, showbiz.

I was wise-cracking, he laughed and said, "You're very funny. When I get my own show, you'll be one of the first on it."

I laughed and said, "Sure…and when are you getting your own show?"

He said, "Soon, soon."

We had a nice time and I forgot about it. Sure enough, he got *The Tonight Show* after Jack Paar left in 1962. He called me and said, "I want you to come to New York and do the show."

I was flabbergasted—he had kept his word. He was so nice to me. Every time I had to go to New York, I would do his show. When he came out to California to do two weeks, I would do his first and last show. Then when he moved to California, I did a lot of his shows. Bobby was on staff at NBC, so he did *The Tonight Show* all the time. Of course, Carson would mention him. But Carson didn't become an angel to me until later on.

Noop was doing very well in her own right too. While she was going to Egremont, they would have a horseback-riding day. Noop would come home and say, "The other kids go on Saturday too so they can ride the horses." Bobby started taking her on Saturdays.

Then it became, "All the kids have their own horse."

I said, "No, no, no. I don't want her jumping and falling and breaking her neck."

Bobby said, "It's not English riding where they jump, this is Western saddle."

I was against it, but they both paid me no never-mind. That was *their* thing together. Both of them got hooked on horses. One Sunday—I'll never forget it—Bobby came in to the kitchen. They had been out all day looking at horses. I was making dinner and Bobby backed me up against the sink and said, "We found the horse."

I said, "No! No! No horses!"

He said, "When you hear the name of the horse, you'll have to give in."

I said, "What's the name of the horse?"

He smiled and said, "Chubby." Well, Noop was a little chubby, and I had to smile.

Bobby said, "I'll be with her all the time, so you don't have to worry and I'll pay all the expenses out of my record dates."

What could I say? They were so happy with finding the horse and it was really between them, so I said, "Okay."

That's how Noop got started with horses. Through the years, she was National and Pacific Coast Champion many times. She was president of the Pacific Coast Horse Shows Association for two years, and is currently vice president. She was the first woman to be president of the PCHA in its 45-year history. She really got involved with the horses and showing them. She breeds them, and at the moment she has five. Right now she has one of the best reining mares in the country, Rona Doc.

I named the ranch. We call it the Residual Ranch. One of her horses is called Residual Chex, and Rona's daughter is called Rona's Residual. The daughter of Rona's Residual is called Our Emmy. Noop has won a lot. She has hundreds of ribbons, and she has won everything in silver you can think of. She loves it and has gotten quite a reputation as a horsewoman. After all, she started when she was eleven years old.

One day at the studio, Dick Van Dyke came over to me and said his daughter Stacy wanted to learn to ride and wanted a horse. I said, "Call Noop, that's her department. I know nothing about the horses." So he called Noop and she said she'd love to help Stacy get started and there was the beginning of a beautiful friendship. I guess kids with famous parents all feel the same way—that people are nice to them to get to their parents. Noop was like that in the beginning, but she finally got over it. I guess Stacy was going through the same thing.

So Noop was in her glory. Looking at horses, getting the proper clothes—it's really very involved. Noop was now handling Stacy because she could help avoid the mistakes Noop had made with the horses, the wrong turns, and so on. Noop's trainer was Bill Corey, a real honest-to-God cowboy. He doubled for John Wayne in a lot of early Westerns and now had a ranch so he could train kids and horses.

Bill had about eight kids in training for horse shows. It was a nice group that would ride and learn and go to horse shows. Noop took Stacy under her wing and taught her everything she knew. It was great for Stacy and wonderful for Noop, who felt like a mother hen. Bill Corey became a part of our family. He and Bobby became good buddies, and Bobby helped Bill in more ways than one. I didn't find out until much later that Bobby bought Bill a *truck* because he needed one to haul the horses to the shows.

Stacy became one of the group and wasn't treated in any special way, even though her father was on the number-one television series and was the costar of *Mary Poppins*.

That lasted for a few years and at the final award dinner, which Dick and Marge attended, Marge came over to me and said, "I will never forget what Noop did for Stacy. I am most grateful to her. Stacy is another person, and it's all thanks to Noop." I was quite proud of my wonderful daughter. I've been very proud of her in many ways. She's a great gal with a great sense of humor. I never had a bit of trouble with her—no drugs, no booze. She's someone her father would have been very proud of too.

When Dick and Marge decided to move to Arizona, Marge and Noop discussed purchasing Stacy's horse Regret. She made a deal with Marge to purchase the horse and pay it off with payments over time, which she did. Regret was a wonderful horse and Noop continued to win with him.

Chapter Twenty-Three

When "Tom" Became "Tim" Conway

June 1961 was a big month in more ways than one. On June 19, we filmed the pilot of *The Dick Van Dyke Show*. It was perfect from the opening scene. We did it with a live audience, and when the filming was over, Sheldon Leonard, our executive producer, told us that the show had been sold! Representatives from Procter and Gamble had been in the audience and had loved the show. They said they would sponsor it.

In those days, the sponsors were the important ones to please, not the networks as it is today. We were all so thrilled knowing we would be on the air in the fall of 1961 on CBS! Jim Aubrey, president of CBS at the time, decided to do a promotional tour for the three new shows going on in the fall season. I was chosen to represent *The Dick Van Dyke Show*. Tony Martinez would represent *The Real McCoys,* and Sterling Holloway, the great British actor, would represent *Our Man Higgins*. The latter show was about a butler and Sterling was the star.

We were to go from town to town to promote the shows—Milwaukee, Denver, Cincinnati, Cleveland, and five other cities. We would be wined and dined by the manager of each station, after which we would go to the TV studio and do local promos. In one town, the station manager took us to dinner and said he loved *The Dick Van Dyke Show* and *The Real McCoys,* but he didn't buy *Our Man Higgins*.

I asked him, "Why not?"

He said, "I don't think the people of this town would like that show, so I didn't put it on the fall lineup."

I was shocked! I said, "*You* didn't think the people of this town would like the show? *You* think for all the people in this town, this state?"

He said, "Yes, I know what they like!"

I couldn't believe it. Here was a man who could make or break a situation-comedy show. He could ruin the career of an actor starring in a sitcom. That one man could ruin so many lives. Good God! I don't know why I dwell on this. Perhaps it is because the networks are doing the very same thing today and, as a result of this kind of thought process, very few shows on television are even worth watching. It's unbelievable what know-it-alls *think* they know.

In any event, we went to Cleveland to the TV station and started our promos. Tony went first for *The Real McCoys*. Mr. Holloway stayed at the hotel. After Tony, it was my turn. They put the chair in front of the camera and I heard, "Action."

I started, "Hello, my name is Rose Marie."

A voice from somewhere said, "Is that Baby Rose Marie?"

I started to laugh and then said, "Okay, I'll start again. 'Hello, I'm Rose Marie and I'm going to be on a new show called *The Dick Van Dyke Show*.'"

This voice came on again—from God knows where: "Dick Van Dyke….Is that a big star, or a new star? What *is* a Dick Van Dyke?"

I laughed again and said, "Who is that?"

"The director in the control room!"

I said, "Let's get this over with, I want to meet you."

He said, "Come on, honey, I want to meet you too."

We started the promo again. This time I got through it without any interruptions from the control room: "Hello, I'm Rose Marie. I'm going to be on a new show called *The Dick Van Dyke Show*. It will be on this channel at 9:30 P.M. Wednesday evenings. You'll love it. Be sure and watch it."

I heard, "That's it."

I said, "Where is this guy? I want to meet him."

Out came Tim Conway, a short, balding, cherub-faced man with a big smile. We shook hands and I said, "You're very funny."

He said, "I hope I didn't hurt your feelings, but I knew you'd have a great sense of humor."

I said, "I hope so. Tell me, what do you do around here beside trying to be funny in the control room?"

He said, "A little of everything. I direct, write promos, and work with Ernie Anderson. We do all the lead-ins on the show. We host a horror show one night a week, and we do some radio."

I said, "Wow! Do you have anything I can see?"

He said, "I don't have any video, just audio."

I said, "Let me have at least one. I can't promise anything, but I'm going to see what I can do. You're really very talented."

He thanked me, gave me his home address, phone number, and one audio tape. That was it.

I finished the rest of the promo tour and got home to California. I told my husband about meeting this "funny little man."

He said, "Let me hear the tape."

I had never heard it, so we sat down and listened to it. It was hilarious. It was about two sportscasters at a baseball game that was rained out. They keep trying to sign off and have the guys in the studio take over, but everybody at the studio has left, so there's all this dead airtime that needs to be filled. You have to understand that when broadcasters "are out in the field" doing their broadcast, from time to time they will send the viewing audience "back to the studio" for news or other sports. These guys kept talking about anything and everything they could think of. It was brilliant.

My husband said, "Sign him up."

I said, "What?"

He said, "Sign him up. You can do wonders for him."

I said, "I don't know anything about being a manager. I'm lucky I can handle my own career, much less someone else's."

He said, "You know enough about this business to handle him. It's always easier to handle someone else! *Do it.* You can give him the biggest break of his career."

I said, "I'll try."

I didn't do much of anything for about a week. Then I heard that Steve Allen was doing a new show and was looking for some new guys. He had Don Knotts, Louie Nye, and Tom Poston. He had already made them famous and he was now looking for *new* guys. I heard he was at the theater across from the old NBC on Vine Street, so I went over.

Steve was there, along with a lot of people walking around and looking quite busy. I saw Steve sitting in the audience, so I walked over and said, "Hi, Steve."

He said, "What are you doing here?"

I said, "I heard you were looking for some new talent and I think I found a great hunk of it in Cleveland."

He looked at me as if I was crazy. I had never done anything like this before, so I was a little apprehensive. I continued, "I have an audio tape of his, please listen to it and let me know what you think."

He said, "Okay." I went home feeling funny about the whole thing.

By the time I got home, the phone rang and it was Phil Weltman from the William Morris Agency. He said, "Steve liked the tape and wants the *one* guy." (Tim had done the audio tape with Ernie Anderson. I thought about the old show business curse—we like you, but not your partner!)

I said, "He has to come from Cleveland, so let me call him and see what he says." So I called Tim.

Tim was thrilled and said, "You take care of it."

I said, "I'll call you back."

I then called Phil and said, "He'll come out for the show. $1,000 and a first-class roundtrip ticket from Cleveland. After all, he might not want to stay here, since he has a good job in Cleveland."

Phil was furious. He said, "$1,000? Are you crazy? Nobody knows him."

I said, "*You* do and you want him!"

I then called Tim back and made the arrangements. He came out, did the show and was terrific. God bless Steve Allen. He knew talent, and he was always willing to help anyone he thought might have some.

Let me explain—Tim's real name is *Tom* Conway, but George Sanders, the British movie star, had a brother named Tom Conway who was also a prominent actor, so we changed Tom's name to Tim Conway.

Everything went well, and Tim returned to Cleveland after the show was done, back to his old job. Phil Weltman called a few days later and said, "Steve wants Tim for the next six shows."

I said, "Fine. Same deal—$1,000 a show and first-class transportation for *two!*" Tim wanted to bring his wife, Mary Ann.

Of course Phil fumed and barked, but finally he said, "Okay."

So Tim and Mary Ann came out to California. Now, I had something else to worry about—two people instead of just one. Where would they stay? How would they move around? I had to look after them.

Thank God things worked out. Tim and Mary Ann found a place to stay and quickly learned their way around town. Tim did the six shows with Steve and was even better than before. Everything was happening so fast.

I told him he had to sign with an agent. I, as the manager, cannot get the jobs for him. The agent has to do that. A manager only handles the deals and makes sure that the performer stays "a nice guy." It's always the manager who is "the louse"—which didn't bother me at all. I told him to sign with the William Morris Agency. We called a meeting at the Morris office and I told Phil Weltman to look after Tim and take him on personally, but to check with me on everything that came in for Tim. Phil didn't like the idea, I'm sure, having to take orders from me on Tim's career, but that's the way I wanted it.

A call came in from Max Liebman from New York. They wanted Tim for some big variety show. Phil Weltman called me and I said, "Fine, but I want to see a script to see what they have in mind for Tim."

Max Liebman sent a wire back saying, "Tell Rose Marie not to worry about the script. I'll make sure he's taken care of properly."

I had to laugh, because Max Liebman had been the producer of *Your Show of Shows* with Sid Caesar—and here I was, asking for a script. Talk about a smartass. At any rate, the deal was made. If memory serves me correctly, they paid him $1,500 plus first-class fare. (I always ask for that!) Of course, Tim was wonderful on the show and he was really starting to make a name for himself.

One day while I was working on *The Dick Van Dyke Show,* a call came from Phil Weltman. Universal Studios was doing a new series called *McHale's Navy* and they wanted Tim. I read the script and thought it would be great for him.

I okayed it and told Phil, "*Don't* sign him to an exclusive contract with Universal. Just get a contract for the show itself, because if anything comes along like a movie and he's signed with them, they can get away with paying him the same money he's making on the series. If he just has a contract for the series itself, he's then in the position of a free agent and can negotiate the price for a movie." That was exactly what happened. For once Phil didn't balk at my request, and he signed Tim to a contract for the series only—for about $1,250 a week. When the movie was discussed, Tim was in the perfect position to name his own price, and he did— $25,000! I was so proud of him. He was doing just great.

On top of all this, Tim and Mary Ann became parents! Mary Ann gave birth to a healthy baby girl and they honored me by asking me to be godmother to Kelly, a beautiful baby who grew up to be a very lovely young lady.

When everything is going well, something always happens. My husband got sick in December 1963. It was the roughest time of my life. This horrible time is explained in another chapter. Bobby remained in the hospital and he was getting worse instead of better. I was trying to work on *The Dick Van Dyke Show,* having Tim's career in my hands, and worrying about my husband. I was truly overwhelmed and unable to handle all of this.

I talked with Tim in detail and explained to him why I couldn't be his manager anymore, but I assured him that, thank the Lord, he had a good agency in William Morris and—I thought—a good agent, Phil Weltman.

Who, I'm sorry to say, turned out to be the biggest S.O.B. of all time. I called Phil and explained to him why I couldn't be Tim's manager anymore.

All he could say is, "What about the contract?"

I said, "Tim can have it. I don't want anything. Just make sure you treat him right."

The next thing I knew I got a check for about $800 as a settlement for Tim's contract. I thought nothing of it at the time, and just said to myself, "Okay." Sadly enough I never saw Tim again. Never heard anything about him, and we didn't keep in touch. Even to this day I don't know what happened…it just ended.

In the meantime, I was so wrapped up with my husband's illness. When he passed away in May of 1964, it felt like the end of my world. I still had another year of *The Dick Van Dyke Show* to do, and I don't even remember half of what went on during the next year.

At some point, I got a call from Mary Markham, who was booking a lot of game shows and who was wonderful to me. She kept me doing game shows to keep me busy, because when *The Dick Van Dyke Show* went off the air in 1966, I didn't want to work anymore. I thought I couldn't sing anymore or do any of the things in my career that I had done prior to my husband's passing. I think I was in a state of shock for over a year, but Mary, God bless her, kept me going by making me do game shows. They were easy and kept me from going bananas.

One day she called me about a new game show called *The Hollywood Squares.* They wanted me to be one of the six regulars—the show would have three guest stars each week. I did the first two pilots of that show. One had Bert Parks as host, the other had Sandy Baron. They finally decided on Peter Marshall as MC, which was the best idea yet. We went on the air and the show turned out to be very successful.

I was on the show for fourteen years. It kept me alive and brought back my confidence, as far as working was concerned. It was an easy show to do. I didn't have to sing, I didn't have to do my act, I just had to answer some questions and maybe try to be clever and funny.

In any case, every once in a while, Harvey Korman would be a guest on *Squares* and he would say to me, "What's with you and Tim? Why don't you get together?" By this time, Tim had become a big star on *The Carol Burnett Show.*

I said, "I'd like to talk to him, I'd love to see him. I'm so proud of him, but I don't know where to reach him. I haven't seen him in years, and I always thought it was so strange. I honestly felt he understood my reasons for no longer being able to manage his career, but now it begins to appear to many other people and to me that we are angry with each other and no longer on speaking terms. None of this is true. It was necessary at the time for us to go our separate ways.

When they did his story on *This is Your Life,* Phil Weltman said that Steve Allen discovered Tim. This made me furious, but I didn't say or do anything. I figured that in the end, the truth would come out.

Then, in 1999, as fate would have it (as fate always does), I got a call from the writers of *Caroline in the City.* I had done two shows for them. We had become friends, and they liked my work. *Caroline in the City* had been cancelled and they were now working on *Suddenly Susan,* starring Brooke Shields. They called me for a guest shot. They had written a big part, which they had to cut down because of time, but they still wanted me to do it. They told me that Tim Conway and Harvey Korman would be on the show as well. When I heard this, I said, "You bet! I'd love to do it." I figured I finally would see Tim and get this misunderstanding straightened out once and for all.

The day arrived. I drove to the studio, parked my car and went into the soundstage. People were milling around, reading, drinking coffee and in general just trying to look busy. I didn't stop to say hello to anyone.

I walked right over to Tim and said, "Have I ever done anything to hurt you?"

He said, "No."

"Have I ever said anything bad about you to anyone?"

He said, "No."

I asked him, "What's all this talk about you and me not speaking to each other? Why don't we get together and straighten out this bad feeling between us? What's all that about?"

He said, "Phil Weltman did that! Let's forget it. Let's forget the last twenty years!"

I said, "That's easier said than done. We had a wonderful friendship and I was so proud of you. All of a sudden I hear all these things about why don't we get along."

He smiled and said, "Forget it. It's over." He hugged me.

I said, "Okay. You know damn well I only wanted the best for you. I was thrilled with what you had accomplished and felt pride in the fact that I had a little bit to do with it!" We laughed and hugged again.

By now everybody was listening to us and we laughed. Tim turned to the group and said, "Yes, she discovered me! If it wasn't for her, I wouldn't be here." More laughter from everyone. I realized that the problems were over. After all these years of a friendship lost.

We went to work on the show. It was such a pleasure working with Tim and Harvey. The set was always crowded. Everybody came to watch the rehearsals. Even our cameraman was there every day. He wouldn't miss a rehearsal, and he often said, "It was so wonderful to see professional people who knew what they were doing and enjoyed working so beautifully together." Brooke Shields has said many times how much fun this particular show was. Everybody enjoyed it.

The taping was good and went well. When it was over, I walked into Tim's room to say good-bye to Tim and Harvey and thank them. A bunch of kids ran in—they were all of Tim's kids—and Kelly, his firstborn, came over to me and said, "Hi, I'm Kelly." God, what a beautiful young lady she turned out to be. We hugged and I apologized for being such a lousy godmother. I told her I would try to make up for it.

The show was over, and I felt better knowing that so much had been cleared up after so many years and that Tim and I were able to straighten out the mess—whatever it was—and settle it once and for all.

Everyone raved about how great the three of us worked together and how maybe we could do another show or two, but alas, *Suddenly Susan* ran for one more season and then went off the air.

October 3, 2001, was a special day for me. (I've had a few of those through the years!) I got my star on the Hollywood Walk of Fame. I was so proud of this accomplishment, but the most touching part of the day was receiving a beautiful letter from Tim. It truly warmed my heart and told me what I had known and felt all along...that Tim Conway is one wonderful guy.

CONWAY ENTERPRISES INCORPORATED

October 3, 2001

Dear Rose Marie:

Congratulations on a Star for a Star. I'm sorry I could not be there, but it is your fault. If you hadn't discovered me in Cleveland, I wouldn't be working in Vegas and I could have made the ceremony.

I thank you so much and think often of how lucky I was that you took an interest in a guy like me and brought me to this wonderful world of magic.

Your kindness and generosity in and out of the business has been a constant companion with me. I love you for it.

Love,

Tim Conway

TC:pd

Letter from Tim Conway

Chapter Twenty-Four

Life Is a Three-Legged Chair

Have you ever thought that everything that happens to you in life has been planned? In other words, that there's a book already written when you're born saying all the things that will happen to you: good things, bad things, big events like marriage and children. Everything has already been planned for you in life, and there's nothing you can do to change it. And everything is not always perfect, because if it were, you wouldn't strive to do better. So you go on and you survive and you finally appreciate what you have…when it's too late.

Look at my life—Bobby and I were very happily married—at this point for nineteen years. We had a lovely home all paid for, and a beautiful child. I was on a hit series and Bobby was top man in his profession. Everything was perfect—then one of the legs of the chair breaks and you have a three-legged chair. And everything falls apart. This happened to me in December of 1963.

I had a club date to do in Bakersfield. It was on a Saturday night. Bobby was tired and said he wouldn't go with me, which was unusual. He said, "You and Buddy Freed go. I'm going to try and get rid of this cold." I knew that he must really not feel good, because a cold would never keep him away. So he stayed home. On Monday, I called Bill Loeb for a good doctor. Our doctor had lived on our street but moved away. Let's face it: You don't look for a doctor when you're feeling good. I called this doctor that Bill told me to call, who was in Beverly Hills (of course), and we made an appointment for Wednesday. Bobby was feeling awful and I was worried because he was a healthy man. He didn't smoke, or drink—he drank milk. He was a meat and potatoes man. He played golf, went bowling, and generally took good care of himself. But I was sure it wasn't just a cold—he was tired all the time.

So Wednesday came. Bobby had a record date with Bing at one o'clock, and I was due at the studio at eleven o'clock. I called Sheldon and said I was taking Bobby to the doctor and that I might be a little late. He said, "Not to worry, come in when you can." So we went to this doctor. I don't even remember his name. We sat down in his office. Bobby told him he was tired all the time, and that this cold was getting to him.

The doctor said, "Do you drink?"

Bobby said, "No."

The doctor asked him, "Do you smoke?"

Bobby said, "No."

So with my big mouth I said, "What, are you going to tell him to give up?" The doctor said he would have to take blood and do some tests and so on, and it would be a few hours.

Bobby said, "I have a record date at one."

The doctor said, "Cancel it." He told me to go to the studio, Bobby would call me. Since we only had one car and I would have to pick him up, I went over to the studio.

Morey, who knows me so well, said, "What's wrong?"

I said, "I don't know. Bobby is at the doctor's and he's going to call me."

Bobby called about 1:30 and said, "I cancelled the record date…the doctor is putting me in the hospital."

I said, "Why? What's wrong?"

Bobby said, "He thinks it's hepatitis."

I said, "Sure, that's the popular disease this season. Let me talk to him."

The doctor got on the phone and said, "I *think* he has hepatitis and *you* have to get a gamma globulin shot."

I said, "I'll be right over. I want to talk to you," and I hung up.

I told Morey, "I have to leave—they're putting Bobby in the hospital."

He said, "Why?"

I said, "The doctor thinks he has hepatitis."

Morey said, "I don't believe that, that's a liver disease."

I said, "I know, and I have to get a shot."

Morey said, "I'll tell them when they come back from lunch."

I said, "Thanks, Morey," and I was off to the hospital. It was a little hospital on Beverly Glen and Santa Monica Boulevard—it's not there anymore. I think it was just a hospital for facelifts, nose jobs and so forth.

When I got there, Bobby was in a room with a hospital gown wrapped around him and the doctor was there. I walked in loaded for bear—I was so mad. I said to the doctor, "What makes you think he has hepatitis?"

He said, "His blood count is down and we have to try and bring it up."

I said, "He doesn't have yellow jaundice, which goes with hepatitis. He seems fine."

The doctor said, "I want to keep him a few days and we'll try and build up the blood. Meanwhile, you have to get a shot." So he gave me the shot and I went back up to Bobby's room and stayed with him until six o'clock. I went home and couldn't sleep all night. Somehow this all seemed so wrong!

He was in the hospital for about six or seven weeks and he wasn't getting any better. If he were home and not getting any better, I could understand, but he was in a hospital. I told everybody that I didn't think Bobby had hepatitis and that I really didn't like that doctor. Bernice and Harry Ince, who were with me, said, "Get another doctor if you're unhappy with this one." I didn't know where to turn. None of us had ever been sick enough to have a regular doctor. I called up the doctor and said that I wanted to talk to him.

I went up to his office to see him. I sat down and he said, and I quote: "I think your husband has cancer of the liver."

I said, "What does that mean?"

The doctor's answer: "He'll die very soon."

I was in shock.

He then said, "I want to do an exploratory and find out what's going on."

I said, "You don't *know?* You just *think?* No, no, don't touch him, I want to get another doctor." And I walked out.

I went to get my car in the parking lot and saw a phone booth. I called my mother. She was in Florida visiting my brother and his family. I told her what the doctor had said and she said, "How dare he talk like that?"

I said, "Mother, you better come out here. I can't handle this alone."

She said, "I'll be right out. I'll call you tonight and tell you what plane I'm coming on."

I said, "Thanks, mother," and hung up.

Driving down to the studio, I never stopped crying. I kept thinking, *Oh my God, what if he does die? No, no, I mustn't think like that, he's too young. He's forty-eight years old. He's never been sick, outside of a cold now and then. He can't have cancer—he lives too well.* Morey was waiting for me— bless him—and he said, "What's wrong?"

I told him what the doctor said and he said, "Jesus, he has no right to talk like that. I'm going to call Jerry Lewis, he must have a great doctor. If anyone has the best doctor, it's Jerry."

So he called Jerry and told him what was going on and Jerry wanted to talk to me. I got on the phone and told him what the doctor had said to me.

Jerry said, "S.O.B., what kind of doctor says things like that?"

I said, "Jerry, I don't know what to do."

Jerry said, "A Dr. Marvin Levy will call you in five minutes. Tell him what you told me. He's your new doctor. You'll like him. Besides, he's the best."

I said, "Thanks, Jerry, I really appreciate it."

He said, "Do you need any money?"

I said, "No, I don't think so, Jerry."

He said, "If you need any money and don't tell me, I'll never talk to you again."

I couldn't help it, I started to cry, and again I said, "Thanks, Jerry." You wonder why I say he's a special angel to me? Just wait—there's more!

Dr. Levy called right after I hung up and he said, "Tell me everything." I started from the beginning and told him what the doctor had said.

After I was through, Dr. Levy said, "He had no right to talk like that. What hospital is he at?" I told him and he said, "Meet me there tomorrow morning at ten."

I said, "Okay, and thanks." The next morning at ten, I was in the hospital. Dr. Levy was there. We went up to Bobby's room. Dr. Levy went in and said to me, "Stay here until I call you."

He walked in and said, "I'm Dr. Levy. Jerry Lewis sent me. I'm so glad you're in California. He usually sends me all over the country for his friends." I heard Bobby laugh, and I knew they would hit it off. Bobby was so disgusted with the other doctors that every time he saw another doctor, he would cringe. Nobody seemed to know what the hell was wrong. I waited outside while Dr. Levy was examining Bobby. Then he called me in and said, "We *have* to get this boy well."

I said, "Yes, and the sooner, the better."

Dr. Levy said, "I want him out of this hospital as soon as possible."

I asked, "What hospital do you want him at?"

He said, "Cedars or UCLA. Which one do you want? I'm on the board at both."

This sounded a lot better to me. Then he said, "I personally would like him at Cedars—it's closer to my office."

I said, "Fine."

So we made arrangements to move him to Cedars. I called the other doctor and told him he was off the case. I felt better having Dr. Levy in charge.

When we got to Cedars, it was so different from that face-lift hospital. I know Bobby felt better about the move, and so did I! I forgot to mention that Jerry Lewis knew Bobby. Bobby played first trumpet on the soundtrack of most of his movies. Jerry Lewis called Bobby every two or three days, and visited him frequently. Jerry kept in touch with Dr. Levy *every day!*

Dr. Levy had everybody at Cedars on their toes. He had his blood checked, and he had specialists look at Bobby. No one could figure out what was wrong. Dr. Levy said it was an overpowering blood infection. Where? Why? When? No one could figure it out.

I asked if it was leukemia.

He said, "No. That's the first thing we look for." Dr. Levy thought that it might be something that had lain dormant for a long time and suddenly popped up. I said that I didn't know. He was a healthy man. I couldn't understand it—nobody could.

I know for a fact that Jerry Lewis told Dr. Levy to get in touch with all of the specialists in or out of this country and to send Bobby's blood to them. Maybe then someone could find out what was wrong. He said that he would pay for it. I only found this out about a year later! I will never forget his kindness and thoughtfulness at the most horrible time of my life. I hear people talk ill of Jerry. I don't care what anyone says to me, he came through when I needed somebody badly. I will be grateful to him forever. He is truly one of my special angels.

They continued to take tests and finally thought that maybe because Bobby had had diverticulitis awhile back, perhaps the poison from that might have gone to the blood. It was like having an earache or a toothache—one thing didn't relate to the other.

So on with the tests, all kinds. I was at the hospital every day. I stayed as long as I could and then I would go to the studio. They were wonderful. They understood that I had to be at the hospital, so when I finally did go into rehearsal, they would tell me when and where I had to move. All of them helped me get through the shows. After taping, I would go back to the hospital and stay until eleven P.M. or twelve midnight and go home. Thank God my mother was with me. She cooked and looked after the dogs. I felt very secure with her at the house. I missed Bobby's mother—she had died the year before. Some days my mother would go with me to the hospital. How I got through the shows, I'll never know. It was like I was in a fog.

Bobby was holding up pretty well. Some days the blood would come up a little and then go down again. Everything connected with the blood—the platelets, the hemoglobin, and so on—was down. They even tried a bone marrow test, but nothing really helped that much.

This went on for quite awhile. Our lives were so screwed up. I didn't know if I was coming or going. I showed up at work on taping day, never rehearsing. I was at the hospital eighteen hours a day. Noop went down to the hospital maybe once a week. She couldn't take looking at her father getting thin and looking awful. They tried *everything*. Finally Dr. Levy said he would operate to see what was going on with the blood. Dr. Levy was keeping it on an even keel, but that wasn't fixing the problem. So they set a date and they were going to remove the spleen. It was taping day for me, so you can imagine how I felt. My mother stayed with Bobby at the hospital and I stayed with him until 6:00 P.M. I raced to the studio, got made up and dressed, went over the script and we did the show. I swear I don't know how I did it. I told everybody that the doctor would call and to please let me talk to him no matter what. Sure enough, Dr. Levy called right in the middle of the show and said that they had removed the spleen and that he had *no cancer* anywhere. That was a big relief. Levy said, "I'll get that guy well, I promise you."

That helped for a little while. Then they decided that they should remove the infected intestine Bobby had from diverticulitis. It really had nothing to do with anything, but they thought if they removed the intestine, the blood might clear up. They planned it for the next morning!

I went to work—I was supposed to do *The Tonight Show* with Carson. When I got to the studio to rehearse, I called *The Tonight Show* people and said I couldn't make the show because they were going to operate tomorrow morning on Bobby and I wanted to be at the hospital with him tonight. We started to rehearse *The Dick Van Dyke Show*, and I got a call from Carson.

He said, "I can't get a replacement. You have to do the show tonight."

I said, "I can't....I'm not in the right frame of mind. My mind is on Bobby and the operation tomorrow."

Johnny said, "You've got to do the show tonight. You're leaving me in a hole."

I said, "Okay, I'll be there."

So after we finished rehearsing *The Dick Van Dyke Show*, I went to NBC to do *The Tonight Show*. Johnny was waiting for me and he said, "I'm glad you came." We did the show and I guess when I don't feel good or when I'm scared, I get very funny. So it was a great show for me.

After it was over, Johnny said to me, "You feel okay?"

I said, "Yes."

"See, I had to make you do the show to get your mind off the operation for a little while. Now you can go to the hospital and stay up with Bobby to watch the show."

I said, "Thanks, Johnny. I truly appreciate what you did."

He kissed me on the cheek and said, "Give my best to Bobby. I'm sure everything will be all right."

What an angel he was to me. I will never forget his thoughtfulness and kindness. He's quite a classy guy!

I went to the hospital. Bobby and I watched *The Tonight Show* and it came off fine. I told him what Johnny had said, and Bobby also said, "He's a helluva guy."

I went home and prayed. I was at the hospital the next morning and Bobby was fine after the operation. Dr. Levy said he might go home soon. They had the blood under control and he'd be better off at home. I was dumbstruck. Nobody had said anything about going home. Wow! I was so happy that he was well enough to go home. We had to go twice a week to the doctor's for shots. As long as he was doing all right and he was home, that's all I cared about. So we made arrangements to come home. It felt wonderful to sleep beside him again.

That went on for about two months. We went out to the movies and we even went to the Grammy Awards, because I was a presenter. And we went to the doctor's office twice a week. The Emmy nominations came out—I was nominated for Supporting Actress in a series. They didn't have separate categories for drama and comedy then. So I was up against dramatic actresses—one of whom was dead! This was my second nomination; I had lost out the year before to an actress who was also dead!

Bobby didn't feel like going. He told me to go with Richard Deacon. I said, "No, I'd rather stay home with you because I am not going to win anyway—I'm not dead yet. Seems all the dead people get the awards." We watched the award show and sure enough, another dead actress won. I can tell you honestly, it really didn't bother me. Bobby was home and getting well and I was happy.

One night we were watching TV and Bobby said, "I'm going to bed, I really don't feel well."

I said, "I'll call the doctor." I called Dr. Levy and told him Bobby didn't feel good and wanted to go to bed and that he ached all over.

Dr. Levy said, "Give him a sleeping pill and make him go to bed early." I told Bobby what Dr. Levy said. He got undressed, but with a lot of pain in his arms and legs. I had to help him. This was something new. He had never complained about pain before. I got undressed and we both lay in bed watching TV, but he was very restless. He couldn't find a position in which he was comfortable. My mother made some cinnamon twists and came into our room and we had tea and the twists. Still Bobby was not comfortable, and he was getting edgy. I gave him the sleeping pill, put out the lights and we kissed good night. I wrapped myself around him, but it hurt him to have me touch him. It was like his nerves were on edge. So I went over to my side of the bed and he was still restless. He moved from one position to another, he tossed and turned—the sleeping pill was not working.

I called Dr. Levy again and he said, "Give him another sleeping pill and keep me posted. I got him well once before and I'll do it again." The sleeping pills didn't work. We were up all night. Finally at 8:00 A.M., he was in agony.

I called Dr. Levy again and he said, "Get him to the hospital."

I said, "He can't walk—everything hurts him."

Dr. Levy said, "Call an ambulance."

So I called and told my mother to go with him in the ambulance and I followed in my car. We went to Cedars Sinai. It was 12 noon.

At 1:30 P.M., Levy came out to me and said, "I need you." He took me to Bobby's room. There must have been seven people in that room working on him.

He looked at me and said, "Hi, Mommy."

I said, "Hi, sweetheart....You do what they tell you."

He said, "I will Mommy....Sure do love you."

I started to cry and Dr. Levy pushed me outside and said, "I needed you—we were losing him. He's fighting now."

I went back to my mother and told her what was happening. She said, "He'll be all right, don't worry."

All of a sudden Bill Loeb came to the hospital and sat with my mother and myself. At 5:10 P.M., Dr. Levy came out and said, "We lost him. It was an overpowering blood infection."

I yelled and screamed and said, "I want to see him!" He took me into his room. I kissed him and I passed out. The date was May 27, 1964.

The next thing I knew, Bill Loeb said he'd drive us home. I was in shock. I didn't know what was happening, nor did I care. I had lost the love of my life. What was I going to do without him? I couldn't stop crying. We arrived home and Noop was doing her homework.

I took one look at her, grabbed her and said, "Daddy's gone."

We both cried and my mother said, "You go to bed. Dr. Levy gave me these pills for you, so I'll make you a cup of tea and you lie down and take these pills."

I remember thanking Bill Loeb and he said not to worry, he would take care of things. I didn't know what he said or meant—I was starting to get very groggy. I didn't want to go into my bedroom, so I went in the back bedroom and lay down.

I woke up about 9:30 and my mother made me something to eat. I couldn't even think about food. I was all sleepy and dopey, so I went back to bed and fell asleep. I didn't sleep in my own bedroom for a year!

Everyone was so kind. The flowers were unbelievable—from everyone we had ever known. Bill Loeb and Harry Ince took care of the funeral. They laid out the money for everything. I couldn't think or talk. I just wanted to be left alone. I guess my mother helped them with the information they needed and she took care of all the social things. I didn't want to see anybody or talk to anyone.

I must say everybody from *The Dick Van Dyke Show* was there and they were just wonderful. They called and came over to try and talk to me. I tried to cope with it all and just couldn't. Even Morey, bless him. He and his wife Kay were traveling in China, and Kay's father called them and told them about Bobby. Morey wanted to know if I wanted him to come back and whether he could he do anything. I said, "No, stay in China. Don't come back just for me."

I was glad when it was all over. I couldn't stand talking to people. I just wanted to sit and cry. Even my mother could not shake me out of it. I was lost. I had decided I couldn't work anymore. I had a mental block with my throat; I couldn't sing, I could hardly talk…and I just wanted to be left alone.

I called Sheldon Leonard and said I couldn't do the last year of *The Dick Van Dyke Show*. (We had been informed before going off for the summer that the coming year would be the last year.) Dick wanted to do movies and Carl thought we should quit on top. Sheldon was angry—he said they would back up the Brinks truck if Dick wanted it. So we never made a show in color…we could have gone two years on that alone. In any case, I didn't think it was a big deal not to do the final year. John Rich called and said he wanted to come over and talk to me. I said, "Sure." I had no idea what he wanted to talk to me about.

He came over one night at 8 o'clock and talked until 1:30 in the morning. My mother came out and said, "Don't you think it's about time you left?"

He said, "Have I convinced you?"

I said, "Yes."

He said, "Then I've done my job."

He had talked me into doing the last year of the show.

He said, "What are you going to do?"

I said, "I don't know what I want to do. I may just quit everything—period."

He said, "You have to finish the last year. It would look very bad if you didn't do it. You'll need to do it to keep your mind going." He was right, I knew that—but somehow I couldn't see myself as I was before, working, joking, coming home—and no Bobby. It all seemed so unreal! I agreed to do the last year and John went home. Dear John, another one of my special angels.

Chapter Twenty-Five

❧

Hollywood Squares

I wore black for a year. That was *my* way of showing respect for my husband. Everyone looked at me like a woman from the old country. I didn't care. Everyone at the show was just great. Richard Deacon told everybody, "Don't put your arm around her or she'll start to cry. Don't bring up any subject relating to Bobby—if she wants to talk about it, fine." They changed lines in the show that would remind me of anything…they were absolutely the best!

We went on to do the last year of *The Dick Van Dyke Show*. I've already told you about the last day of shooting. Even though everyone went his or her own way, we remained good friends and still see one another all the time, usually at parties or award shows. Morey and I were very close. I'm his daughter's godmother. I was and am very honored that they asked me. Cathy, my godchild, is a beautiful young lady who just got married. We're family! Carl and Dick and I see each other every once in a while. When Mary comes into Los Angeles, we sometimes see one another.

For about a year after the end of *The Dick Van Dyke Show*, I did *nothing*. I couldn't sing or even think about working. But then I got a call from Dinah Shore. She was doing a teenage special show and wanted Noopy and me to do the show. I didn't want to, but Noopy wanted to do it and she begged me to please do the show. So we did. Dinah and her daughter Missy, Noopy and I. We sang, we danced. It was a great show, and Dinah was wonderful to me. She told me to get off my ass and go to work. I said, "Yeah, it's not that easy."

They called me to do *The Dean Martin Show* and sing a ballad. I said,

"I can't sing. It doesn't come out right." Guess what song they wanted me to sing? "Little Girl Blue," a real tearjerker if there ever was one. Greg Garrison, the director, called me and said he wanted me to sing a straight song and not do comedy. Greg was Milton Berle's director on the old Texaco TV show, and he knew Bobby. They had talked cars all the time. He said he wanted to show the dramatic part of me—whatever that meant.

I finally said, "Okay," and went to the studio to record the song, with Les Brown's Orchestra. I couldn't go through with it. I broke down and cried and ran into my dressing room. I had never done anything like that in my life, and I felt like an idiot. Greg didn't come to get me—he let me cool off and just waited for me to go back to the mike and record. All the guys in the band knew. They had all known Bobby, so thank God, they understood.

The Dean Martin Show was great. They did all kinds of effects for my number and it was nominated for an Emmy. Then Dean sang, "When You're Smiling" to me and I couldn't help it, the tears began pouring down. Then Dean kissed me and held me in his arms. It was quite a memorable moment. I did Dean's show three more times. Of course, I knew Dean when he was with Martin and Lewis. It was always special to do his show.

I got a call from Mary Markham. She used to book all the talent for the game shows, and we were good friends. I had done all the game shows: *Password, You Don't Say, Pantomime Quiz,* and so on. I was getting to be known as the Arlene Francis of the West! She said they were doing a pilot for a new game show called *The Hollywood Squares.* They wanted me to be a regular. There were to be five regular squares and four guests. The regulars were Morey Amsterdam, Wally Cox, Charlie Weaver, Abby Dalton, and me. We made a pilot with Sandy Baron as the host. Nothing happened. We made another pilot with Bert Parks and that didn't sell. I understand Morey spoke to the producers and suggested Peter Marshall as the host. We never made a pilot with Peter—we just went on the air. I was with the show for fourteen years, and boy, I saw a lot and heard a lot!

We did five shows in one day, once a week. Heatter and Quigley were the producers, and Art Alisi was in charge of the prizes and distribution. We were the top daytime show for years, and we had the greatest stars as guests. In time, Morey left because he could make more money on the road, which he liked, and Abby Dalton left too. Charlie Weaver (played by Cliff Arquette), Wally Cox, and I stayed. We also started doing the nighttime *Squares.* The money was lousy, but it was home and I didn't have to

Some of the regulars and a few guest stars who appeared on *Hollywood Squares* during its fourteen-year run: Host Peter Marshall, Rose Marie, Tony Randall, Shelley Fabres, Dennis Weaver, George Gobel, Susan Clark, Jack Albertson, Paul Lynde, and Robert Goulet

sing. Just sit in a square and answer questions once a week. With the night-time *Squares* coming on the air, I worked twice a week. The schedule for the daytime shows remained the same. The nighttime *Squares* was only seen once a week, however, so on the one day we taped nighttime *Squares*, we taped five of them, which would be seen for the next five weeks. We would arrive at the studio shortly before 7:00 P.M., get made up and dressed and the first audience would arrive. We'd do three shows and break for dinner. They always had a nice caterer come in. After dinner, we'd have the second audience come in and we'd tape the last two shows. I would usually get home about 10:30 or 11:00 P.M. It varied sometimes because of techni-cal mistakes, of which there weren't too many because we had a great direc-tor, Jerry Shaw. Don't forget: He had *nine* people to cover, and when Peter would ask a question, Jerry would have to be ready to put the camera on *that* person, as well as to anticipate a joke from one of the other squares. He did a brilliant job—he's a great friend too.

Since *Squares* was seen every weekday plus one night a week, they tried to introduce variations on the original theme once we'd been on the air for a while. "Storybook Squares," where we all had to dress up as fairy-tale characters, was one theme they tried. It really didn't work and it was soon abandoned. The big hit was the "original" *Squares.*

We had some great people on. Carol Channing did the show a few times. She would arrive with her own food in a little carrying case—I think it was buffalo meat! Karen Valentine was a particular favorite of mine. I love her like a second daughter—she did the show many times. I also worked with her in *Bus Stop,* with James Naughton, on the Kenley Circuit in Ohio. During the hiatus periods I would do many plays around the country: *Everybody Loves Opal* in Chicago; *Bye Bye Birdie* in Dallas and Los Angeles; and *Everybody's Girl* in Chicago, Dallas and Seattle. While I was in Seattle doing *Everybody's Girl,* I became good friends with Bob Nichols, who was the director and also had a part in the show. He told me I needed a good show written especially for me, and he wrote *Up a Tree,* which is now known as *Ring Around Rosie.* I did the play in Chicago and San Antonio. It was a big hit, and I'm still working on getting it on TV as a sitcom.

Back to *The Hollywood Squares.* The producers were all right guys—Bob Quigley and Merrill Heatter. Bob was in vaudeville at one time, so we got along great. As to who picked the guests, well, we never knew. We had people on who couldn't spell "cat," but if they were in a series or very hot at the time, they got on. Thank God for Peter Marshall. He knew how to get in and out of some awkward situations. Really, he's the greatest straight man to help you get a joke across.

Paul Lynde joined the show later as a regular and always sat, of course, in the center square. Most of his gag answers were written for him, but the *real* answers were never given to anybody. Some of Paul's written jokes were hilarious. Peter once asked him, "Why do motorcycle riders wear leather jackets?"

Paul answered, "Because chiffon wrinkles."

Or, "When does a lamb become a sheep?"

And Paul answered, "That depends on the shepherd."

But my favorite was, "If you're doing seventy miles an hour on the freeway and your brakes give out, what would you do?"

Paul's wonderful answer was, "Honk if you love Jesus!"

Don't misunderstand, Paul had a fantastic sense of humor. One night after taping the third show, we went in to dinner and they served wine. Paul drank a little more than usual that night, and the last two shows had to be cut to ribbons because of the things Paul said. The next day Paul told us what happened on his way home the night before.

He was driving on the sidewalk, so a cop stopped him. Paul stayed in his car, and the cop got off his motorcycle with his ticket book in hand ready to write a ticket. Paul pulled the window down and said, "I'll have a cheeseburger, hold the fries." The cop laughed and realized it was Paul Lynde, and said, "I'll escort you home, Mr. Lynde."

Vincent Price was almost a regular. He was on quite a bit—there never lived a sweeter man. Vinnie had a great sense of humor, and when people would ask him why I wore the black bow in my hair, Vinnie would say, "She has to—it's nailed into her head."

I threw many dinner parties. I'm quite a good cook and that's the only thing I brag about. One particular evening, I had invited everyone from *Squares* for a big Italian dinner. They were to arrive at 7:00 P.M.

At 5:00 P.M. the doorbell rang. I was just starting to get dressed. Noopy yelled in to me, "Mom, it's a Rolls-Royce and it's Vincent Price."

I said, "What in the hell is he doing here now? I said 7:00 P.M., not 5:00 P.M."

I grabbed my robe and went to the door. Vincent was standing there with two cartons and asked, "Where's the kitchen?"

I said, "What are you doing here now?"

He walked into the kitchen, put the cartons down. One contained white wine and the other contained red wine.

I said, "Don't you think I know enough to serve wine with my dinner?"

He turned around, went to the door, turned to me and said, "I'll see you at 7:00 P.M.," and left.

By the way, it was a helluva party, with people like Jonathan Winters, George Gobel, Cliff Arquette, Peter Marshall, Steve Allen, Paul Lynde, and darling Vincent Price.

One more cute story about Vinnie. I had just gotten my Rolls-Royce, and I drove it to the studio. I parked in my space, got out and went to the trunk to take out my clothes for the show. Vinnie saw me and started to run toward me, saying, "Anybody who owns a Rolls-Royce shouldn't carry their own clothes." I loved him for that.

Speaking of wardrobe, it took me awhile to realize that sitting in that square, we could only be seen from the waist up. I stopped bringing five complete wardrobe changes and began to just bring blouses or sweaters and change my top for each of the five shows.

Whenever Phyllis Diller did the show, I shared a dressing room with her. This one particular night I came in a little late and I walked into *our* room. Phyllis had every inch covered with feathers, beads, cigarette holders, bracelets, and so on. There wasn't any space left for anything. I looked at her arranging all this stuff and said, "When are you putting the pool in?"

She laughed and said she was sorry, she'd move a few things. From then on, whenever she did the show, she used only a small corner of the dressing table.

I roomed with a lot of the stars. A couple of times I shared the room with Pearl Bailey, who was just wonderful. I met my dear friend and secretary, Dodi Williams, when I shared a room with Pearl. She was Pearl's secretary for years and years. We took a liking to each other right away, and I said, "If you ever need a job, call me."

To my surprise, she called me that week and said, "I can help you out, maybe two days a week, if you want, because Pearl goes out of town a lot."

I said, "Great. I really need some help with the fan mail."

So dear Dodi started doing the mail for me. We've known each other for twenty years, and she's always been there when I needed her. When Pearl died, Dodi started working for me on a regular basis. I'd be lost without her.

I roomed with Ethel Merman. She and I were good friends from the time I was a kid. I went to see all of her Broadway shows and she always called me "Baby." I did a week of *The Mike Douglas Show* and asked her if she would be one of the guests. Mike used to do an entire week with one guest, and have all the guest's friends, family and so forth. So my dear mother went on and showed the world the dress I wore when I was three. Merman was happy to do the show with me. We sang the duet from *Call Me Madam*, "You're Just in Love." That was one of the thrills of my life—to sing with Merman.

She wanted to do *Squares* in the worst way—and I had to *convince* them to put her on. They only used her about two times, and she was great on the show. She was a great lady and I loved her very much. When she came out to do *Squares*, I threw her a party at the house and she asked me to invite Paul Lynde. She just loved him. Jonathan Winters was there, Pe-

With Ethel Merman

ter Marshall, Vinnie Price—what a party! I became the Perle Mesta of the San Fernando Valley!

When *Squares* started its downward slide—after fourteen years, a pretty good run—I wasn't on the show every week. I would be on about once a month, so I started doing some dinner theater. Just straight plays...no musicals. Then my mother had to have a gall bladder operation, so I had to go back east to Jersey. My brother came in from Florida, and we were there with her. While I was back east, I did *The Tonight Show* with Johnny— bless him—and some other guest shots. I got a call from Bill Loeb saying they wanted me to do *Bye Bye Birdie* in Dallas.

I said, "No, I don't want to sing."

He said there was no singing in the part of Mama. It was for two weeks, with Roger Smith, Ann-Margret's husband. I told Bill I didn't want to do it.

He said, "I've already okayed it."

I said, "Then you play it!"

What I didn't know was Dr. Levy had told Bill to put me to work and keep me busy. *Squares* wasn't enough. I was still going home alone and remembering. It had been over a year by this time. Anyway, he talked me into it and I said, "Okay."

My mother's operation went well and I stayed a few extra days. Then I went back to California and got ready to go to Dallas. Mary Markham and her husband, Gary, gave me some beautiful luggage for the trip. I loved them for thinking of me. I took the wardrobe lady from *The Dick Van Dyke Show*—she was called Margaret—with me and took my secretary at that time, Bill Kouski, whom I always called "Kuz." I didn't even think about doing this show alone—I was scared stiff.

We rehearsed for a week, and Noop, Bernice, and Bill Loeb came to the opening. It wasn't bad, but I wasn't happy with it. I finally discovered a few little tricks I needed to make the part mine. It worked, so I was finally happy with it.

I was staying at a residential hotel and hating it. Then Ben Gold called me. He was the CEO of Nardis Clothes; they had supplied most of our clothes on *The Dick Van Dyke Show*. Margaret, the wardrobe lady said, "We have to meet him and thank him." If we ever liked any of his clothes we wore on *The Dick Van Dyke Show*, he let us keep them. Because of him, I had a wonderful wardrobe.

So two nights before I opened, he and his wife called and took me out to dinner at another hotel. They were very nice to me, and the manager of the hotel came over to say hello.

He sat down and started talking—I kept saying to myself: "When is he going to leave?" Little did I know it was the beginning of an affair *not* to remember!!

Chapter Twenty-Six

An Affair Not to Remember

He was Danish, he was a hotel manager, he was five foot ten and a half inches tall, he was blonde, slight of build, had enough of an accent to be charming, and very, very romantic. Let's call him Peter.

I met him that night with Ben Gold and his wife, Tina. After dinner, while we were watching the so-called stage show, I said I had to get up early for rehearsal, and Peter said, "Let's go to my room for a nightcap."

We all agreed, so we went up to his room in this hotel. It was a very large suite of rooms. He was looking at me and looking at me. I felt very uneasy. Eventually we left. Ben Gold decided that we would all have dinner at his house that Wednesday (this was Sunday) and then they would drive me to the airport. I would miss one day of rehearsal and go home for Noop's graduation, and then come right back.

I decided I hated where I was staying and I called Peter about getting some rooms at his hotel, telling him that my daughter was coming, as well as my manager, Bernice, and of course I needed rooms for Margaret, the wardrobe lady, and my secretary, Kuz. Talk about star play!

Anyway, we all had dinner on Tuesday night. Ben always invited Peter. So Peter drove me to my hotel and said, "I'd like to see your rooms, because you dislike them so much." So he came up in the elevator with me and we went to my door. I opened it, he took a look around and said, "I see what you mean."

I said, "Good night....I have to get up early."

He looked at me (oh yes, steely blue eyes!) and said, "Thank you for making me live again," and out he went.

Well, I wondered what that meant. I put my phone on "do not disturb" and went to bed, never figuring he would try to call when he got to his hotel. The next day I got the message that he had called. Wednesday night came and Peter picked me up at this dreary hotel. I had packed all my bags and put them in Peter's car. I packed one bag to take with me to Noop's graduation, and the rest Peter was going to take to his hotel. I would check in when I got back.

We had a nice dinner at Ben's house. We talked about them coming to the opening of the show. Ben had given them all the clothes for the show. *Bye Bye Birdie* has a lot of young people in it, so I told him that was very nice and he said, "I love doing that." He was a very special man. We had a nice time and said good night and Peter drove me to the airport. I told him I would be on the late afternoon plane the next day coming back, and he said he would pick me up.

I went home and told Noop about him. She wasn't too thrilled. We had a cup of tea and then the phone rang. It was Peter. Did I arrive okay? What time tomorrow should he pick me up? He also said he missed me already…and that was that.

The next day I went to Noop's graduation. It was lovely, and I was quite proud of her. She was always a good student and that year she had the lead in the school play, *Wonderful Town,* and she was great in it. She sings very, very well, but she never really pursued it.

If it hadn't been for Noop, Dolores Gray would not have been the tremendous hit she was in London with *Annie Get Your Gun.* I was working Vegas and got a call from Frederick Brothers, which was a big agency at the time, asking me to call them—important! So I called. It was for *Annie Get Your Gun,* in London.

I said, "When?"

They said, "July or August." I was pregnant with Noop and I said I'd call them when I came back into town.

I told Bobby about it and he said, "Take it. If it starts in July or August, you'll have plenty of time after the baby."

So I went up to see them. Irving Berlin was there. We all shook hands and Irving said he was a big fan and thought I would be just great for the part. I said it was my favorite show—which it is. I never mentioned that I was pregnant. I didn't look it, and when they said July or August, I said, "Fine. I would need an apartment and a nanny for the baby, my secretary, and so on." They said fine to everything and the money was great! So I signed the contract. Then in March they called and said something about the theater. They were having trouble and would have to move up the date to *May!* I said I couldn't do it in May—I was pregnant.

They said, "You can't do that. You signed a contract."

I said, "Act of God [well, Bobby anyway] and I'm due in April."

So between phone calls and letters, I got out of the show. Dolores Gray got the part and was one of the biggest hits in London. I had my beautiful daughter and I wouldn't exchange that for anything.

After the graduation we went out for a bite to eat. She took me to the airport and said, "I'll see you in three days." She was coming to Dallas for the opening. Peter met me in Dallas and I went to the hotel. My bags were in a beautiful suite of rooms. I unpacked and we went out to dinner. He was charming and had that lovesick look in his eyes. Hey! I loved it, but I wasn't taking anything too seriously. I still felt married to Bobby. Ben Gold called every day and the four of us went out to dinner every night after rehearsal. Ben would pay the restaurant owner to stay open and if they had an orchestra, he paid for them to stay until we left. He was too much!

Opening night was great. Roger Smith, who played Albert, was wonderful and Raul Julia was Birdie. I think it was his first comedic part. Noop, Bernice, and Bill Loeb came in. Margaret, the wardrobe lady, was with me at the theater and Kuz was with me backstage. I got lots of flowers and three dozen red roses from Peter.

Bill Loeb looked at the card and said, "What's this?" The card read, "My dearest darling: Know you will be great. My love always, Peter." I looked at Bill and smiled.

He said, "Serious?"

I said, "I don't think so, but I love the attention!"

They had a big party after the opening. It was the Dallas Summer Musicals, and of course it was all so chichi. I wore one of the gowns Ben Gold made. It was powder blue with pearls and white sequins. I wore my little white mink jacket. Bernice said I looked like a princess. We went to the party—Ben, his wife Tina, Bill Loeb, Noop, Peter, and me. It was so crowded that we left early and went to some restaurant and had our own little party.

The show was going well and I would see Peter at the hotel during the day, go shopping, things like that, and then go to the theater. Ben, Tina, and Peter would pick me up at the theater after the show and we'd go out for a bite to eat. I can't eat before a show. I feel bloated and can't breathe properly, so I have some toast and tea about 4:00 P.M. and eat after the show.

I started to like Peter. He was very kind and tender. But I felt like I was cheating on Bobby. I still felt married.

Closing day we had a matinee at 5:00 P.M. and no night show. I decided to throw a party for the cast. I dumped it all on Kuz to take care of. I told Ben the night before that I wanted him and Tina at the party.

He said, "Maybe." He didn't want to interfere with the entire cast. He felt like an outsider.

I said, "Baloney, it's my party and you're my friend. I want you there."

He said, "We'll see, but regardless, we'll go out after and celebrate on our own."

Closing day arrived. I went down for breakfast with Peter. Kuz was running around like a chicken without a head. He was so nervous.

I said, "What's the matter?" He said he was worried about the party and the caterers.

I said, "It will be all right," and gave him a blank check to pay for everything.

I had my light snack and Kuz drove me to the theater. Peter would come down for the party and so would Ben and Tina, I hoped. We did the show at 5:00, and it went well. Elaine Dunn, who played Rosie, came to me after the first act and said, "What's wrong with Kuz?"

I said, "He's nervous about the party." By the end of the second act and finale bows, I saw Peter in the wings and ran into the dressing room. Peter sat to the left of the dressing table and I started taking off my makeup to get ready for the party.

I said, "I bet Ben didn't come, I knew he wouldn't from the way he talked yesterday," and Peter looked at me really strangely.

Kuz was in the doorway and said to Peter, "I didn't tell her."

"Tell me what?" I said.

Kuz said, "She had a show to do."

"Tell me what?" I yelled.

Peter said, "Ben played golf this morning and when he was through, he backed out of the driveway at the country club and a big truck hit and threw him sixty feet!"

I said, "Oh my God! I can't believe it. Is he all right?"

Kuz said, "He's in the hospital. I've been keeping in touch with Tina. That's why I was so nervous."

I said, "Let me get dressed and we'll go to the hospital."

Peter said, "You can't, you have a party and you must be the hostess."

I said, "I can't host the party."

Kuz said, "Tina said she'll call and tell us what's what. There's really nothing any of us can do."

So they got out of my room. I cried and got dressed and the three of us went to the garden in the back of the theater, where the party was. I said good-bye to everyone, had some iced tea and said, "Let's go."

We went back to the hotel and Kuz kept calling the hospital. Dear Ben was holding on. There was really nothing we could do but wait. It was early, so we ate at the hotel and by 1:00 A.M., Tina had called and said he was the same. If anything happened, she would call.

So we went to our rooms to go to bed. I know that I didn't sleep. I was up at 8:00 A.M. I called Kuz—he had heard nothing. I said, "Meet you downstairs for breakfast." I called Peter. He was in his office. He hadn't heard anything either. The three of us tried to eat breakfast and at 10:00 A.M., the call came. Ben had died. I couldn't believe that this had happened. Tina called and asked me to stay a few extra days, just to be with her. I said I would. Kuz and Margaret went back to California. Bernice, Bill Loeb, and Noop had gone back after the opening—so there I was, going through another death of someone I cared about.

I stayed at the hotel and stayed with Tina most of the time during the days. Peter would take us out to dinner, and then we'd spend most of the evening with her. I stayed for about a week, but then I had to get home.

Peter and I talked to each other every day, and we would write every day. I think it was getting serious, but what a situation—him in Dallas, me in California, although he wasn't happy with his job running the hotel. But it paid well, and it was a job. His parents were in Copenhagen, retired and not doing too well. So there we were. I called Tina every other night to check up on her. She said she would sell their beautiful house and get a small apartment. Ben's two grown sons from another marriage ran the business. I guess Tina was sort of an outsider. After all, Ben had been seventy-five or eighty and Tina was in her early forties.

Peter kept asking me to come up for a weekend. I wasn't sure. I loved being with him and he was really romancing me—flowers, gifts, Elizabeth Barrett Browning poems in a beautiful book, European beaded evening bags. As I say, very romantic.

I decided to go up for a weekend. I had a great time. He was devoted.

We went to great restaurants...different affairs that were going on. He was very well liked by "the right people" in Dallas.

I was doing *Squares,* so I had to be home most of the time. One weekend I went to Dallas. He met me at the airport and said, "We're going to New Orleans."

I said, "What?"

He said, "We'll transfer your bags to the New Orleans flight!"

I was floored, but it was exciting. We got to New Orleans about 8 o'clock and the town was jumpin'—my kind of town. He had booked rooms at the New Orleans Hotel, right on St. Charles Street. It was like a fairy tale. He booked two rooms, but they were connected, which worried me. I hadn't let him kiss me yet. Well, on the cheek, yes—but nothing else! The rooms were beautiful, with a wrought-iron balcony overlooking the city. You want to talk romantic? Of course, we went out for dinner—during our time there, we hit every well-known restaurant and tried every house specialty. We went to Brennan's for Sunday breakfast, which is a must. We went to Pat O'Brien's for his hurricane drink, and we went to the Court of the Two Sisters, which was just wonderful.

He never tried to come to my bed; he came close, but no cigar! Yes, I finally did let him kiss me, but on the first kiss, I pushed him away. It was stupid, but it felt strange to kiss someone else. We had a great time and then we went back to Dallas. I stayed overnight in Dallas and went home the next day. I had to, I had to go to work.

I went to Dallas about once a month, and then finally he came to L.A. He stayed at a hotel even though I had a guest room. I didn't think it was a good idea for him to stay at the house. Noop was still living at home. While in L.A., he came to *Squares* with me. I introduced him to everyone, and everybody seemed pleased that I had someone. Art Alisi, with whom I got to be very close, said, "He seems very nice. I'm glad you met him. Now have a good time."

Of course, I had to meet his friends—I called them "the Danish Mafia." Scandia, a very famous restaurant on the Sunset Strip, was their hangout. The owner, Kenneth Hansen, and his wife, Mousse, owned the place, and every Dane in Hollywood hung out there. It was a nice restaurant. I met Carl Anderson and his wife Caroline, whom I liked very much. But I really couldn't "cotton" to the others. I was pleasant and all that, because of Peter.

I found out that Peter had worked at the Beverly Hills Hotel as the food and beverage manager a few years earlier, so I figured he must know his business. But, to me, they treated him like they were doing him a favor, and I didn't like that. He looked up to them as if they were the only people in the world. I think they tolerated me because, after all, I was in TV—an actress! But I went along with it. *The Dick Van Dyke Show* was in reruns and I was doing *The Dean Martin Show* and *The Red Skelton Show*, so that kind of impressed them. We went on like this for about a year. I went to Dallas—he came to L.A. We'd go out and have wonderful times, but he always stayed at a hotel while in L.A.—and we did get together in Dallas.

He finally got so disgusted with what was going on with the hotel owners in Dallas that he quit and came to L.A. No—he didn't stay at the house. I thought it would be wrong, and it would mean that maybe we were living together. I didn't want that for Noop. He thought it was silly, but I stuck to my guns.

By now he had asked me to marry him. He bought me a beautiful engagement ring. It was a cluster of diamonds on a wide gold band—an antique. I wore it on my right hand! Of course, the Danish Mafia kept egging him on: When are you going to get married, and so on. I really think they thought that I was very rich and that I would support him. But they didn't know *this* gal.

I kept saying, "When he gets settled with a good job, then we'll get married." He got many jobs, but he only stayed with each one for about three months, which bothered me. Even Lucy Ball, one night at *Squares,* said to me, "What are you waiting for?"

I said, "I want him to get settled with his own job."

She looked at me and said, "You're not ready yet," and she was right.

As I said, he had many jobs, but never really settled in with anything—this went on for five years! In the meantime, I was doing *Squares,* guest shots, and then I got *The Doris Day Show!*

Chapter Twenty-Seven

Doris Day and Australia

Doris had just lost her husband, so I sort of felt a kinship based on that alone. She was wonderful to work with and we became very good friends. She's so good that people take her for granted, as far as her talent is concerned. She's really very, very professional and she knows what she's doing, plus she's got a way about her that you just like her immediately. We worked well together. I would always tease her about her dogs—she had twenty-six at that time!

I would also make fun of her that she always got up so early. She's a morning person and I'm a night person; when I would go to work, it was dark, and the CBS gate man would always say, "Good morning," and I would always say, "Looks like last night," and he would always laugh.

I used to tell Doris, "I'm going around shaking trees so no birds will sleep."

She'd laugh and say, "Oh, you."

But she'd always ask me if I had seen the show on the night it was on, and I always had. I told her what I thought of the show and she'd say, "I know I can always count on you for an honest answer." We had a ball for three years. I loved working with her. She's quite a gal!

After my poodle, Pete, died, I didn't want a dog for a while. I'd always had dogs, but my life had changed so much and I didn't think I wanted one. Doris, found about this and nagged me until Noop went to the pound and found me a bearded Collie called Scruffy. He looked just like his name…a great dog. Noop would never let me go to the pound for fear that I would bring ten dogs home. I used to bring Scruffy to the studio every

With Doris Day

once in a while, and I made Doris his godmother. Doris would bring three or four dogs a day—every day different dogs, but they were so well behaved. She kept them in her bungalow and they never barked while we were shooting.

I love anybody who knows his or her craft, and Doris is one of the best. We would get different directors and she could size them up the first day.

She'd say to me, "Watch."

She'd say to the director, "I think this should be a two-shot," and if the director said, "Oh yes, sure dear, whatever you want, dear," she'd say, "Oops." She would lose respect for him.

If the director agreed with her and said, "If you want a two-shot, fine, but I was going to do two close-ups," she'd say, "He knows what he's doing." I learned a lot from her too, and I'm forever grateful.

One day I carried my alligator bag in a scene. She noticed it and said, "I sure hope that's not real alligator."

I said, "For what I paid for it, it better be."

She looked at me as if I had killed the alligator personally. Then I said to her, "Did you know that the female alligator lays three hundred eggs at a time and that the male alligator eats two hundred and seventy five of those three hundred eggs?"

Doris said, "Really?"

I continued, "If the male alligator didn't eat two hundred and seventy five of those three hundred eggs, then you'd be up to your ass in alligators."

She looked at me and again went, "Oh, you."

I have to say again, she was wonderful. We still keep in touch with one another.

After the first year of working with Doris, I decided to do a play at the Pheasant Run Playhouse near Chicago. I did a play called *Everybody Loves Opal.* I took Joy Tierney with me, the wardrobe lady on *The Doris Day Show.* Joy and I became very good friends, and we still are to this day. I would always try to take her with me—it was fun to be with her and she took care of me like a mother hen. Her husband Johnny was the dearest man I ever knew. Joy is English and Johnny was Scottish. They looked like the couple on top of a wedding cake...adorable! Joy was with me for the Pheasant Run show. In it, I had a very quick change, which we did backstage in forty seconds! She's great as a wardrobe lady, but she's the best friend you could ever have. I'm very lucky to have her as a friend.

On opening night, Doris sent flowers and a telegram. In fact, most of the people from *The Doris Day Show* sent wires; they were a nice bunch of people. I played the show for six weeks, we did good business, and then we went back to California. Peter came up one weekend to see the show and we were together for three days. It was nice. It was nice to have someone, *period.*

The second year of *The Doris Day Show* went well, and we were in the top ten that summer. I went to Sydney, Australia, for four weeks to play the Chevron Hotel. *The Dick Van Dyke Show* had been a big hit in Australia. Morey had played there and was a smash. My act was in good shape and I took the date. It was the biggest mistake of my life! I took Donn Trenner with me. Buddy Freed was working with Dorothy Shay. As long as I wasn't doing too much club work, I told Buddy to go with someone who was working a lot. When the Australia date came up, I called Donn. He was just great, and he kept my morale up when it was the lowest. Donn had worked with Lena Horne, Ann-Margret, and Shirley MacLaine. He was one of the top conductors in the business. Peter saw me off at the airport and off we went. I was supposed to play four weeks and do two TV shows. It was a *long* flight, and we arrived about 7:00 A.M.

Was I shocked when Gordon MacRae met me at the airport—at 7:00 A.M. I was so glad to see him. We hugged and all that, and he rode with Donn and me to the hotel. He kept warning me about this date, which I thought was strange. He said he didn't go over too well, because they expected him to do what he did in the movies with Doris Day. So he was a little disgusted. He said the audiences were nice, but the critics rapped the hell out of him and cancelled *his* two TV shows. I said, "Great—what did I get myself into?"

He introduced me to some lovely people and they were most kind to me and told me not to worry. Everything would be fine. We had a little party for Gordie and he went back to California. The publicity was great for me, because *The Dick Van Dyke Show* was a big hit in Australia—pictures, interviews, the works. The band was good. At rehearsal, they were amazed that I had book covers for the music. Everyone had a part and I had good arrangements. I told them, "Who have you had here, Bozo the Clown?" We rehearsed well and I felt pretty secure. The manager of the hotel watched the rehearsal and wanted to talk to me after I had finished.

I sat down and he said, "How long is your show?"

I said, "How long do you want it?"

He said, "Forty-five minutes."

I said, "Fine."

He said, "Do you do anything from *The Dick Van Dyke Show*?"

I said, "Like what?"

He said, "You know, scenes with you and Buddy."

I was floored. I said, "How can I do that without Buddy?" I figured he didn't know him by his name, Morey Amsterdam—so I said to myself, *I'm dealing with an idiot.*

He said, "Don't talk to the audience—they don't like that."

I said, "What if they talk to me?"

He said, "I guess you'll have to answer them."

I said, "Make up your mind."

Then he said, "No kangaroo jokes and don't say you're happy to be here. The people hate that and think you're making fun of them."

I said, "Why don't I just fall off the roof and you can cancel me?" He thought I was an idiot.

Opening night. Flowers from Bob Crosby, who had a TV show in town. Peter sent flowers, of course, as did the people I met with Gordon. Gordon sent a wire that said, "Screw 'em, Baby."

Well, I opened. It was about half a house. The band was good, my songs went over, the jokes went over, and it seemed to go very well. The audience started yelling, "How's Dick Van Dyke?" I had to answer. I said, "He's fine, and sends his love to all of you in Australia." I realized I had broken two of the so-called "rules"—talking to the audience and mentioning Australia. But I figured, *What the hell, I didn't start it, the audience was yelling up questions. What could I do?* I tried to make a joke out of everything and it seemed to go over. I got a nice hand and that was it.

Donn thought it was great. What was I worried about? We did the second show and it went about the same—I got a good hand. I went upstairs to my room to get undressed. The manager called me to meet him downstairs in the lounge, which I did.

The greeting I got was, "Didn't I tell you not to talk to the audience? And you talked about Australia."

I said, "I couldn't help it, the audience started asking me questions."

The publicity gal was more of a publicity *man,* and she said, "Why do you wear such sexy gowns?"

I said, "Me? Sexy? I'm wearing ballerina full skirts ankle length, short sleeves or long sleeves— whichever gown I was wearing—and no cleavage. What do you mean, sexy?"

She said, "They're too sexy. You should wear street clothes like you do on *The Dick Van Dyke Show.*"

I got up from the table and said, "You people are impossible. Why don't you cancel me?" They didn't say a word and then I said, "I don't want to throw countries at you, but in America, if you do a show like *The Dick Van Dyke Show,* you play a character. If you do a nightclub act, you'd better have an act—and I have a good one! If you are a panelist on a game show, you act like a panelist, and if you're in a movie, you play another character. I'm doing my nightclub act as Rose Marie—*me*—if you don't like it, cancel me." And I went to my room.

I called Donn and said, "Let's go someplace for coffee."

He said, "Okay."

We met in the lobby and went to some joint and I had my tea. I'm glad I didn't cry telling Donn what happened, I was so damn mad. I talked it all out. He was amazed that they could be so stupid. I went up to my room and wrote Peter, trying to explain what happened. Now I was waiting for the reviews!

They weren't good and they weren't bad. They said I sang well and was dressed beautifully and had a few funny things to say, but I really wasn't what they expected. I looked like I was a nice, friendly person and all that, *but* they wished that America would stop sending over acts that aren't what Australia wants or expects. Well! Now they were making me a bad ambassador of America—and I really got mad.

Donn called and said, "Fig 'em. What do they know?"

I said, "Yeah, but I've got to go through four weeks of this jazz."

When I went down to do the show that night, the band applauded me backstage. "Don't pay attention to them, honey, you've got the best act we've had here in years," one of them said, obviously on behalf of the whole band.

I said, "Thanks, but I've got to go through this for four weeks."

One of the guys said, "Do the show for us—we love doing your show."

I didn't want to cry, but it was rough going on to do the show that night. I went out and did Australian jokes, I talked to the audience, I did everything they told me not to do—and by God, the audiences loved it! I mentioned the critics and said that they watch too much TV—that they should get out more often. I had a ball and felt a hell of a lot better. When I came off stage, even the band applauded—and they never do that!

I got a call between shows from the manager, saying he thought I was very rude. I told him I thought he was stupid and maybe he should get a job as a butcher. I went to my room and I never spoke to him again or to that so-called publicity wo-*man*.

I called Bill Loeb and begged him to get me out of the date. I couldn't go on like this for four weeks. I'd be a mental case. He said he'd try. He had never heard me talk like that before—and oh by the way: I was told that I had been nominated for an Emmy for the last year of *The Dick Van Dyke Show*. That made three nominations. Maybe this year a living person would win it, but I was too upset to think about that.

I called Peter and told him how miserable I was and that as soon as I got home, we would get married. He was happy and just said, "Do the best you can and forget it." Which wasn't what I wanted to hear.

Donn Trenner and I were together all the time, and thank God for him. We had a few laughs and tried to make the best of this mess. Bill Loeb called and said that they couldn't get anyone to replace me. The hotel would not permit it. So I stuck out the four weeks. They cancelled *my* two TV shows—just like they had with Gordon—so I didn't do them. Great country, Australia. When you get your visa, it's made from the time you arrive and the exact date of your departure. You can't stay fifteen seconds over. They're funny people. Nice and all that, but very leery of anybody who isn't Australian and who says they love or even like Australia.

I couldn't wait to get home. Bernice, Harry, and Noop met me at the airport, and I did what the Pope does—I bent down and kissed the ground of America. Things hadn't changed with Peter and me, and again that inner voice said, "Don't get married." I can't tell you why I felt like that, but as I said before, I wanted him to get settled first. He was hanging out with the Danish Mafia and drinking too much. They were egging him on about getting married, which I knew bothered him, but I wasn't going to get into something I knew wasn't right. We went on as before, only this time he wanted to go to Denmark to see his mother. His father had died the year before, and he hadn't gone back for the funeral because he was working at the Travelodge in San Diego, which I thought would be the answer to all of this—but he quit there too. So he thought he should go see his mother.

I said, "That's fine—maybe you can get yourself set with something there. Then I'll sell the house and move to Denmark." Yes, I really said that. I figured I could be a producer or director for Danish TV. It was about ten years behind time and maybe I could really do something like that. It sounded good, but we would just have to wait and see.

He went to Denmark. I finished the last year of *The Doris Day Show* and was doing some *Squares* here and there—enough to keep busy. Peter's letters from Copenhagen were a lot different this time. He was staying at a hotel owned by a family that he had known as a kid. The daughter was running it now, and she was also a heavy drinker and had been married many times. Peter didn't particularly like her—he told me all about her—but he knew that he could stay at the hotel for free.

He was gone about two months, and he said he was coming back to get the things he had stored in my garage because he *might* get set up with being the manager of *seven* hotels in and around Copenhagen—which sounded good. He came back—and he was another person. I knew something was up. He said this woman who ran the hotel was really out of her mind and that he was helping her try to run the hotel! But he wanted to see if he could get that job with the seven hotels.

I said, "Let me know. Noop has moved out on her own, has a job at NBC on the *Tomorrow Show* and is doing great. So I can do what I want."

Peter just looked at me and said, "Would you really sell the house and move to Copenhagen?"

I said, "Of course. If you're set with something good, we can get married."

I don't think he believed me...and frankly, I didn't believe myself! But never say die. I think we both didn't want to admit it was over. He went back to Copenhagen and again his letters were strange.

I wrote to his mother, whom I had met that first year when we went to Copenhagen to celebrate his father's 80th birthday and their 50th wedding anniversary. They were dear people, and I know they liked me. So I wrote her and asked her what was going on; I told her that if Peter got set up with this job, I would move to Copenhagen and we would get married. She wrote back telling me to wait and see what happened with the job, because she didn't like the idea of him being at that hotel with that woman. She didn't like her at all! That's about all she said, except that she would love it if I moved to Copenhagen. She sent me some beautiful linens that she had. She said she wanted me to have them.

Things went on for about another month...letters, no phone calls. I got an offer to do a Broadway show, *Fun City,* with Joan Rivers. I didn't want to do it. It would mean being away for Christmas and I didn't like that, but Joan Rivers and Alexander Cohen, the producer, came out to California to talk to me and tell me I had to do this show...that I *needed* it!

I said, "Why? I'm working on *Squares,* I do a lot of guest shots like *Kojak, Adam-12, Mod-Squad.* I had the ideal way of working! Home and still working!"

But they convinced me I should do a Broadway show. I finally said, "Okay."

I called Peter that night and told him about the show: "Should I take it?"

He said that was up to me. He told me that his mother had died—he had never mentioned this before! And he was now running the hotel—which I'm sure he loved.

I said, "Are you sleeping with her?"

He said, "Well, you kept saying we'd get married when you came back from Australia."

I repeated, "Are you sleeping with her?"

"You never said when we would get married and you kept putting it off."

I said, "Are you sleeping with her?"

He said, "Yes. I've known her for years and she needed help, so I started running the hotel."

I said, "You're not a man, you're a male whore. You just wanted someone to support you, which is something I would never do. So now you have what you wanted—a drunken broad who'll drink with you and who'll support you. I feel sorry for *her*," and I hung up!

Chapter Twenty-Eight

❧

The Theater—Dinner and Otherwise

I was glad it was finally over between Peter and me. We really were getting no place, but for six years, it was very romantic and something I guess I needed at the time.

Bobby was a hard act to follow!

I did some more dinner theater engagements. Joy Tierney was with me on all of them. We went to Pheasant Run again and did a show called *Everybody's Girl,* by John Patrick. He also wrote *Teahouse of the August Moon. Everybody's Girl* was originally written for Vivian Vance—she had played Ethel on *I Love Lucy.* I don't think it ever opened on Broadway, but it was a good show for me.

I played it in Chicago, Dallas, and Seattle. Curtis Roberts was the producer. In Seattle, ours became a great friendship—he knew theater *inside and out.* Joy, Curtis and I would go out every night after the show. We'd talk showbiz and theater all night. *Everybody's Girl* did well, but it really wasn't that good of a play. Robert Nichols, whom I had met when I did *Bye Bye Birdie* in California (only this time with Dick's brother, Jerry Van Dyke), played the part of the father. When Curtis called on Robert to direct *Everybody's Girl* in Seattle, I was thrilled. He also played the stranger in the show. He not only is a very fine actor; he's a helluva director and really made something out of *Everybody's Girl.*

One night he said to me, "This play is all right, but you really should be doing a good play. I'm going to write one for you."

I said, "Fine, go ahead," never figuring that in two weeks he'd show me a script.

The show was called *Up a Tree*. He said, "It was taken from a true story, and it just wrote itself."

I said, "Okay, one night we'll get the kids from the show and Curtis and we'll sit around my suite at the hotel, order some pizza and drinks and we'll read the script," which is exactly what we did.

The script was wonderful—fresh, funny, and very well written. I told Bob Nichols, "We're gonna do this show someday, I promise you," and we did. But more on that later.

I went back home and got a call from Sammy Lewis, who had booked me at the Band Box. They were doing *Call Me Madam* in Anaheim, at a theater in the round. Merman was all set to do it, but then she backed out. They called Kay Starr and she turned it down. (The wheel goes around: years later I would work with Kay in *4 Girls 4*...for eight years!) They had had Merman's clothes custom made and they fit me beautifully—a little nip and tuck here and there and I was all set.

I loved doing that show. After all, how can you go wrong with a Merman show? It's all laid out for you. The whole gang from *The Dick Van Dyke Show* came down, except for Mary—she sent a wire. Dick, Morey and his wife Kay, Richard Deacon, Larry Mathews and his mother and father, plus most of my friends. To top it off, Merman sent flowers and a wire.

The show went well! It only played for two weeks, but it was good for me because it was home and the reviews were great. You always like to be a hit at home!

I then had to go to New York to start rehearsals for *Fun City*, the Joan Rivers show. I was to play Joan's mother. It was madness. She and her husband Edgar and Les Colodny were down as writers, Alexander Cohen was the producer, and Larry Adler was the director—no, not the harmonica player. It was a mish-mash from the beginning, but we did have a terrific cast. I met Renée Lippin, who was in the show. She became like a second daughter to me. She is married to a wonderful writer, Allan Leicht. We became good, good friends. So at least something good came out of that show.

We rehearsed every day, and they would change it every night. We never knew what we were doing. We went to Washington, D.C., to break it in. As before, we rehearsed every day and they would rewrite that night and we'd rehearse the new lines the next day. Gabriel Dell, who was the male lead, played the part differently every time he did it, which is very

With Ethel Merman and Richard Deacon

hard to follow. You never knew which way he was going to go on any particular night. Joan didn't have too much theater experience and had her back to the audience a lot of the time. She was really working hard trying to make it right. We got along all right, but it was hard to talk to her.

I would say, "You can't do joke after joke after joke. You have to give the audience time to catch a breath and *hear* the next joke." She couldn't understand that. I told her, "Neil Simon takes five pages to tell one joke, but when it comes, it's a big one."

I asked her to write normal dialogue, like "Hello, how are you?"

She'd always say, "I'll write you some better jokes."

I said, "I don't want better jokes, I want dialogue leading up to the good jokes you wrote."

Well, we opened in Washington D.C. The show was not bad—better than I had expected. I got a good hand and I thought I must be nuts, they liked it. The reviews came out and they lambasted it. It's funny, they never even mentioned the other actors, including me. The reviews were all about Joan: how badly written it was, and that it was not a good show.

So once again we would do the show at night, they would rewrite that night, and the next day we'd rehearse what they had written. At one point, we did the first act of one show and the second act of another show. I think Joan was used to working alone as a stand-up, and it was hard to change her style.

Ethel Merman called me one day. She said she was in Washington, and that she was coming to see the show that night. She wanted me to meet her at the stage door, in her limo. She didn't want to come backstage. So we did the show that night, I got dressed and ran out to the waiting limo. I got in and the driver started driving. Ethel was sitting there and I could tell she was angry.

I said, "Hi," gave her a hug.

She looked at me and said, "How dare you do this show? It's not good. You have nothing to do in it. Don't open in New York like this." Talk about being hit with a baseball bat.

I said, "They're rewriting every night and we keep changing every night. Maybe they'll get into shape. We've got to try. I know Joan is trying so hard to make it good. She has everything wrapped up in this show."

Ethel said, "What about you? You're going on Broadway. The last time you were on Broadway, you were in a big hit, *Top Banana,* and you were great in that show. Now you go in with this?"

I said, "Well, I'm trying!"

Ethel said, "You can't do anything unless they write it for you...and they have written nothing for you to do. They're wasting you."

By now the limo had arrived at some apartment building—I figured Ethel was staying there. The apartment belonged to a friend of hers, and Ethel used it while she was in Washington.

We walked in. I was floored: Maureen Stapleton, Jason Robards, and George Grizzard were sitting in the living room having a drink. They all looked at me like I had killed somebody.

Maureen said, "You know better than to be on stage for fifteen minutes and not utter a word. What's the matter with you?"

I just stood there, with my mouth open.

George Grizzard said, "You can't open in New York with that show as it is."

Then Maureen started to talk about the "takes" I did on *The Dick*

Van Dyke Show. One in particular—I call it the "priest take." I walk into the Petrie house and say, "Where is this tall, good looking..."—and I see that he's a priest—"...*priest* you wanted me to meet?" It was a great take and I knew what Maureen meant.

I felt so foolish, because I knew they liked me and wanted the best for me! So we talked and had a few drinks—I had my iced tea—and Ethel said, "I'm going to write Alex Cohen a letter and tell him to take care of my baby. Maybe it will help."

I said, "Would you do that?"

She said, "Why not? He knows you know what you're doing or he wouldn't have put you in the show...but you've got to do more in that show. You're wasted. If they don't do something, *quit!*"

I said, "Okay," and I hugged them all and thanked them. They were so great to say those things...especially Ethel.

We played two weeks. Never the same show—new lines, new scenes every night, and it went on like that until we got to New York. We never "froze" the show, as they say.

Renée and I became very close friends, and we'd have lunch and dinner together. I was staying at my mother's in New Jersey, so I would drive in every day. We started doing previews, and for some reason the show was actually getting to be something. They extended the previews, because we were sold out every night and it looked like it would make it.

Ethel called me every day at the theater to see if my part was getting any bigger or better. The first time she called, the doorman called me and said, "Some nut on the phone wants to talk to you, says she's Ethel Merman."

I said, "It *is* Ethel Merman." He almost died.

One day she said, "I'm having some work done on my teeth, I don't think I can make the opening."

I said, "Oh! You have to!"

She said, I won't be able to smile, it's my *front tooth.*"

I said, "Look, you do what you think best. I don't think you'll have to worry about smiling—it ain't that funny."

So we finally opened. Every comedian in the world was there, and all of them came back to my dressing room. Ethel was there, of course, as well as Kay Medford, Betty Bruce, and on and on. What a night. There was an opening-night party at Benihana's. The invitation said, "You and a guest are invited..."

I said to Bill Loeb, who had come in for the opening with my friend

Vince Miranda, "What the hell is that? 'You and a guest'? My name is above the title. I'm one of the leading stars. My mother and daughter are here for the opening, my friends are here. What am I going to do?"

Vince said, "Take it easy. You and I will go to the party and Bill will go to my hotel and get an open bar and some food sent up and you can invite anyone you want. You'll have your own party."

I looked at him and said, "Thanks, Vince, I owe you a big one."

My mother didn't like the show. Noop thought it was all right. Vince and Bill thought it wasn't bad…but you could tell, it wasn't all that great.

I got dressed and told everybody about *my* party…gave them all the information. And I left with Vince to go to the so-called cast party at Benihana's.

Ethel was there with two guys, and we sat with her. I think we stayed about a half hour. We told Ethel about *our* party, and she said, "Let's go!" So we went to the Park Lane, where Vince was staying. He had a very large suite. Bill Loeb was there overseeing everything. Food was there, an open bar and pretty soon it was jammed with all the kids from the show. It was a helluva party.

When Ethel left, Vince and I walked her to the door. She looked at Vince and said, "Don't you hurt my baby in any way or I'll cut your balls off!" Poor Vince, he didn't know what to say or do. We all hugged one another and went back to the party and listened to the radio reviews—which were bad. Again, they seemed to just pick on Joan, never saying anything about the rest of the cast. Finally everybody left and Vince drove me home to my mother's house in Jersey in the limo.

The reviews came out in the papers the next day and they ripped it apart. So we knew it was a matter of time. I felt sorry for Joan and Edgar, because they had worked so hard and tried their best to keep it running. If I remember correctly, I think we played two weeks and that was that.

Noop and I went back to California and we were glad to be home…so was Vince!

Chapter Twenty-Nine

❧

The Pussycat Theaters and Vince

I met Vince Miranda when I got home from Pheasant Run in Chicago. Barbara Corday, who was my publicity girl—one of the best—and later went on to be the head of television programming at Columbia Pictures, called me to go to an opening in San Diego at a little theater called the Off Broadway. She was doing publicity for the theater, which was owned by Vince Miranda.

I said, "Okay," and drove to the Los Angeles airport. This man met me at the parking lot of the airport and hurried me to the gate. He was about five foot four, dark hair, kind of wiry, about 45 years old, kind of Italian-looking—it turned out he wasn't Italian. Martha Raye was at the gate, Audrey Christy, Harry Guardino and lots of actors. There were about thirty of us. We got to San Diego. The flight took about fifty minutes. When we landed and went out front, there were limos waiting to drive us to the theater. The guy from the parking lot came into our limo. I found out that he was the owner of the theater and that he owned all of the Pussycat Theaters in California—there were about nineteen of them at that time. He was very pleasant, charming, had a good sense of humor…and he was short! But I liked him.

We went to the theater. It was an adorable little theater, about five hundred seats. We saw *Cactus Flower*. After the show, we went to some big hotel where Vince had a large buffet set up. It was a very nice evening, but I had to take the last flight home, which meant I had to leave fairly early. Vince said, "Don't worry, I'll drive you to L.A. so you can pick up your car." So I stayed another hour and had a lot of fun with everybody. I said good night and told Vince again that I didn't want to stay too late.

We got in his car and chatted about everything on the way back to L.A. He loved theater—although he owned the Pussycat Theaters, his real love was legitimate theater. To him the Pussycat Theaters were a business and that was it...even though they had made him a millionaire. But he was a great sport and, as I always said, "the last of the big spenders."

He drove me to the airport parking lot. I got my car, thanked him, and drove off.

The next day Barbara Corday called and said Vince wanted to ask me out on a date.

I said, "Why doesn't he call me himself?"

She said, "He's kind of shy."

I said, "Get out of here!"

She told me that he really was shy.

I said, "I have to go to a premiere tonight. Ask him to call me and we'll go to this thing together."

She said, "Great. I think he likes you."

I said, "Swell."

I told Noop. All of a sudden she got very excited that I was going out on a date.

After a few minutes, Vince called and said, "We'll go out and have dinner."

I said, "I have tickets for a premiere tonight at the Pantages. Why don't we go to that and then have dinner?"

He said, "Fine," and told me that he'd pick me up at 7:00.

By 6:45, Noop was looking out the window for Vince to see what kind of a car he was driving. At 6:55, she yelled, "He's here and he's driving a Jag!" So I guess that made it fine with her.

He rang the bell and I answered it. He dressed very well...and he was short! I figured I'd better wear flats, so we wouldn't look like Mutt and Jeff. We drove to the theater. It was jammed with photographers, fans, and, of course, Army Archerd at the mike introducing everybody. Archerd is the official MC at all premieres.

He called me up to the mike. Vince sat back and of course Army said, "Who's your date?"

I said, "Vince Miranda."

Army said, "Oh! Hi, Vince." And that was that.

After the premiere, we went to Dan Tana's for a bite to eat, and we talked and talked. He was great to talk to, and he loved the idea that we were going out together. He took me home and we said good night...no kiss, no nothing. I relaxed. We became very good friends...no romance, and I was grateful for that. We liked being together and he loved the idea that everybody knew me and came over for autographs. He was out with a celebrity. Best of all, we went to all of the big affairs, the $1,000–ticket dinners, like the Thalians annual affair and the St. Jude Hospital affair that Danny Thomas always did.

We were getting to be known as a couple. Little did everybody know that we were like brother and sister, but we had fun. Once in a while, a kiss on the cheek, but that's all...and again, I was grateful. I didn't have to worry about a thing.

He was very involved with the Variety Club, which helps crippled children. When they had a big affair, he would buy two or three tables at $2,500 a table and give the tickets to some of the people who worked for him. He did it because he believed in the charity, not to be a show-off, and I loved him for that. Every Christmas he would take twelve boys from the Variety Club Boys Club in the worst section of L.A. He would take them in cars to a wonderful restaurant for dinner and give them each a radio, a $10 bill (so they could buy their parents something), record albums, and candy. Then, after dinner, he would take them to a men's clothing store and they could pick out two complete outfits: shirts, shoes, socks, jackets, and pants. He did it with love.

He took pride in running the Pussycat Theaters. Although they were porno theaters, he ran them as a business. They were cute little theaters that were kept in shape. Sometimes when we were out, he would stop at one theater or another and make sure everything was being run right. I met everyone at the office, including his cousin Jimmy. His publicity man Don Haley kept our names in the columns. Everyone liked him, and, as I said, we had a lot of fun together.

He loved the little Off Broadway Theater, and brought a lot of stars there to do plays. He asked me if I would do *Everybody's Girl* there. I said, "Why not?"

I asked Joy to come with me, although we drove home every night. During the weekend, we'd stay at the hotel in San Diego because of the matinee.

I must say that Vince took care of everything. Jim Burrows (son of

Abe, the movie writer) and Brian Avnet were working for Vince as director and producer. We all had a good time doing *Everybody's Girl*. Even Noop came down a lot. We'd all go out to dinner and have a great time. Jim Burrows went on to become a very successful television producer and director. My birthday came while I was doing the show—and what a party he threw. After the curtain came down, everyone piled up on the stage. One gag after another, including a muscular guy jumping out of a cake (because I was always looking for a guy...ha ha). I told you what he did in New York after *Fun City*. He was always coming to my rescue.

When I was asked to host a telethon in Hawaii, they said I could ask anyone I wanted—free hotel suite at the Ala Moana Hotel, airfare, and food. So I called Merman, Paul Lynde, Jessica Walters, Richard Deacon, and Jane Dulo. I called Frankie Ortega, who became my piano player, conductor, and arranger for the next eleven years. He got some of the local musicians to fill out our orchestra—about six guys. We also had some kid stars from different kid shows.

I had done the telethon two years before when Arthur Godfrey was the host. He was on the air for twenty minutes, and then he ducked out. I sort of took over. They liked what I did, and two years later they asked me to host. I was thrilled. We had our private Western Airlines plane and when we arrived, there was a mob there, plus a parade band and leis by the dozens. It really was lovely. We went to the Ala Moana Hotel and we all had the same suites on different floors.

I brought Joy with me—God, she was wonderful. Knowing me as she did, she did things before I could even ask her to do them. Our first night we had dinner at our hotel in the big dining room. They introduced us and told everyone about the telethon we were doing the next day. Jessica Walters had some friends in Hawaii and wanted to leave. Merman told her, "How dare you leave? You have a job to do here. When we're through with that, then go visiting!" Jessica quietly sat down.

After dinner we all went to Al Harrington's nightclub. He is the most popular and most beloved man in Honolulu. We had a long front table, saw the show, and then Al introduced us. When he introduced Merman, they screamed for her to sing and, bless her heart, she got up and looked at me and said, "What will I sing?" I said, "'Show Business,' what else?" She got up on the stage and said she'd have to bring up *her* conductor, Frankie Ortega.

Frankie got up and said, "What key?"

She said, "Anything."

Well, Frankie was just about the best, so he kind of knew what key, and she sang "There's No Business Like Show Business." We all got goose pimples. She was just great, and she brought the house down. But before she sat down, she talked about the telethon and told everybody to send in money. What a night!

Back at the hotel, I called Vince to tell him about what had happened and he said it sounded great. He also said he was coming to Honolulu the next day, in case I needed any help. Bless him. So the next day, Ethel, Joy and I went down to the airport and picked up Vince. And, who else was there? Johnny, Joy's husband!

It was going to be a ball. Back to the hotel to get ready for the show. We were to rally in the lobby of the hotel at 6:00 P.M. They had convertibles with our names on them at the door. We got leis again, which I loved. We got in the cars and drove down the main street to the Kaiser Dome, where we were doing the telethon.

The main guy, Dick Peicich with Easter Seals, did a helluva job of arranging everything. We had food backstage with soda, juices, coffee, tea—and they kept bringing more in. Vince and Johnny were out in the Dome with baskets, collecting money. The two of them were wonderful, and they helped out a lot. We were to start at 7:30 P.M. The announcer came back for the script and I said, "No script. We open with Ethel on stage, nobody else, nobody at the phones. We say nothing. The minute we're on, Ethel will sing 'The Star Spangled Banner.' Then the announcer says, 'Welcome to the Easter Seals Telethon.' People will go to the phones, and the band is playing 'There's No Business Like Show Business,' he introduces me and I go on and we start."

Everybody said, "Great," and that's the way we opened. I was on the air for twenty-one hours! Al Harrington came down and cohosted. It was just great and we made $260,000, which is the highest they have ever made.

When the telethon was over, we went to the hotel, sat in the coffee shop, and finally went to bed. We had the poster boy and his girlfriend with us, they were named John and Joanie. John had been the poster boy ten years earlier, when he was sixteen. He was now twenty-six and in love with Joanie. They were to be married in October. Richard Deacon said, "Why don't you get married here in Hawaii?" They said they had to call their parents, which we all thought was adorable. We said we'd pay for everything, so they called and the parents said, "Yes." So we planned the wedding for the next day in Merman's suite. She acted like the mother of the bride. She was so excited. We all bought things for the wedding. I bought the dress, Merman bought the shoes and the guest book, Richard Deacon paid for the groom's suit—everybody bought something. The hotel heard about the wedding and sent up a beautiful wedding cake and Vince bought the champagne. Joy dressed our bride.

It was the most beautiful wedding I have ever been to. Joy and Johnny got all the flowers to decorate Merman's room. Merman was at the door as people came in. She said, "Please sign the guest book." The champagne was on ice and there was a table set with glasses. Another table for the three-tiered wedding cake. Everyone came. We started the wedding. Both the bride and the groom wore wedding leis and, while the minister said the service, Merman sang "They Say That Falling in Love Is Wonderful," a cappella. There wasn't a dry eye in the house!

When we got home, Merman went to New York, and most of the gang went back to their normal routines, but I don't think any of us will forget that wedding.

Vince and I went out a lot—any big charity, premieres, and sometimes, just dinner. When Merman played L.A., Vince got tickets and we called Merman to let her know we'd be at the theater. Now, normally you don't go backstage *before* the show, you wait until after the performance. But she said, "Come backstage before the show."

So I went backstage (Vince said he'd see her later), and there she was, in this large dressing room, doing needlepoint. We hugged and I said, "How are you?"

She said, "Fine. I have a present for you," and she handed me a package. She said, "Open it."

I did and it was a pillow she had needlepointed for me, with her initials on the side. I was floored.

She said, "It's for your dining room—I remembered the colors."

I said, "Oh, Ethel! It's the best gift I ever received," and I hugged and kissed her.

They announced that it was fifteen minutes until curtain, so I went out saying, "I know you'll do it anyway, but knock 'em out."

She smiled and said, "I will."

We saw the show, which was sensational, and picked her up for night lunch. It was great, and Vince couldn't believe that he could be that close to Merman. She liked him, so all was well.

Chapter Thirty

Up a Tree, or Ring around Rosie

I got a call from Bill Loeb. It seems that Tony DeSantis, from Drury Lane in Chicago, wanted me to do a play for six weeks. "What play would you like to do?" asked Bill. They always do the same plays over and over, only with different stars, and I didn't want to do that.

I told Bill, "I have a new play that was written for me and I want to do that."

He said, "I don't think they'll go for that."

I said, "Then forget it."

He called me back in about an hour and said, "What's the name of the show?"

I said, "*Up a Tree,* and I want the guy who wrote it to play my husband in the show."

Bill said, "He won't do it, you'll lose the job."

I said, "Fine, so I'll lose the job."

He called back in about twenty minutes and said, "Tony DeSantis says they have good actors in Chicago."

I said, "I'm sure they do, but it's a new play and if it needs fixing, the writer is right there."

An hour later, it was set!

I had made friends with a wonderful astrologer, Angela Gallo. She became my best friend and lived about two blocks away from me. We met on *The Merv Griffin Show* and hit it off immediately. She was from New Jersey and lived across the street from my girlfriend Gerri's husband. So we talked Jersey, and things we remembered as kids, and we became very close.

And as an astrologer, she was the best. When I said I would do the show, I was really sticking my neck out. I asked Angela to do a chart on *Up a Tree* and how I would do in it. She came over to the house and I taped what she said. She said that it would be a smash, that I would stay longer than six weeks, and that I was going to call her on July 4 and tell her about the extension. She also said that this would not be the end of it. It would go on and on, which I didn't understand until later. She also said that a Cancer in the cast would cause some trouble. Nothing big, but annoying. So we laughed, had a cup of tea and that was that.

I left for Chicago with Joy and was met at the airport by Robert Nichols, who had written the play. We were to play Drury Lane South, which was outside of Chicago. Drury Lane was one of many Drury Lane Theaters in and around Chicago, but I think South was the best.

We started rehearsals, and I found out we had a helluva cast. When we broke for lunch, I invited all of them to a restaurant for lunch. I wanted to find out who the Cancer was. I asked all of their signs and the only Cancer was the girl who played my daughter. That knocked me out. She seemed pleasant and nice, so I didn't think any more about it.

Rehearsals went well—very well—and after four days of rehearsal, I knew we had a helluva show. I met Carol Saenz, who played the reporter and doubled as an old lady. She was unbelievable. I told her if she didn't get a hand as she walked off every night, I'd kill her. She got the hand every night! Bob Nichols played my husband, and even though he wrote the part for himself, he was great and super to work with. I don't remember the girl who played my daughter. She was all right, but very odd at times. The other actors were Otto Schlesinger, Tom Elrod, and Dick Stadleman. Just about the best you could get.

We opened and we were a hit. DeSantis threw a party in his suite and the raves were nonstop. They even called Bob Nichols "the new Neil Simon." We did great business, the reviews were outstanding and I became very good friends with Carol, her husband, Ralph, and their two boys. I even cooked an Italian dinner for everyone.

DeSantis was opening another theater in downtown Chicago, a beautiful little place right next door to the Ritz-Carlton Hotel. He was opening with Raymond Burr in *The Good Doctor.* They opened on our night off, so the cast went to see the show. It wasn't very good, and Raymond was actually holding a clipboard with the script on it—we were all in shock. The next day Tony DeSantis wanted to see me. We met and he asked me to stay five more weeks. He was having trouble with Raymond Burr, and he didn't want to open a new show at Drury Lane. Plus, we were doing sell-out biz. Believe it or not, it was on July 4! I called Angela, forgetting that she told me I would do that! She was amazing. So we stayed the extra five weeks. I asked Tony DeSantis if he had watched our show. He said he never watched a show, except for *The Odd Couple.*

I said, "Well, you're gonna watch our show."

He said, "I know you're doing great business, and that's all I care about."

I said, "No, you're gonna watch our show," and he did…that night. He loved it, *but* he didn't like the girl who played my daughter.

He said, "Get rid of her. Get somebody else."

I said, "Not me! You fire her, I won't," and by God he did. We had to get another girl. But as I said before, Angela had called all of this.

One afternoon, Ethel Merman called me and said that she was going to L.A., but she wanted to stop in Chicago to see my show, was that all right?

I said, "Are you kidding? I'd love it."

She said she would be there the day after next. She had a friend pick her up. She was going to stay at the Ritz and he would drive her to the theater. As it was, I knew the guy who was bringing her. Let's just call him Eddie. I told the cast she was coming and they were all excited. I got her the best seats in the house and we did a helluva show that night. I kept looking at her to see if she was laughing, and she was. Of course, I introduced her and she took a bow and came back to my dressing room after the show.

She said she loved it; she thought it was funny and *clean.* She said, "I went to see a play in Chicago and you know what some broad says right in the beginning? She says, 'I gotta pee!' Isn't that awful for a musical? Broadway is not Broadway anymore."

So I said, "I'll get dressed and we'll go downstairs and have a drink and talk. The cast wants to meet you."

She said, "Fine."

So she and Eddie went to the lounge and our entire cast came down to meet her. We all talked and told stories. She was just wonderful and the cast loved her. She was something else. She left for L.A. the next day.

My birthday came in the middle of the run of the play. We did the show that night and at the end of the curtain call, I did a little "after piece."

I would talk about how we got the play going, thanks to Mr. DeSantis. I'd tell some little jokes and talk to the audience. This night Bob came on stage and said, "We have a surprise for you." He told the audience that it was my birthday and that Ethel Merman was visiting me a few days before and she had *made me a tape!* They played it. It was Merman who said, "Happy Birthday dear Roe. The kids asked me to do a little birthday tape for you. Have a happy, happy birthday. I send you all my love, Ethel." She started to sing "Happy Birthday" and everyone joined in. Talk about a thrill—it was wonderful. Carol told me they asked her to do this when she came down to see the show and she said, "Of course." The cast threw a party for me, and I got some beautiful gifts. One was a bracelet I truly treasure; it has charms and each charm had the name of one of the actors. It was a birthday to remember.

I went home, and in three weeks Tony DeSantis called and wanted me to do *Up a Tree* in Chicago at the new theater *and* that he wanted me *in two weeks!*

He said, "I have twelve people on stage and nine people in the audience! I'll get you a big suite at the Ritz-Carlton. It's right next door to the theater."

I said, "You have to get the same cast."

He said, "I'll get them."

I said, "Okay, I'll see you in two weeks."

I called Joy and said, "We're off again," and then I realized what Angela had said: "The show would go on and on." She was right again!

Joy and I arrived in Chicago and again Bob Nichols picked us up and drove us to the Ritz. The suite was unbelievable. It had *three* bedrooms, a kitchen, a dining room, and a living room. I think it took the entire floor. It was fantastic. I arrived on Saturday night and told Bob to call the cast together for Sunday in my suite. They arrived and we sat around and went over the script. We all remembered the show and we breezed through it. We opened the following Wednesday. It was a sellout for six weeks. Thanksgiving came while I was doing the show, and Tony DeSantis brought over boxes of pots and pans, dishes, and silverware, because he knew that I wanted to cook Thanksgiving dinner in the suite.

Angela came to Chicago to see the show and stayed with us in the suite. She loved the show and said it should be a series. I said that was a great idea and spoke to Bob Nichols about it. He wrote a presentation and I called Bill Loeb to see what we could do. In the meantime, Bob wrote a pilot and three story lines for future shows. It was great.

We came back to California and I know Bill was trying to sell the show, but the studios said it was too political—they were afraid of it. So we kind of gave up on it for a while.

I did the play again in San Antonio, at a theater that Earl Holliman had bought. I tried to get as many of the original cast as I could. Carol Saenz was signed, but Bob Nichols couldn't do it. We got a guy to replace Bob, but it wasn't the same. It was all right. We got Otto to play the principal again, and instead of Dick Stadleman, we got a great guy named Don Marston. It came off very well. I did a lot of publicity. I went to the Alamo again and signed the guest book again. Carol and I stayed together at some apartment, and I even brought my dog Scruffy along because there was no one at the house. Noop had moved out into her own apartment. Carol and I became good friends, and it was such fun to work with Carol. She was great!

Vince decided to come to San Antonio and we had a ball while he was there. The whole cast loved him. We'd go out every night after the show and he'd spend money like it was going out of style. I think he enjoyed it too, because I think he had always wanted to be in show business.

When our show closed in San Antonio, I came home to California for a few days and then went to do a TV movie called *Bridge across Time* with David Hasselhoff in Arizona. David had played one of my sons in *Everybody's Girl,* in Chicago. Robert Urich was another son. They were doing all right, bless them. David kept calling me "Mom," which was kind of cute. I had about two days on the film. In the middle of the second day, Angela called me on the set and told me that Vince had died of throat cancer and wanted to let me know before I heard it someplace else. He was 53 years old. He was one helluva guy. He was a dear and wonderful friend, and I think about him very often even to this day.

Chapter Thirty-One

4 Girls 4

Bill Loeb called me one day and said, "How would you like to do your act with Rosemary Clooney, Margaret Whiting, and Barbara McNair?"

I said, "What are you talking about?"

He said he had an idea about putting the four of us together, each doing our own act.

I said, "That's fine, but you have to have a finale—something to tie it together."

He said, "We can come up with something."

I said, "When would we open?"

He said, "In about a month or so at the Wilshire Theater in Beverly Hills."

I said, "Let me think about this, I'll call you later."

Six weeks before this happened, I was booked on a cruise to do my act. I called Frankie Ortega to play for me. Our group was Frankie and his wife, Maxine, Bill Loeb and his wife, Pinky, Joy and me. I was really breaking in my new act. Frankie made the arrangements. I asked Anthony Newley if I could do his song "Funny Man." He was so kind. He sent me a lead sheet and lyrics and asked me if I needed anything else. What a dear man.

The cruise was wonderful. The show was a big hit and Frankie did a concert of his own on another night. We had a great time and I felt a little better about doing my act again. After doing all the TV and Australia, I wasn't so sure about my act. The cruise convinced me again that it was a good act. I had all new numbers and did quite a few bits with Frankie at the piano. So I called Bill and told him I would do it. The money was all right, not great. We would each do about twenty-five minutes apiece. I said, "*And* a finale. I want Frankie to do the show too. He can conduct for all of us."

Bill said, "Fine."

I really wanted to make an impression because this was Hollywood and my home. By this time, it seemed like everybody only knew me from *The Dick Van Dyke Show*. It seemed no one knew I had an act, or that I had worked in all the best clubs across the country for years. So I was out to prove I was something *before* I did *The Dick Van Dyke Show*. I had two gowns made by Michael Travis and I called Sammy Cahn to write a parody of "I'm Glad I'm Not Young Anymore." He said he'd love to do it. I could use a clip from *International House* as my intro—nobody to introduce me, just put the film on and play about one minute, have the band pick up the music from the film and I would walk out, beaded dress and full-length fur to match every gown. It was a helluva entrance.

I told Dodi, my secretary, that we needed a finale and she wrote parodies based on "Together," "Side by Side," "There is Nothing Like a Dame," and "There's No Business Like Show Business." She was a whiz at writing parodies. We used her "Together" parody, and I walked into rehearsal with the finale all written out and said, "This is the finale we're gonna do."

They said, "Fine."

I told Frankie and he wrote out some kind of music so we wouldn't sound like amateur night. We all rehearsed our acts and then we rehearsed the finale. It was good—not great, but good.

We opened and we were sensational. The reviews the next day were unbelievable. On the entertainment page of the *L.A. Times* they had a picture of us taken during our finale! We played the week and we were the talk of the town. Bill Loeb was excited and thrilled and said we should go on with this. He spoke to us about the Huntington Hartford Theater in Hollywood. Barbara McNair didn't want to go on, so we had to think of another girl. I suggested Kay Starr, but Frankie, who had worked with Kay for years, said he didn't think she would do it. So we thought and thought, and somebody, I don't remember who, said Helen O'Connell and we all said, "Great!"

Bill wanted to "four wall" the Huntington Hartford Theater. For those of you who don't know what "four wall" means, it means you pay for everything, the musicians and the acts (us girls), and you pay a percentage to the theater, like a rental.

I said, "We can't make any money."

Bill said, "Even if we fill half the house, we can come out with a little something."

I said, "No, we won't, but I think we should play the date—right in Hollywood. It would be good for all of us."

We got Helen. She was just right and God, she was beautiful—dimples and all. She looked like she was thirty—and she was the oldest of the group!

We decided to rotate each night. I would open, then Helen, then Clooney, and then Margaret. The next night, Helen would open, then Clooney, then Margaret, and then me. It all seemed to work okay, but it still didn't feel right. We needed to really have a good finale. We took our bows to "Together, Wherever We Go." Every night we would add little bits and gags that just seemed to happen on stage. We'd come off stage saying "Leave that in." It worked well for a while, but we really needed a song written for us to make it a solid finale.

We got some great publicity and we opened. It was one of those star-studded openings. Everybody and his brother was there. *Free,* of course, but it was a helluva opening and the reviews? Raves again!

Now we all started thinking about doing this on a tour. Bill would set up the dates, we'd split the money four ways, and we'd each pay Frankie one-fourth. In fact, we'd split everything four ways, including Bill Loeb's commission. We started getting dates. The first one would be New Orleans about two weeks later at the Fairmont Hotel.

I was happy to have a little time to spend at home resting, relaxing, and getting ready for our opening in New Orleans. Noop and I spent a lot of time together during those two weeks. She had been going out with Steve Rodrigues, a KNBC director, for about a year. Noop was producing *The Saturday Show* on KNBC. She had quite a career as a producer. She started on *The Tomorrow Show* with Tom Snyder thanks to Rudy Tellez and Joel Tator. She produced a game show called *Are You or Aren't You?* She was currently doing *The Saturday Show,* producing a live remote every Saturday.

Steve Rodrigues and Noop met at NBC, and as I said, they went out for about a year. He was a nice young man and I liked him very much. He was a lot like Bobby in build, and he had a great dry sense of humor. Before I left for New Orleans, Steve came over and said they wanted to get married if it was okay with me. He was asking for her hand in marriage,

4 Girls 4: Rose Marie, Helen O'Connell, Rosemary Clooney, and Margaret Whiting

which I thought was very sweet. I said, "Fine. We'll have a nice engagement party here at the house, in the backyard, in June."

I left for New Orleans and the Fairmont Hotel. It was a great date.
We all had played it alone and now we went in as *4 Girls 4*. The publicity
was great and the reviews were even better. I decided to have the invitations made there in New Orleans. I went to Marilyn Barnett, who booked

the Fairmont, and asked her where we should go for the invitations for Noop's wedding party. Margaret and I went to Eaton's Stationery Store. I picked out the card and told the saleslady what I wanted engraved on it.

She said, "You can have this in about eight weeks."

I said, "No, I need them now, the party is in two weeks!"

Margaret and I went back to the hotel and told Marilyn about it. She said her sister-in-law did calligraphy and that she could do them.

I didn't want to look like a cheapskate, but having all the invitations and envelopes done by hand has got to cost a fortune—especially for 150 people and about 50 out-of-towners! Marilyn made an appointment for me with her sister-in-law, Audrey Barnett.

Audrey came over to the hotel the next day and we went to Bailey's, the hotel's little bistro. She was very pretty and charming and carried a little briefcase with samples of her work.

After the usual greetings, Audrey said, "Are you happy about the engagement?"

I looked at her and started to laugh and said, "Of course we're happy."

Then she said, "So now we know what the wording should be."

I liked her immediately. We talked and got everything straightened out; much to my surprise, it wasn't going to cost that much. I told her I wanted her to do the wedding invitations and all the things that had to be printed. She then said, "Give me a list of names and addresses." So every day I'd call Noop, get names and addresses, and call Audrey and give her the information. The next morning, a bunch of envelopes were at the desk in the lobby. That's how the invitations were done. By the time we finished the date at the Fairmont, the invitations for the engagement party were finished!

Dear Audrey and I became close friends. She was married to Marilyn's brother, Bill, who was a very fine and well-known lawyer. Every time I played New Orleans, Audrey would be with me every day. She would take me shopping. One day she took me to see some of the old southern mansions, and we ate fried chicken in the car. We had a great time together.

She did the wedding invitations and we did it all *over the phone*. I think I called her every day. She did such a beautiful job. After she sent the last batch of envelopes, she wrote on a card, "Get pretty stamps....don't get Planned Parenthood stamps!"

After New Orleans, we went back to California and the engagement party was beautiful. The backyard looked lovely: baskets of flowers hung from the trees, tables and umbrellas all matching pink, champagne and tea sandwiches, sugar cookies with their names on them. I tried to think of everything, and I must say, it was lovely.

Bill called a meeting and we all met in his office. He told us about the dates—all the best places, which he and Marty Kummer, a well-known booking agent, had set up. It was summer, so we would be playing all the East Coast places—Valley Forge; Cape Cod; Beverly, Massachusetts; Westbury, Long Island; and so on. The money sounded odd, but good. I am the one who keeps contracts and I keep them with me when I am working, in case I have to refer to anything. The other girls couldn't be bothered with that stuff. I had a business head when it came to working! To me, it's a business, and I treat it as a business, and I love it!

We played a lot of theaters in the round and, as I said, they were all the best places. We got along all right. Clooney and I became good friends, and Margaret has been my friend from the moment I met her. I had heard so many people say we looked alike. We don't, very much—well, if you see us together, there might be a slight resemblance. I like Margaret a lot. You can always count on her. To me, she's showbiz and her knowledge of songs and songwriters is unbelievable. When she wrote her book, I told her, "I know now, if it weren't for songwriters, we would have lost the war."

Helen was something else. She could get you mad at her in a second and then in the next second, she would try to make up. There were many times when none of us were talking to her. At times she just didn't think. She would fail to show up for a press interview and say, "Nobody told me," when we had all talked about it the night before. She had a very dry sense of humor and could write lyrics for us like a poet. But she was difficult to get along with—we never knew if she was in a good mood or not. Clooney and Helen were born on the same day, May 23, but different years. They were both Geminis and that means "two people in one." How true, how true.

Many times I told the girls that we had a good thing going. "Hey, we got another crack at it, let's not forget that!" I said. The show was a big hit no matter where we played, and we played a lot of places two and three times. Each time I would try and change a song or two. I'd go to Morey and ask him to write me some new jokes. Also, by now I had found a great wholesale house in New York for beaded gowns. Ruthie Shapiro and Bobbi Baker had a shop in Brookline, Massachusetts. Ruthie knew many of the wholesalers in New York and told me some places to go where she was sure I would get a break—maybe up to half off. For beaded gowns, that means a lot! I took Margaret up there too. We changed the finale again, because we couldn't do the same thing when we played the same theater two or three times. Clooney said, "Fine," and changed a few songs and even got a few gowns, as did Helen. By now, it was truly time for a new finale, since we were returning to some of the places we had already played. Margaret called Tom Hatten. We all knew him from TV and Broadway shows. She told him we needed a grand finale. He wrote our signature song, "4 Girls 4," and it turned out to be just what the doctor ordered.

Everything fell into place beautifully, but four women on the road together can bring about its own problems. Helen's favorite little "trouble starter" was that she'd arrive at the theater and grab the dressing room she wanted. We had two limos (this was in our contract) that would pick us up at the hotel and drive us to the theater and then home. Margaret and Helen went early, because Margaret opened and Helen was second. (We decided that this order was the best after we played the Fairmont in San Francisco.) The limo would come for them at 7:00 P.M., and then the limo would pick Clooney and me up at 7:30. Helen would call the limo at *4:30* and have the driver take her to a restaurant. She had to eat dinner at *5:00 P.M.* (She would order the same thing every night: two Tanqueray martinis straight up; a salad, which she picked at; steak, which she ate maybe a third of; and a bottle of beer!) She'd have the driver wait for her, then he'd drive her to the theater, while poor Margaret was waiting at the hotel to be picked up. Then Margaret would finally take a cab. This happened many times. I was always the one who tried to straighten things out—it wasn't easy! We played about four years like that, about twenty weeks a year. We met some great people: friends of Helen's, friends of Margaret and Clooney, and friends of mine.

Frankie Ortega was just the best. All of our music was in tip-top shape and he'd rehearse the band. All we had to do was show up. Frankie had mentioned it would be great to have either a regular bass player or drummer on the road with us. Clooney had worked with a drummer named Jerry White from Tennessee. She found him when she went there for a date and liked him. She mentioned him to us and Frankie. Jerry met Frankie and Jerry quickly became part of "the family." Jerry was and is a damn good musician. As Kay Starr always said, "He keeps good time." When we played the Regency in Phoenix, I thought it was about time we had a road manager. I called a friend of mine in New York and asked him if he knew of a good road/stage manager.

He said, "Yes, his name is Allen Sviridoff." He gave me his number and I called him. The girls thought I was crazy, but I said, "We're a big act, getting a lot of money—we've got to go in as four stars." We paid for his fare to Phoenix.

He saw the show and after the show I talked to him and said, "Nobody gets treated in any special way. We're all the same, but it will be up to you to work with Frankie and Jerry."

He said, "Fine," but I had to convince the girls to go for it. We paid his salary, as we did for Jerry and Frankie—each of us one-fourth.

Allen was even better than we had expected. We found out that he had worked with Ginger Rogers and Mitzi Gaynor, so he knew what he was doing, and it made everything a helluva lot easier for all of us. This is how it went. Say we had a date in Boston. The three of us who lived in California would go to the airport and Allen would be waiting for our bags. He'd tag them and we would go to the lounge. Margaret usually came in from New York. When we arrived, two limos were waiting; Clooney and I in one limo, and Helen and Margaret in the other. We'd go to the hotel and check in. In about a half hour, Allen would knock on my door and give me my bags—I always had two, one for the theater and one for the hotel. He would take the theater bag with him and leave my hotel bag. I also had a big carton we called "Baby" to hold the gowns and the furs; he would take that to the theater also. He did that with each of us. Frankie had the music and Jerry had his drums. If there was a rehearsal the next day, Allen, Jerry and Frankie would go do that. Jerry would set up his drums, Allen would take care of the lights for all of us and we would show up for the show—all of the luggage in the right rooms, and so on. Sometimes we'd go over just to see the theater. We could rehearse if we wanted, but we really didn't have to because Frankie and Jerry took care of that. It was a perfect way of traveling and working!

Frankie and I did some great bits together and he never knew what I was going to do, but he was always there. We even worked in bits with Jerry. It was a solid show. Frankie would play an overture of "Tenderly" for Clooney, "Tangerine" for Helen, "Rose Marie" for me, and "Moonlight in Vermont" for Margaret. He'd finish with "There Is Nothing Like a Dame," and offstage they would announce, "4 Girls 4....Ladies and Gentlemen, Miss Margaret Whiting." Then she would do her act and introduce Helen.

During intermission Frankie would play "Satin Doll," the screen would come down and my "Baby Rose Marie" film would start. After a minute the lights would go up and the band would pick up the music from the film. I'd walk out, do my act and introduce Clooney and she would do her act. Then Margaret would come out again and start the "4 Girls 4" finale. It was really great.

We had many funny things happen to all of us. We were in Flint, Michigan, at the Kenley Theater. Margaret had some friends who came in between shows and they cooked us a gourmet dinner backstage. Margaret was our goodwill ambassador. When we were in Milwaukee, she would mention a rib joint every show. They finally called us and said, "Come on over for ribs—our treat!" Also in Flint, one night Margaret did her show, followed by Helen, and then me. I noticed some commotion in the back of the theater. (I see everything when I'm on stage.)

After I was through, Clooney went on, and Allen came backstage and said, "Well, Roe, you can say you really killed 'em."

I said, "Why?"

He said, "A guy had a heart attack while you were on and they carried him out."

I said, "I knew something was going on."

Margaret said, "At least he saw me!"

Margaret was the shopper of the group. She would find all the good places to shop. When we were in Cohasset, New York, she found this store. Everything was wholesale, plus ten percent off. Wonderful merchandise! Allen, Frankie, and Jerry bought Armani tuxedos. I think they paid one hundred and ten dollars! And they had a shoe sale too. In addition to being wholesale, they were on sale. Shoes that were $190 or $175 went for $12. The most expensive ones were $15! You just can't pass up a thing like that. We each bought about twenty pairs of shoes. We had a ball!

As I told you, Clooney and Helen had the same birthday, so Margaret and I would throw them a party. Margaret's birthday is July 22, and mine is August 15, so Clooney and Helen would throw us a party. We had some great parties—in the weirdest towns! For instance, Allen found a restaurant outside of Flint, Michigan, that was an old railroad station and the food was the greatest—talk about gourmet. This was *ten-star* gourmet...in Flint?

Yeah, we had a lot of good times and some pretty rough times, and I was slowly having a nervous breakdown because of all the bickering going on with the show. It was mostly little things that just got on my nerves. I was always trying to straighten them out so that we could do the shows. I didn't realize what it was doing to my stomach. I decided to quit, so I talked to Margaret and it turned out that she wanted to quit too. Helen seemed to think that *4 Girls 4* belonged to her alone. Margaret and I had a meeting and told Helen and Clooney that after this date we wanted to quit. Helen called a lawyer and drew up some kind of papers about owning *4 Girls 4*. She got Clooney to go along with her. I really didn't care, I just wanted to go home. They got Kay Starr and Martha Raye to replace us, and I understand Martha quit after a few dates. She couldn't take the bickering either.

I went on to do *Bus Stop* with Karen Valentine and James Naughton. We played the John Kenley circuit for about six weeks. I loved working with Karen and Jimmy. We had a great time. I also did quite a few guest shots on some of the best TV shows of the times. I spoke to Clooney a lot; we kept in touch because we really liked one another. I loved her kids and she loved my Noop and the kids liked one another, which was nice. And I loved Dante, who traveled with her. He was her fella—a sweet man. He was a dancer in one of Clooney's pictures and they were friends for years and finally got married.

I was happy to be home, all calmed down, and back to normal. I had traveled quite a lot in six years.

My mother was now living with me. When I played Westbury in Long Island, I had a day off, so I went to New Jersey to see my mother. When I saw her crawling on all fours to go upstairs, I said, "That's it. You're coming home with me. We'll sell the house."

She seemed happy about that, so that was good. After the last date with "4 Girls 4," I went to New Jersey and we packed. I got her ready to fly to California. We sold some of the furniture, but had a lot of things left over. I got her settled in my house and it was wonderful to have her with me.

I called Bernice to go with me to Pittsburgh. I was doing two plays for the Civic Light Opera: *Once Upon a Mattress,* with Morey Amsterdam, and *Pippin.* It was about four weeks. Mother was doing fine in California, and when I finished Pittsburgh, Bernice and I went to Jersey to get rid of the other stuff in the house and then sell the house. My mother only wanted to keep a few things and she didn't seem upset when we sold the house. I think she was glad, in a way—it was getting too big for her. She was getting a little deaf and I was always worried about her being alone. She had arthritis in her legs and my house is one level, so that made it easy for her. She had the big room next to mine, with her own bathroom, and she had the dogs—at that time, two—and she had Noop, so she was happy…and so was I.

Chapter Thirty-Two

Noop's Wedding

Noop's wedding was coming up on October 14 and we were having a great time getting prepared for the big event. My brother and his family came out for the wedding. Noop wanted her Uncle Frank to give her away. Two of my girlfriends from Chicago flew out for the wedding, and Gerri Danna and her daughter Maria came from Florida. The house was full. The wedding was beautiful. The colors were brown and beige. The men wore brown tuxedos. Steve's brother, Tony, was his best man, and Pam Glober was Noop's matron of honor. She had six bridesmaids and six ushers. They were married in St. Charles Catholic Church in North Hollywood. Frankie played the organ. Margaret was going to sing, but the church said she couldn't sing the songs we wanted, so Linda Ortega, Frankie's daughter, sang "Ave Maria" and "Oh Promise Me." She did a beautiful job and has a great voice.

We had the reception at Vince's house—this was a year before he passed away. Frankie got the band, and they didn't want to take any money—they did it for free because it was Bobby's daughter! Vince's backyard was twice as big as mine, so Vince said, "Let's do it at my house." And he was running around enjoying every minute of it.

We did it in style. The caterers were great. The flowers were beautiful. We had five hundred hors d'oeuvres, roast beef cut from a cart, salad, and a big wedding cake made by Steve's brother.

The guest list was unbelievabl: Paul Lynde, Richard Deacon, Margaret and her date, Peter Marshall, Joanne Worley, most of the gang from *Squares,* Vincent Price, Karen Valentine…I can't remember all the wonderful people who came. Clooney was out of town and Helen was working.

Noopy at her wedding in 1978

Dodi was my right and left arms. She took care of things and kept a record of everything so Noop would know who was there, the gifts, and so on. Angela took care of the wedding favors. We gave little porcelain jugs with flowers and a tag that said, "Noopy and Steve, October 14th."

It was a beautiful wedding and I was very proud. Now I had a son-in-law. They went to Reno, Lake Tahoe, and San Francisco for their honeymoon, which was a gift from Art Alisi from *Squares*. It was really nice.

I got a call for a cruise to Alaska. Joy was working on TV, so I asked Bernice to go with me. Frankie was out of town, I think with Kay Starr. I was stuck. Then I remembered Michael Feinstein. Richard Deacon had introduced us and we had gone to see him play and sing. He was just great. We became friends, including his parents, who are wonderful. I asked Michael if he would play for me on the cruise. He said he'd love to. We rehearsed and he was great. I even made him sing a song in my act. It was funny, and it was all about Alaska, which fit right in. He was a big hit with everyone on the cruise; they all loved him. It was a pleasure to work with him. He's so talented and we still keep in touch.

Noop and Steve settled in an apartment for a while, which was seven minutes to NBC—good for Steve. But Noop wasn't working as much. She had her horses over at Pam's house and wanted to get a place where she could keep the horses in the backyard. Her friends Pam and Bill Glober were moving, and she had to find another place to board the horses. They went looking for a house. They finally found a place about forty-five minutes from NBC. It was a beautiful little house on two and a half acres, with a riding ring and stalls for four horses. I told them to get it. It would solve all their problems, except for being a long drive for Steve everyday. They loved the house, so they bought it and named it the Residual Ranch. They have been married over twenty years now, and they love that house more than ever. They live about twenty-two miles from me but hate to come to the San Fernando Valley, so I don't see them as much as I would love to. But we're always together on birthdays, anniversaries, holidays; they're always here Christmas Eve, and always here if I need them. No children…just horses. I think that's one of the disappointments in my life. No grandchildren. I would have loved to spoil my grandchildren. Another disappointment is I wanted more children. Actually, I wanted two girls and a boy, but I guess we lost the formula!

Our family has always been animal lovers. I have always had dogs. All my dogs come from the pound. Noop usually has anywhere from one to five horses and cats. I know I mention fur coats a lot, because I have always felt it was very glamorous. But after meeting with animal activists, I don't wear fur anymore. I never knew the pain and suffering of the animals that was involved to get the fur. I thought they were bred for that purpose. Boy, was I wrong!

I belong to five Humane Societies: Actors and Others for Animals, Friends of Animals, People for the Ethical Treatment of Animals (PETA), the Humane Society of the United States, and the American Animal Society. I do a lot of work for those organizations. We've put on shows. Gretchen Wyler does a lot of that and always calls me because, as she says, "You're an animal person." I love my animals. They are treated with love and care. I would be lost without their love and devotion. They all sleep with me and have the run of the house. Of course, they've all been "fixed," and they have a big yard to run around in. I just wanted you to know that I'm on the side of the animals now.

Just to bring you up to date, Steve is still directing the news at KNBC. Noop is now freelancing. She works at home with her fax machine and computer. She also produced a show called *The New Homes Show.* It was a

Noopy and my son-in-law, Steve Rodrigues

show for people thinking of moving to a particular city. She would go to that city with two hosts and find out information on taxes, churches, housing, schools, and so on. Usually one of the hosts would interview the mayor of that particular city about why that city was a good place to live. She wrote and edited the whole thing. It was a popular show and was very helpful to those who didn't know too much about an area. She did a similar show in San Diego called *America on the Move.*

She also writes a monthly column for the Pacific Coast Horse Shows Association and is busy taking care of the horses and going to horse shows. She's won a lot of prizes and is considered a top rider. She's been into it since she was eleven years old.

She's really very good at her job, and so is Steve at his. They help each other. It's nice to see two kids working and helping each other. I'm very proud of both of them.

Chapter Thirty-Three

4 Girls 4, the Second Time

I got a call from Allen Sviridoff, our former road manager and stage manager, who was now managing Clooney and booking the four girls, whenever they could get four girls together. Marty Kummer had passed away and I guess Allen took over. He asked me if I wanted to go on a cruise to Hong Kong with the girls. It had been a few years since I had left. I told him I didn't think so—I didn't want to go through all that jazz again. He promised me that there would be none of that. He'd make sure. The money was great, so I said okay. I called Bernice and she went with me.

The cruise was divine. It was the Holland American Line. They were celebrating their twenty-fifth-year anniversary with a cruise around the world. Our trip was eleven days, to Hong Kong. We flew to Honolulu and met the ship there. Bernice and I went to the ship. The gang went on the town in Honolulu. Bernice and I had a very nice cabin, and Bernice went to make arrangements for the second sitting at dinner for the following evening. She also asked if we could get some dinner that night and they said, "Yes." So we went into the dining room and we were led to a back room dining hall. I guess it was for the *help*—and I blew my stack. I made such a fuss about "not being help, I was a guest, how dare they do that," and so on. Harry Blackstone, the wonderful magician, was having dinner there and he just looked at me, never saying a word, which was the best thing to do. I just kept raving on and on and kept saying, "Take care of this or we won't go on."

The next morning Bernice and I had breakfast in the cabin and then we went out. I was looking for a man named Peter Farranto. Ruthie had told me to look him up and get to know him. She and Bobbi Baker had been on some cruises with him; they got to know him and said he was wonderful guy and would take care of us. He was top man on the ship. He took care of almost everything and the rest of the crew loved him.

We went into the lounge and I walked over to this tall, good-looking guy and said, "I'm looking for Peter Farranto."

He said, "I'm Peter Farranto."

I told him, "Ruthie told me to look you up."

And he said, "Everyone on the ship told me Rose Marie is looking for me. I was scared stiff—I didn't know what I did."

So we laughed, sat down and had a soda and I told him about the dining room and how mad I was.

He said, "I thought you stars like to be left alone."

"Not me," I said, "I want to sit in the main dining room." So unbeknownst to the other girls, we all sat at the captain's table. I thanked Peter and he said the captain was very happy to do it.

We were to do two shows for the two sittings, but eleven days without a stop was starting to wear on everyone. I suggested we do our show the next night. They wanted to put us on the night before we were supposed to land in Hong Kong. I said, "No, put us on tomorrow night. We've been at sea for about four days and people are getting itchy for some kind of excitement."

So we rehearsed the next day. The band was not bad. We had Frankie, Jerry, and Allen, so we were okay. The next night the show went on and it was a smash. I did a good show because by now I knew practically all the people on the ship and called them by name, which they loved. I had done a lot of the activities on the ship, met a lot of people and kidded with them, so I made use of it when I did my show. Kay Starr was with her husband at that time, so we didn't see too much of her. Clooney hung out in her cabin and only came out for lunch and dinner. Helen was with one of her daughters, Duffy, so they were on their own. Bernice and I hung out with Peter and had a great time.

As I told you, Harry Blackstone and his wife were part of the show, and we had some good times with them. I met a lovely lady sitting all by herself in the dining room, next to our table. I got to talking to her, found out her name was Alice Mason and we became friends. She threw a cocktail party for the girls, Frankie, Jerry, and Allen, and our traveling companions. We had a great time with champagne and all the wonderful hors d'oeuvres. She started to hang out with us. She was alone, so we adopted her.

It was getting close to Valentine's Day, and I said to Peter, "We should do another show. Not like we did before, but just clowning around." Kay said she'd sing "Love," and Helen said she'd sing "My Funny Valentine." Clooney didn't want to do the show, so I asked Harry Blackstone to do about five minutes. He said, "Sure." We went to rehearsal that day. I did "Chena Luna" with all the jokes—thank goodness Frankie had the music with him—so we had our little show ready. When we walked into rehearsal, they were rehearsing the choir, made up of people on the ship. They had songbooks. I told Allen to get us three songbooks. When the choir finished rehearsal, they walked, in line, to their seats, like we used to do in school. I told Allen, "Don't announce us. We'll get in back of the choir line and just walk on with the songbooks, as the choir goes back to their seats." The audience loved it, and we were a hit before we started. We did about an hour show in all and it went really great, just clowning around. Peter kept telling me that the people on the ship couldn't get over it—that we did a show we didn't have to do. We had a great time.

We landed in Hong Kong and Bernice, being a travel agent on the side, got us rooms at the Regency Hotel. What a beautiful room we had. We even had *our own bellboy*—he stood outside our door. I turned on the TV and there I was, on *The Dick Van Dyke Show,* talking Chinese or Japanese, I don't know which, but it was fun to watch.

We stayed in Kowloon for about three days. Ruthie had made a list of things to see, buy, and eat. I met a man who made shirts and blouses—*overnight!* We went to his shop and I ordered shirts for Noop, Steve, Bernice, and myself. It was unbelievable. The prices were low and the workmanship was terrific. Ruthie told us about a wonderful Chinese restaurant and told us what to order. We took a cab and found the place all boarded up, so we went next door and it was a family-type Chinese restaurant. I ordered everything I was supposed to.

Bernice said, "I feel like having some soup."

I said, "Bernice, I've ordered enough food for an army—now you want *soup?*" So we ordered the soup and it came in a huge tureen, enough for ten people. She had one bowl and said she couldn't eat anymore.

I said, "Bernice, this is Kowloon; you don't take home what's left, like we do in America!"

Then the food came, and came, and of course it was too much and we had to leave it there. I thought, "I'll probably want some of this about midnight," but we didn't take home any cartons.

Next day we had high tea at the Peninsula Hotel—a classic thing to do in Kowloon. I shopped like crazy and had a good time on Nathan Road, located in the middle of the city, the shopping center of the world! We flew back to California, with a stopover in Tokyo. It was a long trip, and as much as I enjoyed it, I was glad to get home.

Allen called again about some dates he lined up for the girls, only Clooney was out of it. So it was Helen, Kay Starr, Margaret and myself. There were more switches than a railroad yard! But it still worked. I decided we needed a new finale. I remembered a song from *Scrooge* called "Thank You Very Much." I called Frankie and told him to get a copy of the song, come over to the house and we would lay it out.

He said, "Don't you think you'd better check it out with Helen?"

I said, "Why?"

He said, "She'll feel better if you ask her."

I said, "Okay."

So I called her and she said, "I don't think we need a new finale. '4 Girls 4' is still good."

I said, "We're playing the Fairmont in Dallas again, and Phoenix again, the Fairmont in Chicago. We can't go in with the same stale stuff."

She said, "It means laying out more money, the arrangement…"

I said, "Forget it, Helen. I'll do it in my act."

She said, "Well, wait a minute. Why don't we hear it and see what we can do with it."

I said, "I *know* what to do with it, and I can tell you, the audience will sing along with us, we'll shake hands with the audience, and it will be a *smash!*"

She said, "Oh, all right."

I was really upset about this. How dare she get final say? I knew Margaret would go for it, and so would Kay. Helen was always the odd one who had to make a fuss over *everything*.

So I called Frankie and said, "The queen has okayed it." He came over to the house the next day with a copy of the song and we laid out the whole arrangement—and it was great. We needed a few extra lyrics to fit it into our act, so I asked Helen to write some. She was very good, I mean *really* good, at that.

So we went to Phoenix. We couldn't break in the new finale because we were playing Sun City and the audience is a block away from the stage. We rehearsed it and said we'd break it in in Dallas. We then went to Westbury, Long Island, and did a couple of days. Great biz, and the shows were great. I decided to do "I Love a Piano." Michael Feinstein had a good arrangement of it and I asked him to help me do it my way. Frankie made the arrangement, and it was great. I did it at Westbury and it wound up being one of my best numbers, because I sat on top of the piano and moved all over the piano—it was funny as hell. We then went to Dallas. I called my friend Steve Castlebury and we spent some time together. I met him when I was doing *Bye Bye Birdie,* and we became good friends. We did the new finale. Helen wrote some great lyrics. The arrangement was great and, just like I figured, the audience sang it with us and gave us a standing ovation. It went over with a bang. Kay and Margaret loved it. Helen was kind of cool on it. I didn't care. I knew it was right and knew it was going to be a smash. Our next stop was St. Louis, where we played that beautiful theater that they had just redone. It was one of the old vaudeville/movie theaters, and it was breathtaking. We were on the bill with Woody Herman and his orchestra. It was a nice date.

We then went to Chicago's Fairmont Hotel, and we did great business and the show was terrific…*and* my throat was going. I really got scared. I didn't want to go through another operation on my throat. So after the two weeks, I quit again. I could hardly talk. I told the gang "Thank You Very Much" was my gift to them. I paid my fourth *and* they could have it.

I came home and went to the doctor about my throat. He's the best throat man, Dr. Von Leder. He looked at my throat and said, "You have nodes, but we can get rid of them. No smoking, no drinking, and rest the throat as much as possible, and see me in two weeks."

I hardly spoke a word. I didn't have to worry about drinking, but I did quit smoking. It was so damn hard to quit, but I did it, cold turkey!

When I went to see him, he said, "One of the little nodes is gone." (I had had four little ones.) I couldn't believe it. My voice was getting clearer and clearer. It was unbelievable. I didn't dare do any work. I just stayed home and didn't talk, and in three months, the nodes were gone. I was thrilled, but I had to think about going to work, so I did some more guest parts. I got a call for a series. It was called *Scorch,* and I worked with a puppet. God, I've done everything, and now with a puppet. It only lasted about six shows and that was that.

I did Rodgers and Hammerstein's *Cinderella.* I played the fairy godmother. Steve Allen and Jayne Meadows played the king and queen. We played the Pantages Theater in Hollywood. It was wonderful and I loved doing that show, especially since I never got to do that Rodgers and Hart show in New York!

Then Billy Van Zandt called me. He's a wonderful writer and does a lot of writing for comedy series. He and his partner had written a play called *Drop Dead*—a comedy, of course—and Barney Martin told him to call me. Barney and I worked together as Frank's mother and father on *Murphy Brown* (did three of those!), and Barney thought I would like to do it. Barney also played Jerry Seinfeld's father on *Seinfeld*.

Doing the play would mean no money, of course, and we did it in a little theater—it seated about forty-five. I read the script, loved it, and said, "Yes." We had a good cast. Adrienne Barbeau, Barney Martin, and some new kids who were great. We had a lot of fun. I played five weeks and had to cancel the last week, because I did a pilot with Debbie Reynolds called *Esme*. Her daughter, Carrie Fisher, had written it. Damn good show. I don't know why it didn't sell. I love Debbie. She's a real trouper and fun to work with—and Carrie is a great writer. It's a shame that they didn't pick it up. I was also doing a movie and they wouldn't let me out of my contract to do the Debbie Reynolds pilot, so CBS, who was doing the pilot, paid *sixty thousand dollars* to get me out of the movie contract! Talk about star power.... *Wow!*

I did a series called *Hardball*. That too lasted six weeks. They had a great idea, but they never did anything with it and didn't use me at all. One week, I got a full week's salary for saying, "You tell 'em, gorgeous." The day I went into the studio to quit, we were cancelled.

I did a Hallmark commercial. I did a voice-over for a cartoon series called *Freakazoid*, a children's show. You'd be surprised if you knew the different stars who do the Saturday morning cartoon shows. We all make the same salary, and we're through in an hour—really easy and a pleasure to do.

In 2001, I was invited to an AIDS benefit in Sacramento. A group of young doctors started a foundation for AIDS a few years ago. The head of the organization is Mike Lemon. Every year Mike and these doctors run an Academy Awards–type benefit for AIDS. They invite a number of stars to attend. Shirley Jones, Esther Williams, Anita Page, Randal Malone, Virginia Mayo, Margaret O'Brien, and I were the honorees one year. We had a great time for this most worthy cause.

These doctors are wonderful and are considered among the best of the new doctors, especially Scott Christenson, a cancer specialist, who is adored by everyone. Not only are they young, they are up to date on all the new medicinal treatments. There are about five doctors who run this organization, in addition to running their individual medical practices. They do a wonderful job and I respect and admire all of them tremendously.

There is a script for Margaret O'Brien and me for a new television series in the works. At this point, it's taking wonderful shape and we're all hoping one of the networks will buy it. It would make a terrific sitcom.

I guess you could say it's been one helluva life and career. I've lasted a long time. I'm grateful for my life. It's been ups and downs, but I ain't out yet.

So I go on. So many things have changed since I started to write this book. I lost so many good friends. The saddest of all was my dear and beloved mother, who passed on November 6, 2000. She had been in a convalescent hospital for the past six years. I would go and visit her every day, as the hospital was only eight minutes away from my home. The morning of November 6, they called to tell me that she wasn't getting enough air in her blood. I left for the hospital immediately. The doctor was there. She was doing okay. The doctor said, "She's fine, now she'll be all right." I kissed her and told her that I loved her and that I would see her later that afternoon. She said, "I love you too, darling" and kissed me and I left. At 6:00 that evening, they called and said she had passed on. Thank God I was there that day to see her and tell her I loved her, but I was in shock.

Noopy arranged everything for the funeral. I just couldn't do it. I couldn't believe that my mother was gone. Noop had a mass said at St. Charles Church in North Hollywood, where Noop was christened and where 30 years later, my dear mother had the pleasure of attending the wedding of her eldest grandchild, Noopy. I miss my mother very much. Her laughter was so full of fun. She loved life. I miss her just being here to talk to about anything and everything and telling me that everything will be all right, no matter what. I know she was proud of me. I guess God needed someone to have fun with and have a few good laughs, so he called my mother. She passed on at the age of 94 and she certainly had a full life. But I will always miss her. I do feel so alone at times.

Bernice Ince, who I used to call my Jewish mother, also passed on. She was a wonderful friend, and I miss our talks.

Carol Saenz divorced her husband Ralph in Chicago and came out

Mother and me

here. She stayed with me for a couple of weeks and married producer/ director and station manager Willie Olmstead. They have become my dearest friends. We spend a lot of time together. We collect video tapes and I go over to their house for dinner and a movie very often. We throw little get-togethers. When the Northridge earthquake came, I had a lot of damage. I guess I was in shock, because the next thing I knew, Dodi was at the house. Carol and Willie called to see if I was all right and came over to the house and cleaned up all the broken dishes and glasses. I just sat there in shock. Dodi made me a cup of tea. I was in a daze, but I do remember them coming out to help me.

I am very fortunate. I have many dear friends. Joy Tierney is one of my dearest friends. We met when I did *The Doris Day Show*. She was part of the wardrobe department. We traveled together when I did stage shows and we are very close. If I need her for anything, she's with me in a flash. We talk on the phone all the time, and I treasure her friendship.

I see Kay Starr quite a bit and Margaret when she comes to California. We are still close. Clooney finally married her Dante in her hometown

Three generations: Noopy, Stella, and Rose Marie

in Kentucky. It was a beautiful wedding and I was so happy for them. But in June 2002, Clooney passed away from lung cancer. I will miss her, and certainly the music world will miss her. She was something very special and will live on. As long as good music is heard, you'll hear a Rosemary Clooney record.

Allen is now a record producer and personal manager. He managed Clooney and now manages Michael Feinstein among others. He's doing a helluva job.

I lost my friend and piano player Buddy Freed, then Frankie Ortega, but I still keep in touch with his wife, Maxine, and their daughter, Sarah.

Helen passed on before Frankie, and we were all at the church to say good-bye. She had gotten married to Frank DeVol and was very happy for about two years I think. She was working when she got sick with cancer of the liver, and it was fast. She didn't suffer too much, thank God.

My dear Morey Amsterdam passed away from a heart attack. I miss him so. I keep in touch with his wife, Kay. Morey is always in my thoughts.

I have met some wonderful new friends, one of whom is Randal Malone, an actor of many motion pictures. He is so kind and thoughtful and does everything in the world for me. He makes my life a little fuller and happier. He and his friend Mike Schwibs take me out a lot. Between them, they look after me. Randal is really responsible for helping to get this book published, and I will forever be grateful to him for that.

I met the great child star Margaret O'Brien at a party, and we became friends immediately. She looks terrific and is so kind and sweet. We go out a lot—parties and different charities. Can you imagine? Two former child stars going to dinners and parties. People look at us and can't believe their eyes! She is a special friend and I adore her. She and her husband, Roy Thorson, although they've been separated for many years, remain good friends. Roy is responsible for all the pictures that are a part of this book. He took some very old pictures and reproduced them so they could be used. It's amazing what he can do with a camera and computer. I'm very grateful to him for all he's done. I'm glad we're all good friends.

Last, but by no means least: Dodi, my secretary. We've been together about 26 years. She's been a big help in so many ways. She comes over twice a week, and we work on fan mail and important mail that comes in. She really does everything for me, including decorating my house for Christmas. We have become very close friends. She knows me like a book. She knows what I like and don't like and takes care of so many things for me. I would be lost without her. She has been a tremendous help with the writing of this book, and for that I will always be grateful to her. But most of all I value our friendship.

So now, I thank God for all he has given me. Most of all, the gift of entertaining people and making them laugh and maybe forgetting their troubles for a little while. I'm grateful to my mother for the way she brought me up. I'm proud of the way I've lived and conducted myself. I'm so very proud of my daughter. She has a wonderful sense of humor and has led a very productive life. She and Steve are happy, so that suits me fine.

I go on—for how long I don't know. I guess until the Good Lord says, "You've had it girl—bring down the curtain." But until then, I wake up every morning and say, "Thank you, dear God, for holding me over."

Epilogue

❧

Things I Forgot to Tell You

I forgot to tell you about Sophie Tucker being the real reason I eloped! I always wanted to get married with all the fanfare—wedding gown, brides-maids, and all that. I even picked out my wedding gown from a picture in a magazine when I was fifteen. But I eloped and got married in a suit.

What finally made up my mind—I was at the Copa, Bobby picked me up and we went to Madison Square Garden for the big Milk Fund benefit. When we arrived, three guys met us and told us when I would go on, so we sat down and waited. Sophie Tucker came in wearing a floor-length chinchilla fur coat with about two dozen orchids pinned to the coat. They were hanging from chin to floor. She had a diamond necklace and three or four diamond bracelets, three or four rings, all with big dia-monds. Wow! What an entrance. About ten guys huddled around her, getting her a cup of coffee, taking her coat, putting the coat around her shoulders, and so on.

I turned to Bobby and said, "Boy! That's a star."

He looked at me and said, "Is that the way you want to wind up? Diamonds, furs, orchids—and all alone? She has nobody with her, she's all alone. Is that what you want? To wind up being alone?"

I looked at him and said, "No, I want a husband and a family who will always come first," and it always has.

I forgot to tell you about my manager, Bill Loeb, almost getting killed by "the boys," all because of me! I was supposed to play the Flamingo in Vegas again, but I had okayed *Top Banana* and had left for New York. Bill had to go to Vegas and tell them I wasn't going to appear, because I had gone to New York to do the show with Phil Silvers. You should hear Bill tell the story. He went to see Moe Sedgeway and told him I wouldn't open.

Moe said, "Why not? She better be here."

Bill said, "She's in New York opening in a Broadway show. You can't ask her to give that up."

Moe said, "I don't care...she's to open tomorrow night, *here,* and you better make sure she's here."

Poor Bill, he thought for sure they were going to kill him, especially that night when a car nearly missed hitting him. He said, "Moe, I've got a girl who will do great for you, I promise. Her name is Polly Bergen. Don't be upset with Rose Marie. It's a chance of a lifetime for her. This girl will be great, I know she'll do well."

And Bill kept on talking and talking. Moe kept walking away from Bill. Moe finally gave in, Polly Bergen opened, and she was wonderful...and Bill is still alive, thank God.

I forgot to tell you about Noop's accident at a horse show. I almost lost her. She was in a horse show at Los Alamitos. After this show, she and I were going to Hawaii for a little vacation. She had asked me to be a presenter for one of the horse show awards, so I drove down, got there about noon, and the first thing I saw was a big commotion. All of a sudden an ambulance came through, and I saw Bill Corey, her trainer, looking out of the window. I knew something had happened to Noop. I stopped the ambulance and saw Noop on a stretcher. Her face was bloody and dirty.

I screamed, "What happened?" Bill said she was sitting on the hood of a car, in fact there were other kids on top of the car also. They were going about five miles an hour, going from the ring to the stable. All of a sudden, a truck pulled out and the girl driver put on the brakes. Everybody got off. Noop fell down and the car rode over her. Bill Corey rushed to Noop and pulled her out from under the car. Thank God her jeans were tight. Bill kept talking to her. She finally opened her eyes and they called an ambulance. Thank God for Bill. He got her out, gave her mouth-to-mouth and saved her life. I left my car wherever it was and rode to the hospital with Noop and Bill.

We went to Long Beach Memorial Hospital. They took some x-rays. She had a dislocated collarbone, a fractured pelvis on both sides and her shoulder was dislocated. She was a mess. I called Dr. Levy—after Bobby died, he became our family doctor.

He said, "How's her face?"

I said, "It's dirty with some blood."

He said, "Nothing wrong with her face, right?"

I said, "I don't think so."

He said, "Get an ambulance and get her into Mount Sinai. Take the x-rays with you," which we did. When we got to Mount Sinai, they rushed her upstairs and did another examination. The x-rays from Long Beach were compared to the new x-rays. Her pelvis had started to heal and come together. Dr. Levy was pleased. He said, "It's because she doesn't do drugs or drink. She's a healthy girl, everything will be all right. Her face is fine" (he always said how beautiful she was). So they put her in a room with another patient who kept her up all night. I never left the hospital. The next day I told Dr. Levy to put her in another room because Noop's room-mate had kept her up all night. They moved her into another room: the same room Bobby had when he passed away! Imagine how I felt! Bernice came to the hospital and stayed with me all day. I couldn't cry, I couldn't talk…I just stared into space and prayed quietly.

When Dr. Levy came in at six o'clock, he said, "She will be fine, but we have to operate on the collarbone and the shoulder. The pelvis is heal-ing itself." They didn't even put a cast on, but she had to lie still. Dr. Levy said to me, "Go home. We won't operate right away. I've got to call a few orthopedic doctors." So Bernice took me home. I was almost in a coma. I slept a little, but went to the hospital at nine o'clock and stayed with Noop. All the horse people sent flowers, cards, and balloons. They came to see her. Even people from the horse world she didn't know.

So now we had two orthopedic men come in to look at Noop. We had Dr. Levy and Dr. Silverman, Levy's associate, who is now our family doctor. The operation went well, but they told me that she would never ride a horse again. I said, "Don't tell that to her—not yet anyway." She was in the hospital about six weeks and came home in a wheelchair, barely able to walk. She had to learn to get out of the wheelchair to go to the bath-room. It was rough, but she had the will to do it. We'd see Levy every week and she was doing all right. She was walking, but we never mentioned anything about riding. Finally there was a horse show in Rolling Hills Estates in California, and she said she was going to enter, and if she won she would give the trophy to her doctors.

I said, "You'd better check with Dr. Levy."

Levy told her, "Be careful, don't take any chances, and win that damn trophy."

I couldn't believe what I heard. I said, "Is she all right to try and ride?"

He said, "She's fine." She did a helluva job of healing all on her own. We went to the horse show and damn if she didn't win! We went to see Dr. Levy the next day. He said, "She's fine. Now go in and show those other doctors that damn trophy," which she did. They were amazed and so was I. They all had thought she would never walk again! But God bless her, she has a strong mind and she was *in no way* going to give up riding horses...which she never has.

Dr. Levy passed away in December of that year, on December 24. I called Dr. Levy to wish him and his wife a Merry Christmas. His wife answered the phone and I said, "Merry Christmas! It's Rose Marie, is Marv there?"

She said, "Oh! You don't know! Marv died last night. He had a bad heart."

I didn't know what to say, so I said, "I'm so very sorry. I'll call you tomorrow."

I hung up and started to cry. I truly loved that man for what he did to help Bobby and how he took over when Noop had her accident. I went into Noop's room to tell her that Dr. Levy had passed away.

She said, "That's odd, because I dreamt last night that he stopped by my door and said, 'Are you all right?' I said, 'Yes.' I knew it was a dream, but it seemed so real!" I just got goose pimples and walked away.

I forgot to tell you about the Guy Curse. If anybody does anything against us, or tries to cheat us, or hurts us in any way, the Guy Curse automatically goes to work. We don't do anything or say anything, it just happens. An example: Peter. A mutual friend of ours would call me after she received a letter from him. It seems that his girlfriend died, sold the hotel, and left all of her money to her children, and left him a monthly pittance *if* he stayed in Denmark. If he left the country, the money would stop—so he's stuck there! Ah...the Guy Curse.

I forgot to tell you about the time I went to London to do two shows on "the telly." It was a variety show and they didn't know me from a hill of beans. I stayed at the Cumberland Hotel (veddy English...and lovely). Buddy Freed went with me. We were to do two TV shows about two weeks apart. Bobby couldn't come because of his shows at NBC, so Buddy and I went. I loved every minute of it.

If there's anything true about "past lives," I must have once been

English. I seemed to know my way around London better than Holly-wood. I always knew which bus to take, which underground to take—it was eerie. I would turn into a street and say, "There is a little house next to a bakery," and sure enough, I would turn the corner and there was a little house next to a bakery. I was there four weeks and really hated to leave. The shows were very good. I was quite pleased. More so after the first show was on the air and the doorman at the hotel said to me, "Saw you on the telly last night, madam. You were a bit of all right!"

I forgot to tell you about making the movie *Top Banana*. Walter Scharf was the musical conductor, so Bobby was on the recording date. We went to work together. He went to the bandstand, and I went over to the rest of the cast. We were recording all the songs from the show, which we would lip-sync later while shooting the movie. We were going to do it just as in the play and the director, Alfred Green, wanted to see our moves.

The chorus did the first number. Judy Lynn and Danny Scholl did their duet and then I recorded "I Fought Every Step of the Way." My number was made up of boxing terms, and of course, I moved on stage like a boxer, jabbing and dancing around like a boxer would. I did one take and they said, "Let's see how you move," so they played back the song and I moved around like I did in the show. They stopped in the middle of a lyric and I said, "Don't leave me in a position like this." Everyone laughed—joke over. We all took a five-minute break.

The producer walked over to me and very softly said, "If you're really interested in some good positions, I'd be happy to show them to you."

I laughed and said, "Funny, very funny."

He said, "I mean it. This could be *your* picture. I'm the producer and I can see to it that it's your movie, so let me know when you want to learn the new positions."

Now I knew that he wasn't kidding. He meant it. It was the first time anybody ever made that kind of a pass at me. I was embarrassed, insulted, and then I got very angry—and I mean spittin' mad. In front of the whole crew, singers, dancers, and orchestra, I said loudly, "Why, you stupid bas-tard, you couldn't get it up if the flag went by." Everybody laughed like hell. Then the orchestra started to laugh, and it went like a wave…through the fiddles, saxes, trumpets, and trombones. And my husband laughed the loudest! I looked at Bobby and sneered at him. He couldn't stop laugh-ing—which, to me, made it worse.

When we finished, Bobby and I walked to our car, neither of us saying a word. We got into the car and I said, "How dare you laugh so hard? Don't you know what he said to me?"

He smiled and said, "I can imagine. I feel sorry for anyone who tries to make a pass at you."

I said, "*Fine.*"

He said, "You know all your songs will be cut. It will be like you weren't in the picture."

I said, "They can't do that, the duet with Phil is one of the best numbers."

He said, "You'll see." He was right—all my songs and the duet were cut!

About a year later, I was doing a movie at Universal. Bobby and I were having lunch in the commissary and in walks that producer.

I looked at Bobby and said, "What will I do?"

He said, "Do nothing. If he says hello, you say hello and that's it. You're a lady. If he's smart, he'll walk away."

Which is exactly what happened. He passed our table and said, "Hello, Rose Marie."

I said, "Hello," and he walked away.

I forgot to tell you about Carmen Miranda. In 1945, I was to open at the Copacabana in New York, one of the top clubs in the country. Martin and Lewis had played there, Joe E. Lewis, Tony Bennett, all the big stars of the day. So I was quite thrilled when asked to play there. I wanted to look terrific. Lloyd Lambert, who was my costumer, made three new gowns for me, all of which were knockouts. My act was in good shape, so I knew I was ready.

Opening night was unbelievable. All the big stars came to opening night: Sinatra, Sophie Tucker, Tony Bennett, and Milton Berle. Carmen Miranda was a big star working in the Follies at the Winter Garden Theater. She was Broadway's biggest and newest star. Her wardrobe was outstanding, different and wild. She wore shoes that had a platform about five inches high. Even though they looked awkward, they were beautiful and all the rage at that time. To be in style, I went to Saks Fifth Avenue and bought a pair of gold Carmen Miranda shoes. I paid plenty for them too. I wore them in my act.

One night after the show, I was in my dressing room, and there was a knock on the door.

I said, "Come in."

There stood Carmen Miranda in the doorway. I almost died.

I said, "Hello, Miss Miranda, please come in."

She said, "Your show was wonderful. I enjoyed it very much. Your gowns are beautiful. I thought you were just great, but you don't know how to work in my shoes."

I said, "What?"

She said, "Put them on."

So I did. She held me by the waist and made me walk around the room, making my body go from side to side.

Then she said, "Now work like you have nothing on your feet, and take small steps."

So I did what I was told, and she said "That's it, fine." Finally, she said, "Now do it like that when you're on stage."

I thanked her and told her how much I appreciated her kindness and how wonderful I thought she was. She said that she was very happy to meet me and that I was very talented and she hoped I wouldn't be angry with her for showing me how to "walk in her shoes."

I said, "I couldn't be angry, and no one can ever 'walk in your shoes,' Miss Miranda. You're a very special lady," and she was.

I forgot to tell you about Prince Charles. Once, when I was going with Vince Miranda, we went to some big British charity affair. Prince Charles was the guest of honor. There were many British stars there, as well as American stars. They had a presentation line, and I got into it in time to meet the Prince.

Vince said, "Are you going to bow?"

I said, "No, I'm an American. He doesn't run my country." (I was feeling very patriotic.) When it was my turn in line to meet him, we shook hands and his companion said, "This is Rose Marie from the Dick Van Dyke television show."

He smiled and said, "We watch you on the telly all the time, and you're always looking for a boyfriend. Why don't you come to England and we'll find you a nice chap." We both laughed and shook hands again, and then I left. My little brush with royalty.

I forgot to tell you about the night I danced with Fred Astaire. I was asked to dinner at Betty White and Allen Ludden's house. We had been friends for a while and we had worked together. They had been over to my house for dinner, so I was looking forward to a nice dinner and lots of fun. Richard Deacon was there, Fred Astaire and his daughter and her husband, and George Tibbles, who did Betty's shows and who had written some material for me. It was a nice group.

After dinner we played "dirty Password," which was hilarious. Then George went to the piano and started playing. Allen asked me to sing.

I said, "No, I don't sing too much anymore."

Allen said, "I love the way you sing. Sing a song and don't clown around, sing it pretty."

So George played "The Devil and the Deep Blue Sea." I sat beside George and started to sing in a slow tempo and Fred Astaire walked over to the piano—just like in a movie! For the second chorus, we picked up the tempo and I saw Fred Astaire moving his foot back and forth in tempo. He put out his hand to me. I got up and we started dancing. He twirled me around, dips and all that.

We finished the dance and Fred said to me, "I'm sure you know the Shim Sham."

I said, "Yes."

So we started to do the Shim Sham. Betty called into the other room and said to Richard Deacon, Fred's daughter and her husband, "Come in here, you're never gonna see anything like this again." Somehow I followed him so easily and when we were finished, they applauded and Fred Astaire kissed me on the cheek and said, "You're okay, honey. Thanks for the dance!" No, Fred: Thank *you* for one of the nicest memories of my life.

October 3, 2001, was a very special day for me. As I mentioned earlier, I've had many wonderful things happen to me, but this was a *very special day.*

Larry W. Jones, executive vice president and general manager of the cable company TV Land—which still shows *The Dick Van Dyke Show* twice a day, called Barry M. Greenberg of Celebrity Connection—TV Land's PR firm—and said, "I think Rose Marie deserves a star on the Walk of Fame." A call was made to Johnny Grant, our honorary mayor of Hollywood. Before I knew it, I got the call. It was such a great thrill to hear that news. Dick Van Dyke, Carl Reiner, and Johnny Grant were the presenters. Dick—God love him—said so many nice things about me and my comedic timing. He said that he learned a lot about timing from me. What an honor to hear him say that.

Then Carl got up—he's so brilliantly funny. He said he wouldn't be where he is today if it wasn't for me. You have no idea how wonderful it was to hear all of that! Ah yes, I have an ego too, and boy it was really popping that day. Especially since it was from the two people I love and respect the most. Johnny Grant then got up and read a proclamation stat-

Congratulations Rose Marie!

October 3, 2001

Hollywood Walk of Fame

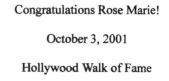

Getting my star on the Hollywood Walk of Fame, October 3, 2001

ing all the things I had done. Even I couldn't remember all the things I've done! It is beautifully framed and says that October 3, 2001, is Rose Marie Day in Hollywood. How about that!

So many people were there at the ceremony. Dear friends such as John Rich, director of *The Dick Van Dyke Show;* Joy Tierney; Barbara Lampson, my hairdresser; Steve and Noopy; Bill Loeb, who was my manager for 26 years; and producer-writer Billy Van Zandt. There were a lot of people I've worked with over the years who took the time to be there. Esther Williams, Margaret O'Brien, Virginia Mayo, and Ann Miller were also there. What a day! What a ceremony! When it was over, there was a beautiful luncheon at the Pinot restaurant in Hollywood, sponsored by TV Land. Everyone had such a wonderful time. It was something I'll never forget.

At the ceremony, I met Steve Cutler and his wife. They brought me a beautiful basket filled with goodies. They spoke to Randy about inducting me in the Las Vegas Hall of Fame on October 12, 2001.

I assume it was because I was one of the first people to play Vegas, with Durante and Xavier Cugat at the Flamingo in 1946. The Flamingo was the third hotel on the strip. I played Vegas at least seven or eight times a year. During those years, aside from the Flamingo, I worked the Riviera Hotel, the Stardust Hotel and the Thunderbird. I was thrilled to be asked to be a part of the Las Vegas Hall of Fame.

Randy made all the arrangements for Noopy, Steve, and me to fly to Vegas. We stayed at the Tropicana Hotel, which is where the Las Vegas Museum is located. The Smothers Brothers were also being inducted, as well as Jimmy Durante. They asked Margaret O'Brien to accept the award because she had been in a few movies with him. They also honored Lt. Governor Lorraine Hunt, who will probably be the next governor of Nevada.

The ceremony was held in the main room of the Tropicana Hotel. It was a full house with about 3800 people. When they introduced me, I walked out to a standing ovation, which was quite a thrill. It felt great to stand on a stage again, in front of an audience! Bob Anderson, the host, did about a 15–minute sit-down interview. After it was over, I walked off to another standing ovation. Steve Cutler and his wife couldn't do enough to make our stay pleasant. Noop and Steve drove me around "the new Vegas." It had changed so much from what I remember. I hadn't been there in years. But it certainly is a kick to know I'm in the Las Vegas Hall of Fame.

To top it off, I got a call that I was to be invited to a luncheon by the California Motion Picture Council, because they were giving me a Lifetime Achievement award at the Sportsman Lodge in Studio City on December 7, 2001. Talk about one thing after another! The luncheon was wonderful. Noopy and Steve came, as did Randy Malone and Mike Schwibs. I sat next to Patty Andrews and her husband. All Patty could say was, "It's about time!"

I guess all the hard work and knocking around the country and entertaining people for so many years pays off. It certainly did for me!

I forgot to tell you about the Black Bow...

It's a Secret!!!"

Lots Love—

Lee Majors

Credits

Television Series

My Sister Eileen, co-star (1960)
The Bob Cummings Show, regular (1961-1962)
The Dick Van Dyke Show, co-star (1961-1966)
The Doris Day Show, (1969-1971)
Honeymoon Suite (1973)
Scorch (1992)
Hardball, co-star (1994)

Television Guest Star Appearances

Drama

Gunsmoke (1957)
The Adventures of Jim Bowie (1958)
The Virginian (1967)
Adam-12 (1972-1973)
Petrocelli (1974)
Kojak (1975)
S.W.A.T. (1975)
C.H.I.P.s (1980)
Bridge Across Time (1985)
Remington Steele (1986)
Cagney and Lacey: Together Again (1995)
Mod Squad
Dragnet
Duet
Heinz 57 Playhouse
Cagney and Lacey (three appearances)

Comedy

The Monkees (1966-1967)
Hey, Landlord (1967)
My Three Sons (1968)
Chico and the Man (1976)
The Love Boat (1978, 1981, 1982)
Murphy Brown (1990-1991)
Herman's Head (1993)
Ultraman: The Ultimate Hero (1993)
Caroline in the City (1996-1997)
Wings (1997)
Suddenly Susan (1997)
The Hugleys (2001)
Dobie Gillis
ESME, pilot
Man of the House

Variety

The Bing Crosby Show
The Bob Hope Show
The Colgate Comedy Hour
The Dean Martin Roast
The Dean Martin Show
The Dinah Shore Show
The Donna Fargo Show
The Ed Sullivan Show
The George Gobel Show
The Jackie Bison Show (1990)
The Jackie Gleason Show
The Jimmy Durante Show
The Merv Griffin Show
The Mike Douglas Show
The Milton Berle Show
Mr. Blackwell Presents (1968)
The Phil Harris-Alice Faye Show
The Red Skelton Show
The Tennessee Ernie Ford Show
Texaco Star Theatre
The Tonight Show (over twenty appearances)
The Wonderful World of Jonathan Winters (1986)

Game Shows

Hollywood Squares, regular (1966-1982)
I've Got a Secret
The New Hollywood Squares (1986)
P.D.Q.
Password
The $25,000 Pyramid
To Tell the Truth
What's My Line
You Don't Say

Broadway

Top Banana
Lunatics and Lovers
Spring In Brazil
Fun City

National Tours

Bye-Bye Birdie
Call Me Madam
Cinderella (Los Angeles only)
4 Girls 4
Once Upon a Mattress (Pittsburgh Civic Light Opera)
Pippin (Pittsburgh Civic Light Opera)
Ring around Rosie

Summer Dinner Theatres

Bus Stop (Ohio)
Drop Dead (Los Angeles)
Everybody's Girl (San Diego, Dallas, Chicago, Seattle)
Everybody Loves Opal (Chicago)
Light Up the Sky (Long Beach)
Up a Tree (Chicago, Dallas, Seattle)

Motion Pictures

Baby Rose Marie the Child Wonder (as Baby Rose Marie)(1929)
Rambling 'Round Radio Row #4, (as Baby Rose Marie) (1932)
International House, (as Baby Rose Marie) (1933)
Back in '23, (as Baby Rose Marie) (1933)

Sing, Babies, Sing, (as Baby Rose Marie) (1933)
Rambling 'Round Radio Row (1934)
Surprising Suzie (1953)
Top Banana (1953)
The Big Beat (1958)
Dead Heat on a Merry-Go-Round (1966)
Don't Worry, We'll Think of a Title (1966)
Memory of Us (1974)
The Man From Clover Grove (1975)
The Honey Cup (1975)
Lunch Wagon (1980)
Cheaper To Keep Her (1980)
Witchboard (1985)
Bridge across Time (1985)
Sandman (1993)
I Saw What You Did Last Summer (1997)
Psycho (voice of mother) (1998)
Lost & Found (1999)

Acts

Caesar's (Atlantic City)
Capitol Theatre (New York)
Chez Paree (Chicago)
Chicago Theatre
Claridge (Atlantic City)
Copacabana (New York)
Fairmont Hotel (Chicago, Dallas, Denver, New Orleans)
Flamingo Hotel (Las Vegas)
Harem (New York)
Harrah's Hotel (Tahoe, Reno)
La Martinque (New York)
Latin Quarter (Chicago, New York)
Loew's State (New York)
Mounds Club (Cleveland)
Pierre Hotel (New York)
Riveria Hotel (Las Vegas)
Sahara Hotel (Tahoe, Reno)
Thunderbird Hotel (Las Vegas)

Record Albums

Hollywood Squares Album (1974)
Rose Marie Sings Italian (Mercury)
Rose Marie Sings Songs for Single Girls (Capitol)
Show Stoppers (Mercury)
Top Banana (Capitol)

Commercials

Bell Potato Chips
Dow Cleaner
Hallmark Cards
Kelloggs
Orange-Sol
Pledge
Tide

Cartoons

Arnold
Betty Boop
Freakazoid
Itsy Bitsy Spider
The Real Ghostbusters (1986)

Documentaries

Added Attractions: The Hollywood Shorts Story (2002)
The Bugsy Siegel Story
The Las Vegas Story
Shriek If you Know What I Did Last Friday the 13th (2000)
Vaudeville: An "American Masters" Special (1997)

Acknowledgments

To Mitch Douglas—Who was the first one to say, "Sit down and write your book." I am grateful to him for pushing me until I finally wrote it. Thanks, Mitch, for having faith in me.

To Randal Malone—My thanks for all of his help and understanding and for being instrumental in getting this book published. He is a dear friend who cares in so many ways. Thank you, Randy.

To Roy Thorson—Who, I said before, did all the restoration of photos that added so much to this book. He was super kind and worked so hard to make them look so good. I am most grateful. Thank you, Roy!

To Bernie Miller and David McFarland—Who gave me friendship when it was needed the most. Thank you both so much.

To Dodi Williams—My secretary for 26 years, who helped me in so many ways. I would write, she would read and then type what I had written. We went on like this for months. She is a super friend and I would be lost without her.

To my wonderful daughter, Noopy—Who gave me the courage to write this book, and who, with her computer, made it all work out correctly. She's a very special daughter and I am so proud of her.

To Larry Jones—President of TV Land, who was the one who made sure I got my star on the Hollywood Walk of Fame. He has always remembered me in so many ways. Thanks, Larry, you are very special!

To Angelique Cain Galskis—Who knew what I wanted to write and guided me through every step of the way. I am grateful and cannot thank her enough—and to everyone at The University Press of Kentucky who helped me, my deepest gratitude!

This book is dedicated to Frank Curley, my brother, who passed away on July 19, 2002. He was a kind, considerate, wonderful husband and father. Everyone loved him. He was an excellent high school teacher whose pupils adored him. He had a marvelous sense of humor and I had always thought that he would have been in show business. I will miss him; I will always love him—he was my brother!

Index

Abbot, George, 67–68
Abbott and Costello, 100
Academy of Music, 5
Actors and Others for Animals, 239
Adams, Berle, 98
Adams, Casey, 133
Adam 12 (television show), 138
Adler, Larry, 210
Adonis, Joe, 82, 83, 84, 85
AIDS benefit, 246
Ala Moana Hotel (Honolulu, Hawaii), 218
Alaska, 238
Albertson, Jack, 126
Alexander, Van, 160
Alice Faye–Phil Harris show, 121
Alisi, Art, 186, 198, 237
Allen, Gracie, 102
Allen, Steve, 168–169, 172, 189, 246
Al Pierce Show, 153
Ambassador Hotel (Coconut Grove), 144
America on the Move (television show), 240
American Animal Society, 239
Amos and Andy, 9
Amsterdam, Cathy, 185
Amsterdam, Kay, 184, 210
Amsterdam, Morey, 139, 176, 184, 185, 186, 202, 210, 231, 235, 249;

The Dick Van Dyke Show and, 151, 153, 155, 156, 157, 158
Anderson, Bob, 260
Anderson, Carl and Caroline, 198
Anderson, Ernie, 168, 169
Andrews, Patty, 261
Andrews Sisters, 24–25
Animal Activists, 239
Annie Get Your Gun (play), 194–195
Antoine's restaurant (New Orleans), 33
Applebaum, Annie, 92
Applebaum, Joe, 91–92
Applebaum, Judy, 90, 91, 92, 128
Archerd, Army, 216
Are You or Aren't You? 228
Arnaz, Desi, 121–122
Arness, James, 118
Arquette, Cliff, 186, 189
Astaire, Fred, 257, 258
Astor Hotel (New York), 66
Atlantic City, 6, 25
Aubrey, Jim, 166
Avnet, Brian, 218

Baby Rose Marie Corporation, 42
"Baby Shoes" (song), 15
Bailey, Pearl, 190
Baker, Bobbi, 54, 231–232, 242
Ball, Lucille, 121–122, 199
Bal Tavern (San Francisco), 125

Band Box club (Los Angeles), 142, 160, 210

Barbeau, Adrienne, 246

Barnett, Audrey, 230

Barnett, Marilyn, 229–230

Baron, Sandy, 171, 186

Baxter, Anne, 13

Bennett, Tony, 256

Bergin, Polly, 252

Berle, Milton, 13, 28, 42, 68, 69, 73, 74, 75, 77, 256

Berlin, Irving, 194

Bernard Brothers, 55, 95

Bernstein, Shapiro, 40. *See also* Shapiro Bernstein Music Publishers

Best Foot Forward (show), 68

Betty Boop cartoons, 42

Beverly Hills Hotel, 198–199

Bianconi, Harry, 149, 150

Big Apple (dance), 51–52

Big Beat, The (movie), 145–146

Billion Dollar Baby (show), 68

Birch, Ruth, 150

Bivona, Gus, 103

Bivona, Ruthie, 130, 160

Blackstone, Harry, 241, 242

Blyth, Ann, 143

Bob Cummings Show, The (television show), 138–139, 148

Bookbinder's restaurant (Philadelphia), 91

Botkin, Ginny, 103, 111, 123, 147, 160

Botkin, Perry, 97, 103, 111, 147, 160

Bowery nightclub (Detroit), 56

boxer dogs, 95, 105

Bradford Hotel (Boston), 53, 54, 73

Brando, Marlon, 129

Brennan's restaurant (New Orleans), 198

Brisson, Carl, 54

Britton, Barbara, 154

Britton, Pamela, 133, 134

Brooklyn Paramount Theater, 12

Brown, Les, 186

Brown, Tommy, 48, 56, 120

Bruce, Betty, 213

Brunswick records, 12

Bucher, Bill, 114, 117

Burns, George, 102

Burr, Raymond, 222

Burrows, Jim, 217–218

Bus Stop (play), 188, 235

Bye Bye Birdie (movie), 158

Bye Bye Birdie (play), 154, 188, 191–192, 194, 195, 245

Cactus Flower (play), 215

Caesar, Sid, 170

Cagney, James, 24

Cahn, Sammy, 227

California Motion Picture Council, 261

Call Me Madam, 210

CALVADA company, 155

Camp Shanks, 80

Capitol Theater (New York), 58–59, 114, 115

Capone, Al, 29–32

Carnation Farms, 105

Carnation Vindicated (show dog), 105

Carney, Art, 161

Carol Burnett Show, The (television show), 172

Caroline in the City (television show), 172

Carrier, Pokey, 96, 97, 102

Carrol, Jack, 29, 35

Carson, Johnny, 161–162, 181, 191

Carthay Circle Theatre (Los Angeles), 133

Castlebury, Steve, 245

Catholic Youth Organization (CYO), 46

CBS television, 157, 166, 246

Cedars Sinai Hospital (Los Angeles), 179, 182
Celebrity Connection, 258
Chandler, Jeff, 139, 140, 141
Channing, Carol, 188
Chase Hotel (St. Louis), 93–94
"Chena Luna" (song), 67, 243
Chevron Hotel (Sidney, Australian), 202–206
Chez Paree nightclub (Chicago), 54–55, 56, 132
child labor laws, 12, 14, 17–18, 21
Christenson, Scott, 247
Christmas, 38, 76, 164–165
Christopher Columbus (show), 68
Christy, Audrey, 215
Ciarleglio, Frank, 53
Cinderella (play), 245
Ciro's nightclub (Hollywood), 97, 99, 121, 123
Civic Light Opera, 235
Claude Thornhill Orchestra, 66
Cleveland Mob, 56
Clooney, Rosemary, 226, 231–236, 237, 241, 242, 243, 244, 248
Clover Club (Miami), 118–119
Coburn, James, 146
Cohan, Alexander, 207, 210
Cohan, George M., 4
Colgate Comedy Hour (television show), 161
Collins, Joan, 137
Colodny, Les, 210
Colonial Inn (Hollywood, Florida), 82–85, 105
"Come Out, Come Out, Wherever You Are" (song), 12
Como, Perry, 158. *See also* Perry Como Chesterfield radio show
Conway, Kelly, 170, 173
Conway, Mary Ann, 169, 170

Conway, Tim, 167–171, 172–174
Cooper, Jackie, 35, 36
Cooper, Neville, 133
Copacabana (New York), 77–78, 81, 251
Corday, Barbara, 216
Corey, Bill, 163, 252
Costello, Frank, 120
Court of the Two Sisters (New Orleans), 198
Cowen, Will, 146
Cox, Wally, 186
Crawford, Joan, 107
Crosby, Bing, 34, 97, 159
Crosby, Bob, 204
Cugat, Xavier, 84, 85, 105, 106, 260
Cukor, George, 145
Cummings, Bernie, 12
Cummings, Bob, 138–139
Cuny, Norma, 46
Curley, Frank (brother), 16
Curtiz, Michael, 136–137, 143–144
Cutler, Steve, 260

Daily, Frank, 59
Dalitz, Moe, 115, 116
Dallas (Texas), 245
Dalton, Abby, 186
Danna, Gerri, 61–62, 63, 131, 237
Danna, Maria, 237
Danny Thomas radio show, 99
Danny Thomas Show, The (television show), 149
Dan Tana's, 217
D.A.'s Man (television show), 138
Davis, Ann B., 139
Davis, Joan, 18
Davis, Sammy, Jr., 140
Dawson, Marty, 92–93
Day, Doris, 136, 200–208
Deacon, Richard, 153, 154, 210, 218, 219, 220, 237, 238, 257, 258

Dead Heat on a Merry-Go-Round (movie), 146

Dean Martin and Jerry Lewis Show, The (television show), 146

Dean Martin Show, The (television show), 185–186

DeCamp, Rosemary, 139

Dell, Gabriel, 210–211

DeSantis, Tony, 221, 224

Desilu Studios, 150

"The Devil and the Deep Blue Sea" (song), 258

Devine, Andy, 123

DeVol, Frank, 249

Diana Ballroom, 4

Dick Van Dyke Show, The (television show), 126, 150–158, 166, 167, 171, 181, 183–184, 185, 202, 203, 205, 213, 243, 257, 258, 260; Earl Hagen and, 98; Nardis Clothes and, 192

Diller, Phyllis, 190

Dinah Shore Show, The (television show), 146

dogs, 200–201, 225, 236, 239

dog shows, 105

Donahue, Jack, 126, 128

Doris Day Show, The (television show), 199, 202

Drop Dead (play), 246

Drury Theaters (Chicago), 222

Dulo, Jane, 218

Dunn, Elaine, 196

Durante, Jimmy, 73, 102, 105, 106, 107, 142, 260

Durbin, Deanna, 47, 52

Earl Theater (Philadelphia), 42

Edelstein, Dr., 104

Egremont Private School, 160, 161, 162

El Rancho hotel (Las Vegas), 106

Elrod, Tome, 222

Emmy Awards, 182, 186, 205

Epiphany Parochial School (New Jersey), 43–46

Esme (television), 246

Etting, Ruth, 16

Everybody Loves Opal (play), 188, 202

Everybody's Girl (play), 188, 209, 217–218

Fairmont Hotel (Chicago), 245

Fairmont Hotel (New Orleans), 228–229

Farranto, Peter, 241, 242

Faye, Alice, 111, 121

Faye, Herbie, 126

Faye, Joey, 126

Feinstein, Michael, 238, 245, 249

Fisher, Carrie, 246

Flamingo hotel (Las Vegas), 105–110, 139, 251, 260

Fonda, Jane, 146

Fontaine, Bill, 102

Forrest, Chet, 68

"Fought Every Step of the Way" (song), 255

4 Girls 4 (show), 226–236

Foy, Brian, 41

Foy, Eddie, Jr., 160

Freakaziod (television), 246

Frechetti, Joe and Charlie, 119, 120

Frederick Brothers agency, 194

Freed, Buddy, 139, 144, 202, 249, 254

Friends of Animals, 239

Frisco, Joe, 160

Fun City (show), 207, 210–212, 218

Funny Girl (movie), 121

"Funny Man" (song), 226

Fun with Dick and Jane (movie), 146

furs, 163–165, 239

Gallo, Angela, 221–222, 223, 224, 225, 238
Garbo, Frank, 56
Garland, Judy, 35
Garner, James, 159
Garoni, Chadwick, 53, 54
Garrison, Greg, 186
Gaukin, Joe, 60
Gaynor, Mitzi, 144
George Gobel Show, The (television show), 146
Gerry Society, 13, 14, 51
Gleason, Jackie, 48, 127–128, 160–161
Glen Island Casino (New York), 52
Glenn Miller Orchestra, 52
Glober, Bill, 239
Glober, Pam, 237, 239
Gluscak, Frank (brother), 49, 69, 70, 77, 82, 120, 131, 132, 191, 237; death of father, 124
Gluscak, Marion, 124, 131
Gluscak, Michael (grandfather), 3–4
Gluscak, Stella (mother), 3, 4, 5, 6, 7, 10, 14, 16–17, 26, 28, 34–35, 38, 40, 41, 42, 43–44, 53, 56, 64, 69, 70, 88, 103–104, 120, 125, 130, 131, 190, 214, 235, 247; birth of RM's daughter and, 113–114; death of Frank Mazzetta, 124; gall bladder operation, 191, 192; Bobby Guy's illness and, 177–178, 180, 182; RM's relationship with Bobby Guy and, 76–77, 80, 82, 86
Gluscak, Ursula (grandmother), 3–4, 7, 38–39, 43
Gobel, Alice, 160
Gobel, George, 159, 160, 189
Godfrey, Authur, 218
Gold, Ben, 192, 193, 194, 195, 196–197

Golden, John, 133
Goldman, Jack, 120, 139
Gold, Tina, 193, 195
Goldwyn, Samuel, 24
golf, 159
Gozzo, Conrad, 98
Grammy Awards, 182
Grant, Cary, 107
Grant, Johnny, 258
Gray, Bill, 142
Gray, Dolores, 194, 195
Gray, Glen, 96
Green, Alfred, 255
Green, Mitzi, 20, 68
Greenburg, Barry M., 258
Greshler, Abby, 48
Grossman, Julius. *See* Julius Grossman Shoes
Guardino, Harry, 215
Gumm, Frances. *See* Garland, Judy
Gunkler, Mickey and Hynie, 103
Gunsmoke (television show), 117–118
Gunty, Morty, 154
Guy Curse, 254
Guy, Georgiana Marie ("Noopy," daughter), 185, 189, 192, 194, 195, 214, 216, 218, 225, 228–229, 236, 237, 238, 243, 247, 250, 252, 254, 260, 261; birth and naming of, 111–114; death of father, 183; horses and, 162–163; nickname of, 121; Sam Levinson show and, 130–132; *The Saturday Show*, 228; schools attended by, 160; Phil Silvers and, 130, 136; *The Tomorrow Show*, 228
Guy, Nan (mother-in-law), 111, 113, 125, 160
Guys and Dolls (movie), 121
Guy, William Robert (Bobby, husband), 59–65, 66, 67, 69–73, 74, 75, 125,

128–129, 130, 133, 136, 139, 143, 251, 252–254, 255, 256; Alice Faye-Phil Harris show and, 121; birthday party for, 123; birth of daughter, 111, 112, 113; Tim Conway and, 168; Bill Corey and, 163; courtship with RM, 76–81, 82–85; death of RM's father and, 123; discharge from the army, 88; dog shows and, 105; domestic finances and, 97–98; elopement and marriage to RM, 85–86, 88–89, 90; Florida vacation, 120; George Gobel and, 159; golf and, 159; honeymoon travels with RM, 90–95; houses in Hollywood, 102–103, 146, 147, 148; illness and death of, 171, 175–184; Kay Kyser Orchestra and, 96; mink furs for RM, 164, 165; RM's attempted suicide and, 87; RM's career in Hollywood and, 99–100, 102; RM's Flamingo engagement and, 106, 107; RM's Mercury recording and, 98, 99; RM's mourning over death of, 185; television career, 146, 149; work in Hollywood, 96–97, 99, 114

Hagen, Earl, 98, 99
Haley, Don, 217
Hallet, Mal, 59, 60
Hallmark commercial, 246
Hanley, Eddie, 126
Hansen, Kenneth and Mousse, 198
Hardball (television show), 246
Harrington, Al, 218–219
Harris, Phil, 111, 121
Hart, Lorenz, 49, 50
Hasselhoff, David, 225
Hatteu, Tom, 232

Hayes, Peter Lind, 75, 116
Healy, Mary, 75, 116
Heatter, Merrill, 186, 188
Heinz Playhouse (television show), 137
Held, Anna, 43
Helen Morgan Story, The (movie), 143–144
Henning, Paul, 138, 139
Herman, Woody, 245
Hill, Virginia, 109–110
Holland American Line, 241
Holliman, Earl, 225
Hollywood Squares (television show), 171–172, 186–191, 198, 237, 238
Hollywood Walk of Fame, 173
Hong Kong, 241, 242, 243
Hope, Bob, 159
horses, 162–163, 239, 240
horse show, 252
Hover, Herman, 123
Howard, Willie, 68
Hughes, Howard, 143
Humane Society of the United States, 239
Hunt, Lorraine, 260
Huntington Hartford Theater (Hollywood), 227

"If I Only Had a Five Cent Piece" (song), 40–41
"I Fought Every Step of The Way" (song), 127, 129
"I Love A Piano" (song), 245
Ince, Bernice, 164, 177, 192, 195, 235, 238, 241, 242, 243, 247, 253
Ince, Harry, 164, 177, 183
Ingo Von Hager (boxer dog), 95
International House (movie), 41–42

Jacobson, Joey, 54
James, Harry, 66

Jazz Singer, The (movie), 11, 136–137
Jefferson Theater, 5
Jessel, Georgie, 11, 25
Jim Bowie (television show), 138
Jolson, Al, 11, 56
Jones, Larry W., 258
Jones, Shirley, 246
Jones, Tommy, 96
Jorden, Jack, 13
Julia, Raul, 195
Julius Grossman Shoes, 14–15

Kaiser Dome (Honolulu, Hawaii), 219
Kanter, Hal, 143
Kaye, Danny, 24
Kenley Theater (Flint, Michigan), 234
Kent, Lenny, 142
Kern, Jimmy, 143
Kingsley, Sidney, 133
Kitel, Clyde, 15
Klein, Dave, 98, 139
Klein, Manny, 98
Knotts, Don, 168
Korman, Harvey, 172, 173
Kouski, Bill, 192
Kowloon (China), 243
Kraft, Hy, 125, 126
Krahulik, Dr., 111, 113
Kummer, Marty, 231, 241
Kyser, Kay, 58, 59, 61, 96

Laine, Frankie, 145
Lakeside Golf Club, 159
La Martinique Club (New York), 134
Lambert, Lloyd, 139, 256
Lampson, Barbara, 260
Lane, Abby, 107
Lastfogel, Abe, 142
Last Frontier Hotel (Las Vegas), 95
Las Vegas Hall of Fame, 260
Lee, Peggy, 137

Leicht, Allan, 210
Leigh, Janet, 142
Leonard, Jack E., 119
Leonard, Sheldon, 121, 140–141, 184;
    The Dick Van Dyke Show and, 150,
    151, 153, 155, 156, 158
Les Brown Orchestra, 186
Lester, Jerry, 102, 119
Levinson, Sam, 130–132
Levy, Marvin, 178, 179, 180, 181, 182,
    192, 252, 253
Lewis, Jerry, 178, 179
Lewis, Joe E., 55, 119, 256
Lewis, Sammy, 100, 142, 210
Liberace, 139
Liberman, Max, 170
Lifetime Achievement award, 261
Lt. Robin Caruso (movie), 158
Lindy's restaurant (New York), 40
Lippin, Renée, 210, 213
Little Care, A (television play), 137–138
Little Club, 6
"Little Girl Blue" (song), 186
Loeb, Bill, 52, 99–100, 101, 105, 114,
    118, 142, 175, 183, 191–192, 195,
    205, 213–214, 221, 224, 226–230,
    251, 252, 260
Loeb, Pinky, 226
Loews State Theater (New York), 56,
    114
Long Beach (California), 253
Long Beach Memorial Hospital, 252–
    253
Long Long Trailer, The, 122
Lopez, Vincent, 9
Lord, Marjorie, 133, 134
Louis, Jean, 143
Lovejoy (Governor of Louisiana), 33
Luchese, Tom. *See* Brown, Tommy
Lucky Strike Orchestra, 58–59
Ludderi, Allen, 257

Lugosi, Bela, 41
Lunatics and Lovers (play), 133–134
Lynde, Paul, 188–189, 190, 218, 237
Lynn, Judy, 255

MacRae, Gordon, 123, 159, 160, 203–204
MacRae, Sheila, 123, 160
Madison Square Garden, 251
Maginie, Doc, 56, 115–116
Mal Hallet Orchestra, 59
Mallone, Jerry, 56
Malone, Randal, 249, 250, 260, 261
Maloney, Jerry, 115
Maloney, Jim, 137–138, 144
Man from Clover Grove (movie), 146
Markham, Gary, 192
Markham, Mary, 171, 186, 192
Mark Warnow Orchestra, 58–59
Marriage Broker, The (movie), 145
Marshall, Peter, 171, 186, 188, 189, 190–191, 237
Marston, Don, 225
Martin and Lewis, 256
Martin, Barney, 246
Martin, Dean, 186
Martinez, Tony, 166, 167
Martinique nightclub (New York), 54, 56–57
Martin, Tony, 53, 142
Marvin, Lee, 138
Mary Jane shoes, 47
Mary Poppins (movie), 158
Mason, Alice, 242
Mathews, Larry, 153, 154, 210
Mayo Brothers, 24
Mayo, Virginia, 24, 246, 260
Mazzetta, Frank (father), 3, 4, 6, 7, 9, 10, 16, 17, 18, 21, 28, 33, 34, 35, 36, 37, 38, 48–49, 50–51, 53, 64, 85, 120; birth of RM's daughter and, 113–114; Al Capone and, 29–32; death of, 123–124; physical abuse of RM, 81–82; RM's attempted suicide and, 87; RM's relationship with Bobby Guy and, 66–67, 69, 70–73, 76, 77, 78–79, 81–82, 86; threats made by, 115
Mazzetta, Joseph (grandfather), 4
Mazzetta, Rose (grandmother), 4
McDonald, Peter, 13
McHale's Navy (television show), 170
McNair, Barbara, 226–227
McNamara, Graham, 9
Meadowbrook nightclub (New Jersey), 59
Meadows, Audrey, 135
Meadows, Jayne, 246
Mecca Theater, 5
Medford, Kay, 213
Mercer, Johnny, 126, 127, 128, 129
Mercury records, 98–99
Merman, Ethel, 129, 190–191, 210, 212, 213, 214, 218–219, 220, 223–224
Mike Douglas Show, The (television show), 190
Miles, Sylvia, 154
Milk Fund benefit, 251
Miller, Ann, 260
Miller, Glenn, 52, 53
Milton Berle Show, The (television show), 146
Miranda, Carmen, 256–257
Miranda, Vince, 214, 215, 216, 219, 220, 237, 257
Miss Lawlor's Professional School (Los Angeles), 35
Montgomery, George, 147–148
Moore, Mary Tyler, 154–155, 158, 185, 210
Moreno, Buddy, 87

Morretti, Willie, 120
Mostel, Zero, 54, 133–134
Mounds Club (Cleveland), 114, 115–116
Mt. Sinai, 253
Movieolas, 157
movie shorts, 11
M Squad (television show), 138
Mullen, Morey, 157
Murphy, Audie, 114
Murphy Brown (television show), 246
Murphy, Scotty, 81, 88, 90
Murray, Jan, 118, 119, 120
Music Corporation of America (MCA), 52, 54, 99–100, 115
"My Bluebird's Singing the Blues" (song), 41
My Sister Eileen (television show), 139

Nardis Clothes, 192
Naughton, James, 188, 235
NBC radio, 9–10, 11, 12, 21, 29, 37, 39, 46
NBC studio, 239
NBC Symphony Orchestra, 12
Nesbit, Evelyn, 6
New Homes Show, The (television), 239
Newley, Anthony, 226
New Orleans Hotel (New Orleans), 198
New Yorker Hotel, 12
Nichols, Robert, 209, 222, 224
nightclubs, 54–57
nodes, 245
Northridge earthquake, 248
Nye, Louie, 168

O'Brien, Margaret, 246, 247, 250, 260
O'Connell, Helen, 227–228, 234, 235, 236, 242, 243, 244
Off Broadway Theater (San Diego), 215, 217

Ohio Villa nightclub (Cleveland), 56
Okun, Jean, 52
Olmstead, Willie, 248
Once Upon a Mattress (play), 235
"One Misty Morning" (song), 160
Orhbach Hour, 7
Ortega, Frankie, 218–219, 226–227, 232–233, 234, 237, 238, 242, 243, 244, 245, 249
Ortega, Linda, 237
Ortega, Maxine, 226, 249
Ortega, Sarah, 249
Our Emmy (horse), 162
Our Man Higgins (television show), 166
Ozzie and Harriet Show, The (television show), 114

Paar, Jack, 144, 145
Pacific Coast Horse Shows Association, 240
Page, Anita, 246
Paget, Debra, 144
Palace Theater (Chicago), 21, 28
Pantages Theater, 216, 246
Pantomime Quiz (television show), 186
"Panzy the Horse," 24
Paramount Studios, 34; RM's appearance in *International House*, 41–42; RM's audition for, 40–41
Paramount Theater (Los Angeles), 33
Park Lane, 214
Parks, Bert, 171, 186
Password (television show), 186
Pastor, Tony, 82
Pat O'Brien's (New Orleans), 198
Patrick, John, 209
Peicich, Dick, 219
Peninsula Hotel (China), 244
Pennsylvania Hotel (New York), 58
People for the Ethical Treatment of Animals (PETA), 239

Perrin, Sam, 114
Perry Como Chesterfield radio show, 77, 78, 87, 88
"Peter" (hotel manager), 192, 193–194, 195–198, 204–208, 209, 254
Peterson, Helen, 53
Pheasant Run Playhouse (near Chicago), 202, 215
Phoenix (Arizona), 244
Pinot restaurant (Hollywood), 260
Pippin (play), 235
Podell, Julie, 81
Poston, Tom, 168
Powell, Dick, 18, 34, 35, 36–37
Prager, Sammy, 144
Price, Georgie, 11
Price, Vincent, 189, 191, 237
Prince Charles, 257
Proctor and Gamble, 157, 166
Professional Children's School (New York), 13, 40
Prosner, Monte, 68, 73, 74, 77
Pussycat Theaters, 215, 217

Quigley, Bob, 186, 188

radio shows, 6–7, 9–10, 12–13, 14–16, 21, 29, 38, 39, 42, 46, 77, 78
Raft, George, 4
"Rain (When Ya Gonna Rain Again)" (song), 35
Raitt, John, 114
Ranger, Ralph, 41, 42
Rapp, Phil, 68
Rase, Betty Jane, 60
Raye, Martha, 119, 215, 235
"Razz-a-Ma-Tazz" (song), 161
Real McCoys, The (television show), 166, 167
Red Skelton Show, The (television show), 29

Regency Hotel (Hong Kong), 243
Regret (horse), 163
Reiner, Carl, 184, 185, 258; *The Dick Van Dyke Show* and, 151, 152, 153, 155, 156, 157
Reiner, Rob, 155
Reisman, Leo, 9
Residual Chex (horse), 162
Residual Ranch, 162, 239
Reynolds, Debbie, 246
Rich, John, 118, 156–157, 184, 260
Rich, Larry, 24
Richman, Harry, 11, 84, 85
Ring around Rosie (play), 188
Rita, Sister Alice, 44
Ritter, Thelma, 145
Rittinshroud, Virginia. *See* Mayo, Virginia
Ritz (Chicago), 224
Rivers, Edgar, 210, 214
Rivers, Joan, 207, 210, 211, 212, 214
Riverside Hotel (Reno), 123
Riviera hotel (Las Vegas), 139, 140–141, 260
Riviera nightclub (New Jersey), 120
RKO pictures, 142–143
RKO Theater of the Air (radio show), 12
RKO theaters: RM's tour of, 16, 17–18, 20, 21, 24–28, 29, 33
roadhouses, 47–49
Robards, Jason, 212
Robbins, Gale, 136
Robert Fulton Middle School, 160
Roberts, Curtis, 209
Robin, Leo, 41, 160
Rodgers and Hammerstein, 245
Rodgers and Hart, 246
Rodgers, Richard, 49, 50
Rodrigues, Steve, 228–229, 238, 243, 250, 260, 261; and KNBC, 228
Rodrigues, Tony, 237

Rolling Hills Estates, 253
Romero, Caesar, 107
Rona Doc (horse), 162
Rona's Residual (horse), 162
Roney Plaza (Miami Beach), 82
Rooney, Mickey, 35, 60
Roosevelt, Franklin D., 88
Rose, David and Betty, 29
Rose Marie: George Abbot and, 67–68; *Annie Get Your Gun* and, 194–195; appearance in *International House*, 41–42; astrology, 221–222, 223, 225; audition for Paramount Studios, 40–41; Baby Rose Marie contests, 26; "Baby Rose Marie" film, 234; benefit performance in San Diego, 149–150; birth of, 3; birth of daughter, 111–114; *Bye Bye Birdie*, 188, 191–192, 194, 195; Capitol Theater engagement, 58–59, 67, 115; Al Capone and, 29–32; Johnny Carson and, 161–162; child labor laws and, 12, 14, 17–18, 21; Clover Club engagement, 118–119; Colonial Inn engagement, 82–85; Tim Conway and, 167–171, 172–174; cooking and, 99; Copacabana engagement, 77–78; courtship, 76–81, 82–85; Doris Day and, 200–202; *The Dean Martin Show* and, 185–186; death of father, 123–124; *The Dick Van Dyke Show* and, 150–158, 166, 167, 171, 181, 183–184, 185; dog shows and, 105; domestic finances and, 97–98; *The Doris Day Show* and, 199; early childhood, 5–6; Easter Seals telethon, 218–220; elopement and marriage, 85–86, 88–89, 90; family history, 3–5; family home in Palisades, New Jersey, 43; Flamingo engagement, 105–110; furs and, 163–165; Chadwick Garoni and, 53, 54; Jackie Gleason and, 160–161; Ben Gold and, 193, 194, 195, 196–197; *Gunsmoke* appearance, 117–118; in Hollywood, 33–37; Hollywood social life, 121–122, 123; *Hollywood Squares* and, 171–172, 186–191; Hollywood Walk of Fame and, 173; honeymoon travels, 90–95; hotel manager "Peter" and, 192, 193–194, 195–198; houses in Hollywood, 102–103, 114, 117, 146–148; Lenny Kent and, 142; Las Vegas shows, 139–141; Bill Loeb's offers for work and, 99–100; in *Lunatics and Lovers*, 133–134; Gordon MacRae and, 160; Mercury Records recording, 98–99; Mounds Club engagement, 115–116; mourning for Bobby's death, 185; movie career, 136–137, 142–146; movie shorts, 11; nightclub dates, 54–57; physical abuse from her father, 81–82; pregnancy of, 103–104, 105; proposal from Rodgers and Hart, 49, 50–51; radio shows, 6–7, 9–10, 12–13, 14–16, 21, 38, 39, 42, 46; RKO theaters tour, 16, 17–18, 20, 21, 24–28, 29, 33; roadhouse dates, 47–49; Franklin Roosevelt and, 88; Roxy Theater date, 51–52; ruby cuff links, 82–85; schooling and education, 13–14, 17, 40, 43–46; Dinah Shore and, 185; sixteenth birthday, 52–53; at Slapsie Maxies, 102; Ruth Snider and, 53–54; *Spring in Brazil*, 68–69, 73–75; suicide attempted, 86–87; television

promos, 166–167; television shows, 137–139; Danny Thomas and, 56–57; *Top Banana* and, 125–130; vocal chord nodes and, 135–136; waterskiing and, 119–120;
Rose Marie Day, 260
Roxy (New York), 125
Roxy Theater, 51–52
Rudy Vallee Show, The (radio show), 12
Russell, Bob, 114
Ryan, Kermit, 111, 159
Ryan, Peggy, 122

Saenz, Carol, 222, 224–225, 247, 248
Saenz, Ralph, 247
St. Charles Catholic Church, 237, 247
St. Louis (Missouri), 245
Sally Swing, 42
Sam Levinson show, 130–132
Sanders, George, 169
Sardi's restaurant (New York), 49, 129
"Satin Doll" (song), 234
Saturday morning cartoon shows, 246
Scandia restaurant (Los Angeles), 198
Scarpelli, Jim and Kay, 93, 94
Scharf, Betty, 121
Scharf, Walter, 121, 255
Schewing, Ed, 9, 42
Schlesinger, Otto, 222
Schoenenbaum, Dottie, 52
Scholl, Danny, 255
Schrafft's restaurant (New York), 80
Schribman, Joe, 60, 66, 72–73, 87
Schubert, Lee, 68
Schwibs, Mike, 249, 261
Scorch (television), 245
Scottie dogs, 105
Sedgeway, Moe, 139, 252
Segal, Boris, 138
Segal, George, 146
Seinfeld (television show), 246

Shapiro Bernstein Music Publishers, 39
Shapiro, Irving, 53
Shapiro, Ruth, 53–54, 55–56, 73, 74, 82–85, 127, 128, 231, 241, 242, 243
Shaw, Jerry, 187–188
Shay, Dorothy, 202
Shields, Brooke, 172, 173
Shim Sham, 258
Shore, Dinah, 148, 185
Shore, Missy, 185
Show of Shows, The (television show), 170
Shubert, Lee, 73
Shubert Theater (Boston), 73
Siegel, Benjamin ("Bugsy"), 105, 109–110
Sliverman, Dr., 253
Silvers, Phil, 102, 132; *Top Banana* and, 125, 126, 127, 128, 129, 130, 252
Silvers, Philadelphia, 136; Georgiana Guy and, 130
Silvers, Sid, 143
Sinatra, Frank, 104, 256
Slapsie Maxies nightclub (Hollywood), 100, 102
Sloan, Mike, 136
Smearer, Lofty, 148
Smith & Dale, 142
Smith, Ethel, 58
Smith, Roger, 191, 195
Snider, Ralph, 53
Snider, Ruth, 53–54. See also Shapiro, Ruth
Snyder, Tom, 228
Song of Norway (show), 68
Sportsman Lodge (Studio City), 261
Spring in Brazil (show), 68–69, 73–75
"Springtime in the Rockies" (song), 26
Stadleman, Dick, 222, 225
Stalmaster, Lynn, 118

Stanley Theater, 18

Stapleton, Maureen, 212–213

Stardust Hotel (Las Vegas), 260

Starr, Kay, 210, 227, 232, 235, 237, 242, 243, 244, 248

Steel Pier (Atlantic City), 6, 25, 28, 42

Steiner, Herbie, 15, 39, 42

Stone, Paula and Mike, 126

Suddenly Susan (television show), 172, 173

Sully, Joe, 52

Sviridoff, Allen, 233, 234, 241, 242, 243, 249

Sylvania Hotel (Philadelphia), 90, 91

Tastyeast, 38, 43

Tator, Joel, 228

television promos, 166–167

Tellez, Rudy, 228

Tennessee Ernie Ford Show, The (television show), 146

Terrace Room (Newark), 59, 60, 63

"There's No Business Like Show Business" (song), 219

"They Say That Falling in Love Is Wonderful" (song), 220

This Is Your Life (television show), 172

Thomas, Danny, 56–57, 99, 102, 136, 140, 149, 153, 155

Thomas, Rosemarie, 56

Thornhill, Claude, 66

Thorson, Roy, 250

Those Whiting Girls, 122

Thunderbird (Las Vegas), 260

Tibbles, George, 257, 258

Tierney, Johnny, 202, 219, 220

Tierney, Joy, 202, 209, 217, 218, 220, 222, 226, 238, 248, 260

Tinker, Grant, 155, 158

"Together, Wherever We Go" (song), 228

Tokyo (Japan), 244

Tonight Show, The (television show), 146, 161–162, 181, 191

Top Banana (Broadway show), 125–130, 135, 136, 251

Top Banana (movie), 121, 255

"Top Banana" (song), 130, 131, 132

Travasoni, Monsignor, 149, 150

Travis, Michael, 227

Trenner, Donn, 202–203

Trilling, Steve, 143

Tropicana Hotel (Las Vegas), 260

Tucker, Sophie, 11, 119, 251, 256

Turner, Lana, 107

TV Land, 260

20th Century Fox, 144–145

2 Girls on Broadway, 122

Two Tickets to Broadway (movie), 142–143

Universal Studios, 145–146, 170

Up A Tree (play), 188, 210, 221–222, 223–

Urich, Robert, 225

Vagabonds, The, 118, 119, 120

Valentine, Karen, 188, 235, 237

Valentino, Rudolph, 4–5

Vallee, Rudy, 9, 15–16, 41

Vance, Vivian, 209

Van Dyke, Dick, 152, 153–154, 155, 158, 163, 164, 185, 210, 258

Van Dyke, Jerry, 209

Van Dyke, Marge, 163, 164

Van Dyke, Stacy, 163

Van Nuys High School, 160

Van Zandt, Billy, 246, 260

Variety Club, 217

Verdon, Dr., 86–87, 103

Versailles nightclub (New York), 54

Vincent, Romo, 93

Virginian (television show), 137
Vitaphone movies, 11
Von Leder, Dr., 245
Von Waldeck, Max, 58, 81, 87, 101–102

Wagon Wheel restaurant (Cleveland), 115–116
Wald, Jerry, 143
Walk of Fame, 258
Walters, Jessica, 218
Ward, Sammy, 39, 42, 46
Warner Bros., 136–137, 143–144
Warnow, Mark, 58, 67
waterskiing, 119–120
Wayne, John, 163
Weaver, Charlie. *See* Arquette, Cliff
Webb, Jack, 138
Welscher, Wally, 25
Weltman, Phil, 169, 170, 171, 172, 173
Wesson, Dick, 138, 139
Westbury, Long Island (New York), 245
"When You're Smiling" (song), 186
White, Betty, 257
White, Jerry, 232–233, 234, 242
White Heat (movie), 24
Whiting, Betty, 122
Whiting, Margaret, 63, 122, 226, 229, 231–236, 237, 244, 248
"Who Will Be with You When I'm Far Away" (song), 106
Wilkerson, Billy, 107
William Morris Agency, 142, 169, 170, 171

William Penn Hotel (Pittsburgh), 92
Williams, Dodi, 190, 238, 248, 250
Williams, Esther, 246, 260
Wills, Si, 18
Wilshire Theater (Beverly Hills), 226
Winchell, Walter, 113
Winter Garden Theater (New York), 11, 56, 129
Winters, Jonathan, 189, 190
WJZ radio station, 14
WMCA radio station, 7, 52
Wolfe, Rube, 33
Wonder, Tommy, 106, 107, 109
Wonderful Town (play), 194
Woodbury, Woody, 119
"A Word a Day" (song), 129
Worley, Joanne, 237
WPG radio station, 6
Wright, Robert, 68
Wyle, George, 139
Wyler, Gretchen, 239

Yacht Club Boys, 143
"You Don't Know What You're Doing" (song), 18
You Don't Say (television show), 186
"You're Just in Love" (song), 190
Yule, Joe, Jr. *See* Rooney, Mickey

Zaccho, Bert and Bob, 95, 97
Zaccho's Kennels, 95
Zevin, Harry, 133
Ziegfeld, Flo, 43
Ziegfeld Follies, The (show), 68

CPSIA information can be obtained
at www.ICGtesting.com
Printed in the USA
BVOW08s1934180118
505449BV00022B/417/P

9 780813 168005